CENTRAL BANK COOPERATION:

1924-31

STEPHEN V. O. CLARKE

FEDERAL RESERVE BANK OF NEW YORK

COPIES OF THIS BOOK are available from the Publications Section, Federal Reserve Bank of New York, New York, N. Y. 10045, at $2.00 per copy. Educational institutions may obtain quantities for classroom use at $1.00 per copy.

Library of Congress Catalog Card Number: 67-17650

To

John Henry Williams

Foreword

THIS monograph is another in the series published by the Federal Reserve Bank of New York on monetary policy, institutions, and techniques. It deals with a segment of history that has special fascination for students of monetary affairs: the efforts of American, British, French, and German central bankers to reestablish and maintain international financial stability in 1924-31 and the frustration of those efforts during the financial crisis at the end of that period. This is a story whose broad outlines are familiar, but the author has used the historical records of this Bank and unpublished papers of various prominent Americans to bring new insight to his description of the dramatic events of those years.

Mr. Clarke's monograph surveys central bank cooperation as it was practiced in an era when the international economy differed in many respects from that of today. In the twenties and early thirties, the world was still feeling the repercussions of the political and economic upheaval generated by World War I. Reparations and war debts were souring relations among the great powers. The United States, having rejected membership in the League of Nations, had retired by and large into isolation. At the same time, the Western democracies were experiencing a reaction against government management of their economies—of which they had had their fill during the war—and a renewal of confidence in the functioning of free market forces. As governments withdrew from economic management, central banks were left to carry virtually the whole responsibility of maintaining economic stability.

Although the contrasts are many, striking parallels with today are also to be found. Mr. Clarke's account of the efforts of the authorities in the United States and abroad to reconcile domestic and international policy objectives has a familiar ring, as does his discussion of the complications that arose from conflicts in the foreign policy objectives of the great powers. This book also focuses on the perennial problem of the policy maker who must be on the alert to adjust economic policies and techniques to changing circumstances. In fact, the study suggests that the failures of 1929-31 can be traced basically to the slowness of the Western democracies to realize that the problems at hand were radically

(Please turn page.)

different and more complicated than those of the midtwenties and that their handling thus demanded major new departures in economic policy and technique.

The problem of benefiting from the lessons of the past, while at the same time discerning where previous events are no longer relevant, is as old as the study of history. How far the experience of 1924-31 can be of help in dealing with present-day international financial problems, and how far it is only a reminder of turbulent days gone by—these are intriguing questions posed by Mr. Clarke's study. At the very least, however, a review of the period provides a vivid reminder of the pitfalls into which an earlier generation fell, and a warning to governments and central banks today.

ALFRED HAYES
President

New York City
January 1967

Acknowledgments

Many persons have given invaluable assistance to the author in the preparation of this monograph. Associates in this Bank, especially Francis H. Schott, have supplied unfailing encouragement and constructive criticism throughout the various stages of the study. The author has benefited from the comments of staff members of the Board of Governors of the Federal Reserve System as well as from the scholarly suggestions of Benjamin H. Beckhart of Columbia University, Arthur I. Bloomfield of the University of Pennsylvania, Lester V. Chandler of Princeton University, and Herman E. Kroos of New York University. Sir Theodore Gregory and Sir Otto Niemeyer made numerous valuable suggestions based on their intimate knowledge of the events of 1924-31. The author is indebted to those who arranged for him to use several important collections of private papers: Dr. Everett Case who arranged for the use of the Owen D. Young Papers, located in Young's former office in Van Hornesville, New York; Thomas S. Lamont for the use of his father's papers, deposited in the Baker Library of the Graduate School of Business Administration of Harvard University; and Richard H. Logsdon, Director of Libraries of Columbia University for the Papers of George L. Harrison. He owes an especially large debt to Mrs. Evelyn Knowlton, who searched through not only these private collections but also this Bank's records and the Library of Congress for the key historical materials on which this study is so heavily based. Mrs. Knowlton also prepared the Dramatis Personae, the Chronology of Important Events, 1919-31, and the index. The author wishes to thank Mrs. Ann A. Goldenweiser for permission to quote from her late husband's papers, deposited in the Library of Congress, and the Macmillan Company of London for permission to quote from Sir Henry Clay's *Lord Norman*. Valuable assistance in the collection and checking of statistical materials was provided by Miss Vincenzina Santoro and Mrs. Rona Lupkin. Many thanks are also due to Miss Gloria Topper who designed the cover of the book, Miss Abigail M. Cantwell and Miss Stella E. Walsh for their painstaking efforts in the final editing and preparation of the manuscript for publication, to Mr. John H. Hendrickson and Mr. Sigurds Vidzirkste for the preparation of the charts, and to Mrs. Marilyn Daniels and Miss Geraldine Barry for patiently providing indispensable secretarial assistance.

Contents:

Dramatis Personae*

Balfour, Lord Arthur James, British Prime Minister, 1902-06; Foreign Secretary, 1916-19; Lord President of the Council, 1919-22, 1925-29; British Representative, League of Nations, 1920; Chief British Delegate, Disarmament Conference in Washington, 1921-22.

Bradbury, Sir John (later Lord), with British Treasury, 1913-19; British Delegate, Reparation Commission, 1919-25.

Brüning, Heinrich, German Chancellor, 1930-32.

Case, James Herbert, Deputy Governor, 1917-30, Chairman and Federal Reserve Agent, 1930-36, Federal Reserve Bank of New York.

Churchill, Winston (later British Prime Minister), First Lord of the Admiralty, 1911-15; Chancellor of the Exchequer, 1924-29.

Clementel, Étienne, French Minister of Finance, 1914, 1924-25.

Coolidge, Calvin, Vice President of the United States, 1921-23; President of the United States, 1923-29.

Crane, Jay E., Manager, Foreign Department, 1919-27, Assistant Deputy Governor, 1928-29, Deputy Governor, 1929-35, Federal Reserve Bank of New York.

Cunliffe, Lord Walter, Director, 1895-1920, Deputy Governor, 1911-13, and Governor, 1913-18, Bank of England.

Dawes, Charles G., President, 1902-21, and Chairman, 1921-25, Central Trust Co. of Illinois; American Member and Chairman, First Committee of Experts on Reparations, 1924; Vice President of the United States, 1925-29; American Ambassador to Great Britain, 1929-32.

Doumergue, Gaston, French Premier, 1913-14, 1934; President of the Republic of France, 1924-31.

Gilbert, S. Parker, Assistant Secretary of the Treasury of the United States, 1920-21; Under Secretary of the Treasury, 1921-23; Partner, Cravath, Henderson & deGersdorff, 1923-24; Agent General for Reparation Payments, 1924-30; Partner, J. P. Morgan & Co., 1931-38.

Goldenweiser, E. A., Assistant Statistician, 1919-24, Assistant Director, 1925, and Director, Division of Research and Statistics, 1926-45, Federal Reserve Board.

Hamlin, Charles S., Governor, 1914-16, and Member, 1914-36, Federal Reserve Board.

Harjes, Henry Herman, American partner in the French banking house, Morgan, Harjes & Co., 1898-1926.

---

* This list, which is provided for reference purposes, includes only the important posts of the more prominent figures mentioned in this monograph.

Harrison, George L., Assistant General Counsel, 1914-18, and Counsel, 1919-20, Federal Reserve Board; Deputy Governor, 1920-28, Governor, 1928-36, and President, 1936-40, Federal Reserve Bank of New York.

Harvey, Sir Ernest M., Comptroller, 1925-28, Director, 1928-29, and Deputy Governor, 1929-36, Bank of England.

Henderson, Arthur, British Secretary of State for Foreign Affairs, 1929-31.

Herriot, Edouard, French Premier, 1924-25, 1926, 1932.

Hoover, Herbert, Director, United States relief program in Europe, 1914-19; Secretary of Commerce of the United States, 1921-28; President of the United States, 1929-33.

Hughes, Charles E., Associate Justice, 1910-16, and Chief Justice, 1930-41, United States Supreme Court; Secretary of State of the United States, 1921-25; Partner, Hughes, Rounds, Schurman & Dwight, 1917-21, 1925-30.

Jay, Pierre, Chairman and Federal Reserve Agent, Federal Reserve Bank of New York, 1914-26; American Member, Transfer Committee, and Deputy Agent General for Reparation Payments, 1927-30.

Kemmerer, Edwin W., Professor, Princeton University, Princeton, New Jersey, 1912-43; Financial Adviser to many governments between 1917 and 1934.

Keynes, John Maynard (later Lord), Fellow, King's College, Cambridge University, Cambridge, England, 1910-46; Editor, *Economic Journal,* 1912-46; Secretary, Royal Economic Society, 1913-46; Author, *The Economic Consequences of the Peace (1919), The Economic Consequences of Mr. Churchill (1925),* and *The General Theory of Employment, Interest, and Money (1936);* Member of the Macmillan Committee, 1929-31.

Kindersley, Sir Robert (later Lord), Director, Bank of England, 1914-46; Governor, Hudson's Bay Co., 1916-25; Chairman and Managing Director, Lazard Brothers & Co., Ltd.; British Member, First Committee of Experts on Reparations, 1924.

Lacour-Gayet, Robert, Financial Attaché at the French Embassy in Washington, 1924-30; Director of Economic Research, Bank of France, 1930-36.

Lamont, Thomas W., Partner, J. P. Morgan & Co., 1911-40; Director, 1940-48, and Chairman, 1943-48, J. P. Morgan & Co., Inc.; Alternate American Member, Committee of Experts on Reparations, 1929.

Laval, Pierre, French Premier, 1931-32, 1935-36.

Logan, James A., Unofficial American Delegate, Reparation Commission, 1923-25.

Lubbock, Sir Cecil, Director, 1909-42, and Deputy Governor, 1923-25, 1927-29, Bank of England.

Luther, Hans, German Minister of Finance, 1923-25; German Chancellor, 1925-26; President, Reichsbank, 1930-33; German Ambassador to the United States, 1933-37.

MacDonald, J. Ramsey, British Prime Minister, 1924, 1929-35.

Macmillan, Lord Hugh Pattison, Chairman, Committee on Finance and Industry, 1929-31.

11

May, Sir George (later Lord), Secretary, Prudential Assurance Co., 1915-31; Chairman, Committee on National Expenditure appointed by the British Prime Minister, 1931.

McDougal, James B., Governor, Federal Reserve Bank of Chicago, 1914-34.

McGarrah, Gates W., American Member, General Council of the Reichsbank, 1924-27; Chairman and Federal Reserve Agent, Federal Reserve Bank of New York, 1927-30; President, Bank for International Settlements, 1930-33.

McKenna, Reginald, British Chancellor of the Exchequer, 1915-16; Chairman, Midland Bank, 1919-43; British Member and Chairman, Second Committee of Experts on Reparations, 1924.

Mellon, Andrew W., Secretary of the Treasury of the United States, 1921-32.

Meyer, Eugene, Member, Federal Farm Loan Board, 1927-29; Governor, Federal Reserve Board, 1930-33.

Mills, Ogden L., Under Secretary of the Treasury of the United States, 1927-32; Secretary of the Treasury of the United States, 1932-33.

Moreau, Émile, Director General, Banque de l'Algerie, 1906-26; Governor, Bank of France, 1926-30; President, Banque de Paris et des Pays Bas, 1930; French Member, Committee of Experts on Reparations, 1929.

Moret, Clément, with French Ministry of Finance, 1908-28; Deputy Governor, 1928-30, and Governor, 1930-35, Bank of France.

Morgan, J. P., Partner, 1891-1940, and Senior Partner, 1913-40, J. P. Morgan & Co.; Chairman, J. P. Morgan & Co., Inc., 1940-43; American Member, Committee of Experts on Reparations, 1929.

Morrow, Dwight W., Partner, J. P. Morgan & Co., 1914-27; American Ambassador to Mexico, 1927-30; Member, United States Senate, 1930-31.

Niemeyer, Sir Otto E., with British Treasury, 1906-27; Comptroller, 1927, Director, 1938-52, Bank of England; British Member, Financial Committee, League of Nations, 1922-37.

Norman, Montagu C. (later Lord), Director, 1907-44, Deputy Governor, 1918-20, and Governor, 1920-44, Bank of England.

Platt, Edmund, Member, Federal Reserve Board, 1920-30.

Poincaré, Raymond, President of the Republic of France, 1913-20; French Premier, 1912, 1922-24, 1926-29.

Quesnay, Pierre, General Manager, Bank of France, 1926-30; General Manager, Bank for International Settlements, 1930-37.

Rist, Charles A., Professor, University of Paris, 1914-26; Deputy Governor, Bank of France, 1926-29; Financial Counsellor, National Bank of Rumania, 1929.

Sackett, Frederic M., United States Senator, 1925-30; American Ambassador to Germany, 1930-33.

Salter, Sir Arthur (later Lord), General Secretary, Reparation Commission, 1920-22; Director, Economic and Financial Organization, League of Nations, 1922-30.

Schacht, Hjalmar H. G., President, Reichsbank, 1923-30, 1933-39; German Minister of Economics, 1934-37; German Member, Committee of Experts on Reparations, 1929.

Siepmann, Harry A., Assistant to Finance Member, Executive Council of the Governor General of India, 1922-26; Head, Central Banking Section, 1926-36, and Director, 1945-54, Bank of England.

Snowden, Philip (later Lord), British Chancellor of the Exchequer, 1924, 1929-31; Lord Privy Seal, 1931-32.

Sprague, Oliver M. W., Professor, Harvard University, Cambridge, Massachusetts, 1913-41; Economic Adviser, Bank of England, 1930-33.

Sproul, Allan, Assistant Federal Reserve Agent and Secretary, 1924-30, Federal Reserve Bank of San Francisco; Assistant Deputy Governor and Secretary, 1930-34, Assistant to Governor and Secretary, 1934-36, Deputy Governor, 1936, First Vice President, 1936-40, and President, 1941-56, Federal Reserve Bank of New York.

Stewart, Walter W., Director, Division of Research and Statistics, Federal Reserve Board, 1922-25; Vice President, 1926-27, Chairman, 1930-37, and President, 1937-38, Case, Pomeroy & Co.; Economic Adviser, Bank of England, 1928-30.

Strong, Benjamin, President, Bankers Trust Co., 1914; Governor, Federal Reserve Bank of New York, 1914-28.

Swope, Gerard, President, General Electric Co., 1922-39.

Theunis, Georges, Belgian Premier, 1921-25, 1934-35; Governor, National Bank of Belgium, 1942-44.

Vissering, Gerard, President, De Nederlandsche Bank, 1912-31.

Warburg, Paul M., Member, Federal Reserve Board, 1914-18; Chairman, International Acceptance Bank, 1921-32.

Young, Owen D., Chairman, General Electric Co., 1922-39; Chairman, Radio Corporation of America, 1919-29; American Member, First Committee of Experts on Reparations, 1924; American Member and Chairman, Committee of Experts on Reparations, 1929; Interim Agent General for Reparation Payments, 1924; Director, Federal Reserve Bank of New York, 1923-40.

Young, Roy A., Governor, Federal Reserve Bank of Minneapolis, 1919-27; Governor, Federal Reserve Board, 1927-30; Governor, 1930-36, and President, 1936-42, Federal Reserve Bank of Boston.

1. Introduction

Like many historical studies, this monograph is the result of an attempt to gain insight into present-day problems by exploring those of the past. The study was initiated in a period when the authorities of the North Atlantic countries were cooperating closely to handle the problems of the international financial system, and was written in order to fill the need to understand the accomplishments and shortcomings of central bank cooperation from 1924 to 1931, the only earlier period during which this type of cooperation was undertaken on a significant scale.

Heretofore no detailed study of central bank cooperation during the 1920's and early 1930's has been published although several authors have discussed various aspects of the subject, sometimes at considerable length, in the course of biographical and other more general economic works. This lack was due partly to the absence, until recent years, of any pressing interest in the subject and partly to the inadequacy of accessible information on the relations between central banks during the period. However, the revived interest in central bank cooperation has been accompanied by a great enlargement in the availability of relevant historical materials. A major portion of the diary of Émile Moreau, Governor of the Bank of France, 1926-30, was published in 1954.[1] Thereafter

---

[1] *Émile Moreau,* Souvenirs d'un Gouverneur de la Banque de France *(Paris: Librairie de Médicis, 1954), hereafter referred to as* Moreau Diary.

15

autobiographies of Hjalmar Schacht[2] and Hans Luther,[3] who presided over the Reichsbank, 1923-39, were published. Equally important, official archives and the letters and papers of bankers and statesmen have become accessible. Of particular interest for this study are the papers of Benjamin Strong and George L. Harrison, who headed the Federal Reserve Bank of New York from 1914 through 1940, of Charles S. Hamlin, a member of the Federal Reserve Board, 1914-36, and of E. A. Goldenweiser, director of the Board's research staff, 1926-45, and the minutes and other records of the Open Market Investment Committee of the Federal Reserve System. In addition, valuable insights into the negotiations to stabilize the German currency in 1924 and to settle the reparation problem are provided by the papers of Thomas W. Lamont of J. P. Morgan Co. and of Owen D. Young, who among numerous other positions served for many years as a director of the Federal Reserve Bank of New York.

Scholars have already begun to exploit this wealth of material. Included among the recently published works are excellent biographies of Montagu Norman, Governor of the Bank of England, 1920-44,[4] and of Benjamin Strong,[5] a monumental monetary history of the United States,[6] and a fascinating history of Germany's role in the 1931 financial crisis.[7] Close study of these recent publications as well as of the abundant literature published earlier on the more general economic and political problems of the interwar years has of course been indispensable in the writing of the present monograph. One important source of information has not been explored: the archives of foreign central banks. The monograph thus tells the story of central bank cooperation on the basis of the voluminous but nevertheless incomplete historical materials available in the United States.

The study is less than comprehensive in another sense too. It focuses primarily

---

[2] *Hjalmar Schacht,* My First Seventy-Six Years *(London: Allan Wingate, 1955).*

[3] *Hans Luther,* Vor dem Abgrund, 1930-1933 *(Berlin: Propyläen Verlag, 1964).*

[4] *Sir Henry Clay,* Lord Norman *(London: Macmillan & Co., Ltd., 1957).*

[5] *L. V. Chandler,* Benjamin Strong, Central Banker *(Washington, D. C.: The Brookings Institution, 1958).*

[6] *Milton Friedman and Anna J. Schwartz,* A Monetary History of the United States, 1867-1960 *(Princeton: Princeton University Press, 1963).*

[7] *Edward W. Bennett,* Germany and the Diplomacy of the Financial Crisis, 1931 *(Cambridge: Harvard University Press, 1962).*

on those developments that are of central importance in the stabilization of the exchange rate structure during the mid-1920's and in the efforts to maintain that structure until the breakdown in September 1931. In these developments the central banks of Britain, France, Germany, and the United States played the major roles. The monetary authorities of these countries did not, of course, discuss their problems only among themselves. There was no exclusive club of the big four. The leaders of each of the major central banks corresponded and exchanged visits with a wide circle of other central bankers. The central bankers of most European and some other overseas countries participated at one time or other during 1924-31 in the granting of stabilization or other credits or were themselves the recipients of such credits. The cooperative activities of the smaller central banks certainly contributed significantly to the degree of international monetary stability that was achieved. Yet any one or several of these cooperative efforts could have failed—as at least one did—without threatening the international financial edifice.

This was not true of the cooperative efforts that involved the major powers. The main pillars of the 1924-31 monetary order were the stabilizations of the currencies of Germany in 1923-24, Britain in 1925, and France in 1926-28. These pillars were based in turn upon the fixed gold parity of the dollar, unchanged from the figure at which specie payments had been resumed in 1879. So long as the stability of the major currencies' exchange rates was maintained, the essential features of the international monetary order were preserved. But, when the pressures loosed in the 1931 crisis overwhelmed both national and international cooperative efforts and forced, first, a resort to exchange controls to protect the reichsmark and, shortly thereafter, the depreciation of sterling, the international monetary system of the 1920's was shattered beyond repair.

The vital role of the major currencies was well understood by the leaders of the American, British, French, and German central banks. Events so moved as to bring these central bankers together, sometimes face to face, more often in correspondence by letter and cable or on the telephone, in repeated attempts to resolve international monetary problems in which some or all of them were vitally concerned. It is primarily the story of their efforts to establish and then maintain the stability of the international monetary system that this monograph aims to tell.

17

2. The Problems of 1924-31

In the history of 1924-31, the relations among the central banks of Britain, France, Germany, and the United States form a relatively small but significant part. To a certain extent the central banks themselves influenced the environment in which they functioned, and part of the story of what they did will be related in subsequent chapters. But to a very large extent the central banks' policies and their relations with each other were determined by international political and economic developments over which they had little control. A brief outline of these developments is set forth in this chapter.

ECONOMIC DIFFICULTIES

The world of the 1920's had changed in many of its fundamentals from the one familiar to the pre-1914 generation. That generation, to which the heads of the major central banks owed their basic outlooks, had known a world economy that was unified to a unique degree. For the most part, exchange rates were stable and the major currencies convertible into gold. Movements of merchandise and capital were on a multilateral basis and were impeded to only a relatively minor extent by tariffs and other barriers. At the center of this system was Britain, still a leading industrial power. London was the world's major financial center, and sterling the world's currency.

To this orderly, integrated, and expanding system, the world of the 1920's bore only a superficial resemblance. In the early 1920's indeed *any* resemblance was hard to find. War and revolutions had weakened both the economies and currencies of Europe. The Austro-Hungarian Empire had been dismembered. Much of continental Western Europe was devastated. The French franc was quoted in the exchange markets at a fraction of its prewar value, the German currency was entirely destroyed, and even sterling, whose stability in terms of gold had been the keystone of the prewar exchange rate structure, was fluctuating at substantial discounts from the 1914 parity (see Chart 1). Of the major currencies, only the dollar remained at the same gold value as before the war.

These monetary changes reflected deeper economic ones. The war had led to major shifts in economic power and competitive strength. British industry, whose primacy had been surpassed even before the war by the United States and Germany, lost further ground during the 1914-18 hostilities as well as in the decade that followed. What had been British overseas markets were now

18

CHART 1

FOREIGN EXCHANGE RATES IN NEW YORK
JUNE 1914 AND 1920-31

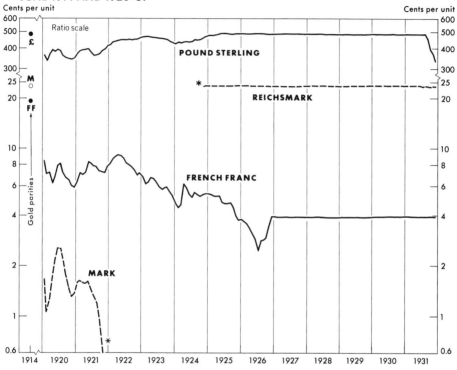

Note: Monthly averages of daily market buying rates in New York at noon for cable transfers.

*The monthly average of daily rates for the mark dropped below 0.6 cents in November 1921. A year later it was 0.0147 cents. In the fall of 1923, the rate was stabilized at 1 trillion marks = 23.8 cents. In October 1924, the old currency was replaced by the reichsmark whose parity in terms of gold was established at the equivalent of 23.82 cents.

Source: Board of Governors of the Federal Reserve System, Banking and Monetary Statistics (Washington, D. C., November 1943).

increasingly supplied by newly established local industries or by industrial competitors abroad. Among the latter, the foremost was the United States, whose international competitive strength had been greatly increased through the development of new products and highly efficient productive techniques. Growing rapidly, the United States had become preponderant in the world economy.

It accounted for almost half of world industrial production in 1925-29; its imports of the nine principal raw materials and foodstuffs in 1927 and 1928 accounted for 39 per cent of total imports of such commodities into fifteen major trading countries. As a source of capital, its weight was even greater—foreign loans floated in the United States during the decade ended in 1929 exceeded the total of similar loans floated in all the other capital lending countries put together.[1] Even in the second rank, Britain experienced sharp challenges from Japan and, once their currencies were stabilized, also from Germany and France. But Britain—its youth decimated by the war, its business leadership complacent, its industry facing stagnant domestic markets and encumbered by heavy taxation, and its labor force often recalcitrant—responded to these challenges only slowly.

Britain's adjustment difficulties were associated not only with rigidities in its internal economic structure but also with the structure of exchange rates adopted by the European countries during the mid-1920's. In Britain, the conviction was widespread that the reestablishment of sterling at its prewar gold parity was a prerequisite for the restoration of London's position as the major international financial center. On the Continent, in contrast, there was less preoccupation with financial status and more with the need to maintain or strengthen the international competitive position of trade and industry. In many Continental countries, moreover, prices had risen so much that it was unrealistic to try to force them back to their prewar levels. Therefore, while Britain accepted strict financial disciplines in order to restore and then maintain sterling's 1914 gold parity, the Continental countries stabilized their currencies at exchange rates that represented heavy discounts from their prewar values.

The international economy was fundamentally changed not only by the relative decline in Britain's competitive strength but also by the development out of the war of a burdensome structure of reparations and intergovernmental indebtedness. Efforts led by the British to cancel these obligations came to naught on the insistence of the United States Government that the European Allies honor their contractual obligations, and the demands of the devastated Allied countries that Germany pay an amount sufficient not only to offset Allied payments to the United States but also to finance at least part of the cost of reconstruction. Accordingly,

---

[1] *United States Department of Commerce,* The United States in the World Economy *(Washington, D. C.: United States Government Printing Office, 1943), pages 29-31.*

20

Germany made reparation payments to the European Allies equal to about 12 per cent of its total exports in 1925-30, while the United States obtained receipts on account of war debts equal to 5 per cent of its total imports, the principal effects being to weaken the international position of Germany and to strengthen the already powerful position of the United States.

POLITICAL TENSIONS

These major changes in the international economy were not necessarily fatal. In more propitious circumstances, any one or all of them could have been handled through some combination of economic adjustment and cooperation among the major powers. In the 1920's, however, the basis for such a solution was weakened by sharp conflicts in the great powers' national aims and also by the bitterness and mistrust that arose among them as the result of the war. To these political difficulties, reparations and war debts of course contributed. A large segment of the German population felt that reparations and the apparatus of foreign control erected to ensure their payment were not only economically but morally wrong. Even those Germans who worked for the fulfillment of the reparation obligations did so only in the belief that this would hasten the day when the Allies would give up their claims. Across the Atlantic, Americans resented references in Allied countries to "Uncle Shylock", while the Allies, bled white by the war, grew increasingly bitter as they felt themselves squeezed between a United States that insisted self-righteously that loans contracted be repaid and a Germany that was determined to escape the reparation burden.

At least as important as the problem of intergovernmental debts in its detrimental effect on international cooperation was the conflict between Britain and France over security against Germany. For France, security meant a Germany confronted on all its frontiers by the allies of France—a Germany economically enfeebled and thus powerless to wage another war. Such a policy was unacceptable to the British government, because it would help perpetuate the dominance of France on the Continent and would hinder the reconstruction of trade between Britain and the markets of Central and Eastern Europe. Lacking Britain's support, France was not in a position to enforce its policy on Germany but had to accept compromises which, to the extent that they fostered the recovery of Germany's political and economic strength, were regarded by many French leaders as involving the sacrifice of French security. Moreover, French fears were only increased as it became clear that the German government had a long list of aims, beginning with the evacuation of the Ruhr and including among other things the dismantling of the Allied control apparatus, the evacuation of the Rhineland, revision of the frontier with Poland, and a customs union with Austria—for the attainment of which it was prepared to press when it felt that the time was ripe. For its part, the United States, disillusioned by Europe's quarrels, eager for "normalcy", and the enjoyment of its rising prosperity, retired by and large into isolation. In these circumstances, there were large obstacles indeed to great power cooperation to deal with the grave economic difficulties of the 1920's.

TEMPORARY SOLUTIONS

Despite these many and fundamental difficulties, it was possible to believe, once the worst of the postwar political upheavals in Central and Eastern Europe had passed, that a stable international monetary system could be reestablished. Such a belief was nurtured in 1924 by the stabilization of the German currency, the tentative settlement of the reparation problem, the successful flotation of the Dawes Loan, and the agreement of France and Belgium to evacuate the Ruhr, and in 1925 by the stabilization of sterling and six other currencies in terms of gold. Moreover, as Europe's political quarrels temporarily abated and the venerated symbols of normalcy and stability were reestablished, investors began to look forward to a new era of international economic growth and prosperity. The outlook appeared particularly bright in the primary producing countries and also on the continent of Europe, especially in Germany, where the demand for capital was huge and prospective rates of return on investment were far above what might be expected in the relatively depressed British economy or even in the United States whose economy in 1925-27 was still expanding relatively slowly.

The American economy responded vigorously to the hopeful outlook abroad. A rising outflow of capital swung the United States balance of payments from a surplus of almost $270 million in 1923 into a deficit of more than $1 billion in 1927.[2] The movement of gold to the United States, which had been a dis-

---

[2] *Throughout this monograph, a surplus or deficit in the United States balance of payments is defined as equivalent to the total of (a) the changes in the United States gold stock and (b) the change in foreign short-term dollar claims. The data used are from the United States Department of Commerce,* Historical Statistics of the United States *(Washington, D. C.: United States Government Printing Office, 1960), pages 562-64.*

turbing feature of the earlier postwar years, was reversed. In mid-1928 the United States gold stock was almost $400 million lower than it had been four years earlier. Moreover, after sterling's return to gold, Britain too resumed its traditional role as a lender of long-term funds.

These mutually reinforcing political and economic developments had striking effects. The economies of Europe were rapidly restored: primary commodity output expanded, and there was a strong revival of international trade. Under the exhilarating influence of market incentives, some essential adjustments were taking place, notably in Germany whose export volume almost doubled in the six years ended in 1929.[3]

TROUBLE SPOTS

While the world economy appeared sound as long as the large outflows of United States and British capital continued, new trouble spots that were to complicate the underlying difficulties began to develop. A significant proportion of the inflow of foreign capital to Germany financed local government projects that could not be expected appreciably to increase the country's export capacity. At the same time, there were signs that foreign investment in certain primary producing countries was being overextended, with the consequence that many important food and raw material prices declined during 1926-29. Financial difficulties also appeared. Short-term inflows formed a substantial part of the foreign capital invested in Germany; they also, in effect, financed much of the long-term capital outflow from Britain. In both these countries, short-term liabilities to foreigners at the end of the 1920's exceeded by several times the gold and foreign exchange reserves of their central banks. Above all, trouble was brewing in the United States where the final stage of the long economic upswing of 1921-29 was accompanied by a variety of speculative excesses, including a stock market boom that saw call money rates in New York averaging 6 to 10 per cent in each of the twelve months ended in October 1929 and occasionally drove rates for overnight money as high as 20 per cent.

The New York stock market boom was only the first of a series of misfortunes that was to lay bare the faulty foundations of the economic structure that had

---

[3] *Angus Maddison, "Growth and Fluctuation in the World Economy, 1870-1960",* Quarterly Review *(Banca Nazionale del Lavoro, June 1962), page 186.*

been so hopefully erected in the mid 1920's. The lure of speculative gains and the high level of interest rates in New York led, not only to a sharp decline in new foreign issues in the United States during the fifteen months ended in October 1929, but also to some flow of foreign balances to America. Central banks abroad countered these flows by tightening credit in their own markets but, despite these defensive measures, foreign countries lost almost $240 million in gold to the United States in the fifteen months ended in October 1929, a sharp reversal from their gold gains of the four years ended in June 1928.

THE ECONOMIC BREAKDOWN

After the New York stock market crash at the end of October 1929, the strains in the world economy intensified. The difficulties resulted from the interaction of many elements of which four major ones will be briefly discussed: (1) the "real" contraction, i.e., the decline in production, trade, and employment; (2) the undermining of the financial positions of individuals, firms, and governments; (3) the renewed disequilibrium in the world economy; and (4) the search for liquid and stable assets that increasingly developed as confidence in banks and currencies declined. The interaction of these elements was not of course in chronological, or any other, order but may best be conceived as part of a deflationary spiral, in each twist of which all four elements operated as both cause and effect.

The contraction of production and trade in the two years ended in June 1931 was the sharpest on record. Industrial production in some countries, notably France, was fairly well maintained, but it declined in Britain by one fifth and in Germany and the United States by one third. In the three latter countries, one out of every four or five members of the labor force was unemployed in mid-1931. With the contraction in incomes and production came a sharp drop in the demand for food and raw materials, which aggravated the preexisting decline in commodity prices. By mid-1931 many of these had fallen to three fifths or less of their June 1929 levels. With both production and prices declining, international trade also contracted sharply, the contraction being aggravated by self-defeating governmental attempts to protect domestic markets through the erection of tariff and other barriers to trade.

The contraction of economic activity had serious repercussions on the financial positions of individuals, firms, and governments. Individuals who had contracted mortgages and borrowed against securities, firms with bank loans and long-term

24

market obligations, and governments with fixed charges including domestic and foreign debt—all were confronted with serious declines in incomes or revenues. Moreover, as the economic outlook darkened, private borrowers found it increasingly difficult to obtain additional credit to cover the gap between income and expenditure or even to refinance outstanding debt. Banks and capital markets became highly selective in their lending. Retrenchment consequently became a byword: individuals pruned consumption, firms laid off workers and reduced investment outlays, creditors decreased their outstanding loans, and governments attempted to cut expenditures in the futile hope of balancing their budgets. But these retrenchment measures only aggravated the economic contraction and in the end worsened the financial problems that they were designed to alleviate. Consequently, financial obligations of all types went into default, from home mortgages to government long-term obligations to foreigners, which led in turn to a further freezing-up in borrowing facilities. Indeed, during the year ended in June 1931 the markets for new foreign issues in both London and New York became almost dead. For the primary producing countries whose borrowing during the 1920's had saddled them with large fixed service charges and for Germany which in effect had met its reparation obligation by borrowing abroad, the difficulties were especially severe.

These problems were compounded by a search for liquidity that became increasingly intense. The gyrations of exchange rates in the early 1920's and the destruction of the German currency were remembered all too well. As the depression deepened, fears of yet another period of currency chaos increased. Confidence was shaken by currency devaluations in primary producing countries. In the industrial countries the financial difficulties of individuals and businesses resulted in a rising number of bank failures, particularly in the United States. These failures in turn led to a disturbing increase in the hoarding of gold and currency that reflected a growing uneasiness about the soundness of the banking system. In the international sphere, the increased uncertainty and the search for liquidity led to disequilibrating movements of balances from countries whose currencies were suspect to centers such as New York and Paris whose positions were regarded as impregnable.

The situation in the early 1930's was thus the reverse of that in the mid-1920's. Just as the expansive optimism of the earlier period had led to a great outflow of American capital, so the deflation and pessimism of the early 1930's slowed down and finally reversed the outward capital flow. The disequilibrium between the United States and the rest of the world that had been bared initially by the

1928-29 boom was now aggravated by the ensuing depression, the consequence being that in the twenty months ended in June 1931 the United States drew an additional $514 million in gold from abroad, largely from primary producing countries. At the same time, capital moved in substantial volume to France, initially for investment in its relatively prosperous economy and subsequently for security. The resulting gold movement to Paris came largely from London and was even greater than that to the United States.

The world economy was thus badly out of balance and one of its major financial centers, London, was enfeebled, when a severe liquidity crisis struck at the weak spot in the network of international financial claims. As already noted, the revival of Central Europe in the mid-1920's had depended heavily on borrowing from abroad, much of it short term. By the early 1930's the short-term component had, if anything, increased. Especially was this true of the Austrian and German banking systems, the bulk of whose short-term obligations to foreigners was held by London and New York. Amsterdam, Paris, Zurich, and other centers in turn maintained large short-term claims on London and New York. Hence the announcements in the spring and early summer of 1931 that the largest Austrian commercial bank and a major German bank were insolvent precipitated a scramble for liquidity which dealt devastating blows successively at the international financial positions of Vienna, Berlin, and London. In each instance the withdrawal of foreign balances, together with the flight of domestic capital, swept away a large part of the gold and foreign exchange that was available to the authorities to support their respective currencies and forced Austria and Germany to adopt exchange controls and moratoria on foreign obligations and Britain to abandon sterling's gold parity.

3. The Role of Central Bank Cooperation

INTRODUCTION

In dealing with the problems of 1924-31, the authorities in the major countries were hobbled by international political conflicts and a dim perception of how much the world had been changed by the wars, revolutions, and inflations of 1914-23. They were also handicapped by fundamental conceptual difficulties. The goal toward which they strove and the norm by which they judged economic behavior were defined by gold standard conceptions that purported to describe the way in which the world economy had operated prior to 1914 and that had a unity and simplicity whose appeal was widespread and powerful. Supported by the great weight of opinion in their countries the major central bankers worked, sometimes with almost moral fervor, to realize the gold standard ideal. But the economic clay was recalcitrant. The vision of a unified world economy, functioning according to accepted rules, could not be fitted to the circumstances of the 1920's. Yet, so influential was the gold standard vision that the few attempts to develop alternative conceptions of the working of the world economy were dismissed or ignored by the authorities. Rather than discard the cherished vision, each central banker sought to reinterpret the traditional theory to suit his country's particular needs. However, as these needs were seldom similar and often diametrically opposed, the reinterpretations resulted in conflicting views about the manner in which the gold standard should operate. The result was confusion and misunderstanding and in the end a failure to deal effectively with the economic difficulties of 1924-31.

THE GOLD STANDARD CONCEPTION OF CENTRAL BANK COOPERATION

Under the gold standard conception to which the central bankers adhered in the early 1920's, the role of central bank cooperation was distinctly limited. Indeed, there would normally be little need for it. This followed because the countries adhering to the system were expected to behave, for the most part, like components of a unified economy. The currencies were to be roughly stable in terms of both gold and each other, fluctuating only within the gold points. Balance-of-payments disequilibria were to be speedily corrected by economic adjustments within the affected countries. The rules of the game by which adjustments were to be achieved and exchange rate stability maintained had been described in countless textbooks and official reports and were well understood by the central bankers. An illustration of the way in which they expected the gold standard to operate is found in a letter that Benjamin Strong wrote in May 1924 to Secretary of the Treasury Andrew Mellon.[1]

> Prior to the war the regulation of both domestic and world general price levels was a more or less automatic affair. The payment of the small net balance of indebtedness between the nations resulting from all trade and services by shipments of gold had the effect of depleting bank reserves in the country where prices had advanced too rapidly and overtrading and speculation had developed, thus forcing advances in the rate of discount of the bank of issue and of interest rates generally, which in turn induced borrowers to liquidate stocks of goods in order to pay loans, so again reducing prices and restoring world price equilibrium. Comparatively slight but rapid advances of prices in one country were automatically corrected by these means and a fairly stable level of world prices resulted. No arbitrary human agency had to be employed. There was no one charged with direct responsibility for regulating prices and the extent to which discretion or judgment entered into the processes of adjustment was very slight. Even the judgment which was exercised was forced upon those responsible by movements of gold which made changes of interest rates imperative and hardly a matter of discretion.

In this conception, the flexibility, the adjustability, of the economic components of the international system made cooperation almost unnecessary. Or viewed from another angle, the adherence of the central banks to agreed rules of behavior, and especially to the principle that the maintenance of exchange rate stability should take precedence over all other economic objectives, was itself a form of cooperation that normally made other forms of cooperation redundant. In exceptionally severe financial crises, it is true, a central bank could legitimately turn to its counterparts abroad for emergency credits. But such credits would be short term in character and would be supported by vigorous monetary measures to restore equilibrium. The unusual character of such cooperation was underlined by the very few occasions on which the British central bank received special credits from abroad during the seventy years following the enactment of the Bank of England Act of 1844.[2]

---

[1] *Strong letter to Andrew Mellon, May 27, 1924, pages 2-3, historical records of the Federal Reserve Bank of New York. All unpublished materials, not identified as from other collections of papers, are from this Bank's historical records.*

[2] *R. G. Hawtrey,* The Art of Central Banking *(London: Longmans, Green and Co. Ltd., 1932), page 229; Arthur I. Bloomfield,* Monetary Policy Under the International Gold Standard: 1880-1914 *(New York: Federal Reserve Bank of New York, October 1959), pages 56-57.*

An important corollary of gold standard theory was that governments normally played an extremely limited role in economic management. They were to provide for the national defense and maintain domestic order so that market forces could have free play. Budgets were to be balanced. While a government might legitimately combat combinations in restraint of trade, the notion that it might adopt policies to counteract the swings in business cycles or to hasten the international adjustment process had yet to be conceived. Overall economic policy, to the extent that it existed at all, was a matter for central banks acting virtually alone.

CENTRAL BANKS AS INSTRUMENTS OF NATIONAL POLICY

The actuality of the central bankers' practice during the 1920's and early 1930's bore little resemblance to the gold standard precepts to which they adhered. In many ways their position was the reverse of that depicted. Whereas the literature assumed that all gold standard countries followed agreed rules and gave priority to exchange rate stability over all other policy objectives, the actuality was that the central bankers disagreed continually about the way in which the international financial system should operate and usually gave priority to domestic objectives over external ones.

Indeed, whatever their hopes about the gold standard might be, Strong, Norman, Moreau, and Schacht were first and foremost *national* central bankers. Although each of their institutions was, in varying degrees, legally independent of its government, this independence in no way reduced the central banker's drive to serve his national interest as he saw it. Sometimes, as with Norman, the view taken of the national interest was a very long-term one that identified the interest of his own country—some would say of his own financial community —with that of the international financial system.[3] In other instances, the central bankers devoted themselves more overtly to national objectives as Schacht did in his perennial efforts to achieve a scaling-down of reparations or Moreau in his attempt to mark out spheres of financial influence in Eastern Europe and thus counter what he felt to be the excessive influence of the Bank of England in that area. Even when they did not fully share the views of their respective governments, prudence demanded that these views be taken into account by

---

[3] *L. V. Chandler,* Benjamin Strong, Central Banker *(Washington, D. C.: The Brookings Institution, 1958), page 261. See also discussion in next section.*

the central bankers. A letter that Strong wrote to Norman in February 1922 illustrates the point.[4]

In the face of a powerfully organized antagonism in Congress, the Federal Reserve System must, to a considerable extent, rely for its protection against political attack and interference upon the present administration . . . .

We cannot afford, practically or politically, to embark upon a course which ignores the policy of the administration, which would possibly antagonize the administration and place us in the position where we would be quite helpless to resist the repeated efforts which have been made in Congress to effect important and possibly vital modifications in the underlying principles of the Federal Reserve System.

Each central banker thus formulated his policies within the framework of his country's needs and political objectives. Within the whole range of these national aims, the maintenance of the international gold standard, however defined, was only one objective among many and one that could not always be easily reconciled with others to which vital importance was attached. In each country the problem that confronted central bankers was essentially the same but took different forms. In Britain there was a perennial conflict between those who advocated an easing of financial policy to relieve the domestic economic stagnation and those who advocated a strict policy to support sterling in the exchange markets. Sometimes in Germany, and more often in France and the United States, the opposite side of the problem appeared in the form of a conflict between the need to ease monetary policy in order to support sterling and the need to tighten it in order to maintain domestic monetary stability.

Although the resolutions of these conflicts varied widely, they had one common element—each central banker sought solutions that were consistent with the needs of his own country as he saw them. When Moreau demanded in May 1927 that the Bank of England raise its discount rate to restrain a heavy flow of sterling to Paris, Norman's response was that, given the condition of the British economy, he could not do so "without causing a riot".[5] The focus of Strong's concern was at least as clear. His views are vividly expressed in a letter written to Norman early in 1923 when the United States economy was expanding rapidly

---

[4] *Strong letter to Norman, February 18, 1922.*

[5] *Confidential minutes of meeting of Friday, May 27, 1927, page 10, sent to Strong by Moreau on June 2, 1927. The background and outcome of this episode are discussed at length in Chapter 6.*

and was at the same time attracting a substantial inflow of gold. Since, contrary to the traditional "rules", Federal Reserve discount rates had been increased to levels well above the Bank of England's, Strong felt the need to explain:[6]

> Never, I suppose, have the factors which should move us in our rate policy been so carefully examined and considered, as recently. The results convinced me that our action was required, and that with our excessive gold stock we must entirely ignore any statutory or traditional *percentage* of reserve, and give greater weight to what is taking place in prices, business activity, employment, and credit volume and turnover.

> Of course we must not close our eyes to the bearing this may have upon Europe . . . . Enlightened opinion on this score must appreciate that should we dissipate our credit resources in speculation and price boosting, in the long run Europe will suffer. The advantage—a very temporary one—of a high price market in which to sell us goods would be more than offset by the ultimate disorders of readjustment . . . .

> You may be sure that inflation has no charms which have not been analyzed by Reserve Bank men and rejected as spurious.

A few months earlier Strong had stated his position in more general terms when he commented on a proposed statement of principles for central bank cooperation that had been sent to him by Norman:[7]

> no "surrender of sovereignty" should be attempted under the guise or through the formalities of this expression of principles. I think you realize, as we have here, and as in later years we may have occasion to realize it even more strongly, that *the domestic functions of the bank of issue are paramount to everything* and that anything in the nature of a league or alliance, with world conditions as they are, is necessarily filled with peril.

As it evolved during the 1920's, therefore, the international financial system lacked the unity, the tendency to move toward equilibrium, that was implicit in the gold standard conception. On the contrary, given the criteria for policy accepted by the authorities, there was no necessary reason, short of the exhaustion of a deficit country's international reserves and devaluation, why disequilibrium could not persist indefinitely. If adjustment policies could not be implemented in deficit countries because of industrial rigidities and unemployment, or in

---

[6] *Strong letter to Norman, February 22, 1923, page 2.*

[7] *Strong letter to Norman, July 14, 1922, page 3. Italics added.*

surplus countries because of the threat of inflation, an impasse was reached. Yet the chances of avoiding such an impasse were greatly reduced because the authorities viewed international financial developments through the distorting lenses of the gold standard conception and of their individual national needs and aspirations. To Norman, viewing his difficulties toward the end of 1926, the international machine was out of gear because the American authorities were acting on gold standard principles different from the orthodox ones on which he felt European financial policy was based.[8] Similarly, the Bank of France absolved itself of responsibility for the heavy flow of gold from Britain to France that threatened the stability of sterling in the third quarter of 1929 by attributing the movement to the free play of market forces under the gold standard.[9] In Berlin, London, Paris, and New York equally, it was always easy both to advise other countries about how their economic policies could be improved and also to find reasons why nothing more could be done at home.

Nowhere is the failure to achieve a consensus on the operation of the international financial system in the interwar years better reflected than in Norman's testimony before the Macmillan Committee early in 1931. He had been asked to discuss the Bank for International Settlements (BIS) and had stated that its monthly meetings had led to extraordinarily good relations among the central bank governors:[10]

> Nevertheless, a Central Bank Governor, when he comes to Basel, is necessarily to a certain extent dominated by the particular state of his own fiscal and economic situation at home, of the mind of his public, of the mind of his Government, and it is a matter therefore, not, as I say again, of establishing personal friendship— which we have done to a marvellous degree, I think, almost intimacy—but of taking up questions which are international and regarding them, as one would say, on their merits. No two or three countries can really regard an international question on its merits. There is no such thing as merits when you come to that. To get the affairs of a country, and possibly the needs of a country, considered on their merits is a thing which has not been achieved, and, I believe, will not be achieved for a very long time. The moment the position of certain countries is mentioned you get a reaction for or against, for particular reasons applicable to the individual in whom the action takes place. There will be a new Europe before we get away from that.

---

[8] *Sir Henry Clay,* Lord Norman *(London: Macmillan & Co., Ltd., 1957), page 224.*

[9] Infra, *page 166.*

[10] *Committee on Finance and Industry,* Minutes of Evidence *(London: H. M. Stationery Office, 1931), Vol. II, pages 298-99 (hereafter referred to as* Macmillan Evidence).

The conflict between the gold standard ideal and the actuality of national central banking led to much confusion in the debate over the appropriate forms of central bank cooperation. To be sure, each of the major central bankers supported at one time or other the principle of cooperation. Moreover, Strong and Norman at least came to understand that the international financial system could not be left to run itself, that there was no automatic means by which exchange rate stability could be maintained, and that, on the contrary, the international system required management which could be successful in the long run only if there were cooperation among the major countries.[11]

But while the central bankers were agreed on the principle that cooperation and management were necessary, it was less easy to agree on any particular plan because each proposal that was officially discussed was designed either to serve specific national interests or at least to be consistent with such interests. Unfortunately for the clarity of the discussions, the proposals were not always put forward in terms of the national interest but in terms of how they would restore or maintain some undefined form of the gold standard. Certainly this was true of the major proposal supported by the British authorities, discussed below. By the same token, it was all too easy for the central bankers to employ the gold standard ideal as a debating weapon against proposals they found unacceptable. Strong did this when he testified against legislation that would have made price stabilization a specific responsibility of the Federal Reserve:[12]

> I keep getting back to the subject of the gold standard, Mr. Chairman, because I have great confidence that when the time comes to conduct these things as they were in former years, a lot of the need for the type of management which has to be applied in the present situation will be eliminated. It will be more automatic. We won't have to depend so much on judgment, and we can rely more upon the play of natural forces and their reaction on price . . . .

Norman employed similar arguments to discourage consideration of a proposal sent to him by Strong on February 7, 1922 for an international stabilization fund

---

[11] *Strong letter to Norman, October 19, 1927.*

[12] *United States Congress, House Committee on Banking and Currency, Stabilization, Part 1, Hearings, 69th Congress, 1st Session., on H.R. 7895 (Washington, D. C., 1927), page 379. Strong's testimony was given on April 9, 1926. See also Strong's testimony on March 19, 1928, United States Congress, House Committee on Banking and Currency,* Stabilization, *Hearings, 70th Congress, 1st Session, on H.R. 11806, page 18-21.*

that would have given the Federal Reserve a central role in the effort to restore the international financial system. Norman wrote:[13]

> Generally speaking, I do not believe that any artificial means for the stabilisation of Exchange would, if ever, be practicable until the [intergovernmental war] debts have been settled, the Reparations adjusted, and free Gold Markets have again become much more general than they are now. And is it not true that when these things shall have happened stability in the Exchanges will be looking after itself in the old-fashioned way and artificial stabilisation will hardly be necessary?

THE GENOA PROPOSALS. Although Norman's arguments against the stabilization fund proposal are hard to reconcile with his position as a major proponent of international currency management, his view is understandable when account is taken of the fact that four days earlier he had sent to Strong drafts of the resolutions that were to be presented by the British delegation to the Genoa Conference[14] and that aimed, as William Adams Brown, Jr., has said, to restore by agreement and management as much as possible of the London-centered international financial system that had existed prior to 1914.[15] It is unlikely, however, that Norman would have admitted any inconsistency between the grounds on which he rejected Strong's stabilization proposal and those on which the Genoa resolutions were based. Looking back on the Genoa proposals it is easy to see how they served the interests of the London financial community and of the Bank of England in particular. But from this distance in time, it is also easy to forget that in the early 1920's London was the center to which the world was looking for financial leadership. The United States had withdrawn into isolation. France and Germany were devastated by war and inflation. London had been the world's financial center before 1914 and, with its famed institutions and skills intact, it sought to resume its historic role. Indeed, central bankers around the world urged Britain to do so and waited with impatience for it to act. In their minds almost as much as in Norman's, the restoration of sterling to its pre-

---

[13] *Norman letter to Strong, February 27, 1922, pages 1-2.*

[14] *This conference, the most notable of a series dealing with international economic and financial problems after World War I, was called by the governments of Britain, France, Italy, Belgium, and Japan and met between April 10 and May 19, 1922. Representatives of thirty-three governments participated, including those of nearly all European countries. The United States was represented only unofficially.*

[15] *W. A. Brown, Jr., The International Gold Standard Reinterpreted, 1914-1934 (New York: National Bureau of Economic Research, Inc., 1940), Vol. I, pages 345-46.*

34

war parity and that of the gold standard were an identity. Given this viewpoint, it required no great intellectual agility for Norman to reject Strong's stabilization proposal because it was "artificial" while at the same time holding that the Genoa proposals were a legitimate means to reestablish the gold standard.

The proposals, which were presented to the Genoa Conference by the British delegation and were adopted by the Conference's Financial Commission, reflected by far the most ambitious official attempt of the 1920's to organize central bank cooperation.[16] In addition to enumerating various economic and political pre-requisites for a return to gold, the resolutions contained three major, interrelated, and controversial proposals. These were to the effect that central banks (1) should so conduct their credit policies as to prevent undue fluctuations of domestic prices in terms of gold, (2) should cooperate continuously with each other, and (3) should be divided into two categories: (a) those in center countries which would hold their international reserves entirely in gold and (b) those of other (unspecified) countries which would hold their reserves partly in gold and partly in foreign exchange, i.e., in short-term claims on the center countries.

Those who drafted the Genoa proposals were aware that they contained many difficulties. Nevertheless, they hoped that, despite the deep-seated political dis-agreements of Europe, central bankers could rise above national preoccupations to cooperate for the attainment of common monetary objectives. For this purpose the Genoa proposals set forth what, seen from the British viewpoint, appeared to be minimum requirements. So long as prices in the major countries fluctuated as wildly as they had in the earlier postwar years, there was little hope for the successful restoration of an international gold standard. Price stability was surely an apolitical aim to which apolitical central bankers could agree. Furthermore, if existing or newly established central banks required foreign financial support to stabilize their currencies in terms of gold, surely it was not unreasonable to expect them to hold a substantial part of their international reserves in the centers from which the support was supplied. In addition, specifically British interests were at stake. Between its peak in May 1920 and the low reached in January 1922, the index of United States wholesale prices had dropped 49 per cent. Over the same period the corresponding British index had declined 50 per cent, but the sterling-dollar exchange rate in January 1922 averaged only

---

[16] *The resolutions are printed in the* Federal Reserve Bulletin, *June 1922, pages 678-80.*

$4.22, still well below the $4.867 parity at which the authorities were aiming. Any further decline in American prices—or, to use the terminology of the Genoa resolutions, any further rise in the gold value of the dollar—would further complicate Britain's problems in reestablishing the prewar parity. Britain's problem would be complicated still further if other countries that were attempting to stabilize employed the proceeds of their stabilization credits, or deflated their prices, in order to build up their gold holdings because, given the nature of the international gold market, most if not all of the metal would be taken from London.

Norman pursued one variant or another of the Genoa proposals throughout most of the rest of the 1920's. Time and again he sought means by which to manage gold flows so that the movement of the metal might be made to support, or at least not interfere with, the aims of British monetary policy.[17] When international commodity prices began to decline in 1926-27, Norman gave at least tacit support to a League of Nations study of whether the decline was the result of a scramble for gold by countries that were stabilizing their currencies and when the results of the study were published he almost certainly approved of the League's reiteration of the Genoa recommendations on the economization of gold and particularly on the gold exchange standard.[18] Norman also made repeated efforts to convene the central bankers' meeting that had been proposed at Genoa. Although the Genoa objective was not attained, Norman was instrumental in bringing the central bankers together to discuss their problems face to face, especially after the establishment of the BIS in 1930 provided them with a monthly occasion on which to meet.

STRONG'S CRITIQUE OF THE GENOA PROPOSALS. A major condition for the successful implementation of the Genoa proposals was of course the support of the United States monetary authorities. Actually the initial reaction of the Federal Reserve was not unfavorable. Strong secured the approval of the Harding Administration to attend a conference of central bankers that was to be called by Norman, but the conference was postponed again and again because of difficulties

---

[17] *Strong, "A Bank Meeting", memorandum of July 22, 1925; Clay, op. cit., pages 224-25.* Infra, *page 114.*

[18] *League of Nations,* Interim Report of the Gold Delegation of the Financial Committee *(Geneva, 1930), page 20;* Report of the Committee on Finance and Industry *(London: H. M. Stationery Office, July 1931), pages 122-23 (hereafter referred to as the* Macmillan Report).

surrounding the settlement of European war debts to the United States and also because the central bankers who were to participate had numerous other commitments. Moreover, as time went by, Strong came to have serious doubts about the substance of the proposals themselves. Although at times he expressed his misgivings in vague gold standard terminology, the basic ground for his objection was that the proposals might impair the ability of the Federal Reserve to fulfill its national central banking responsibilities.

Strong's misgivings centered at first on the proposal that credit policy should be directed to the avoidance of undue fluctuations in the purchasing power of gold, a proposal whose implementation, he believed, could run directly counter to the central bank's obligation to maintain monetary stability within its own market. This proposal, he wrote, had[19]

an ominous sound to me.

Expressing it from one point of view, the regulation of credit for the purpose of maintaining the purchasing power of gold or the parity of currencies would imply that the nation which had a discount on its currency should undertake, through its bank of issue, to bring about a contraction of credit and currency; or, as in the present case, the United States, with its currency at a premium the world over, should undertake, through the Reserve Banks, to so regulate credit policies as to expand credit and currency to a point where the value of our currency would decline and consequently other currencies would approach the value of ours . . . .

From the standpoint of this country, we must be assured that we are not suggesting or recommending a plan which if adopted would be anything in the nature of handing a blank check to some of the impoverished nations of the world, or to their banks of issue, and especially to those whose government finances are in complete disorder and quite beyond control. This is one reason for caution from the standpoint of your country and ours, or at least your bank and ours, in accepting principles which might have far reaching effects in practice.

Strong's opposition to any proposal that central banks should direct their policy to the stabilization of prices in terms of gold became more vehement as time passed. When, as mentioned above, the League reopened the subject in 1927-28 he used his influence to discourage the proposed study of whether the decline in commodity prices was in any way connected with a gold shortage. Strong indicated his skepticism about any such shortage, present or impending,

---

[19] *Strong letter to Norman, July 14, 1922, pages 5-6.*

but he agreed that a purely factual study of the question might be useful. However, his serious concern was that the study would revive criticism along the oft-repeated line that the Federal Reserve was sterilizing gold and might recommend that the United States should follow a policy of monetary ease at a time when the Federal Reserve was struggling to restrain the culminating boom of the 1920's. It was with these concerns in mind that he told Sir Arthur Salter, the director of the League's Economic and Financial Organization and an advocate of the study, that neither the League nor any group meeting under its auspices was in a position to advise central banks on policy and that, in particular, any advice to the Federal Reserve would be very badly received in America.[20]

Strong's reaction against the Genoa proposals on the gold exchange standard did not come until the late 1920's. He did not touch on the subject in his correspondence with Norman during the spring and summer of 1922, it being taken for granted apparently that, in the turbulent conditions of the time, New York and London would be the only centers in which other countries would hold the foreign exchange component of their international reserves. As late as the spring of 1926 Strong did Norman the favor of testifying, albeit somewhat backhandedly, to the effect that India would better serve the cause of international monetary stability if its currency were based, not on gold alone, but on the gold exchange standard.[21]

Indeed, Strong did not turn against the gold exchange standard until he had digested the details of the acute difficulties that arose between the central banks of England and France in the spring of 1927. Thereafter, however, his letters and memoranda expressed frequent misgivings.[22] He was concerned that the gold exchange standard facilitated a pyramiding of credit on small gold holdings in center countries; that the conversion of foreign exchange balances into gold might force the center countries sharply to increase their discount rates and so bring about the very deflation that the advocates of the League study feared; and that the gold exchange standard was, in some undefined way, undermining the

[20] O. Ernest Moore, memorandum of conversation between Governor Strong and Sir Arthur Salter, May 25, 1928. See also Strong letters to Harrison, December 24, 1927 and July 8, 1928 (Harrison Papers).

[21] The Royal Commission on Indian Currency and Finance, Minutes of Evidence (London: H. M. Stationery Office, 1926), Vol. 5, pages 274-330.

[22] Strong letter to Norman, August 30, 1927, pages 2-3; Strong letter to Owen D. Young, June 11, 1928, pages 6-7; and Strong letter to Norman, September 19, 1927.

gold standard. However, what lay at the bottom of these objections was Strong's shock at the discovery that the Bank of France, in attempting to exercise its undoubted right to convert its large London balances into gold, had brought the Bank of England to the point where it had to choose between severely deflating the British economy or abandoning sterling's gold parity.[23] To be sure, he foresaw no immediate danger that the Federal Reserve would face any similar threat.[24] Its holdings of gold above the minimum legal requirements were considered adequate to meet any likely foreign demands for the metal. Even so, Strong could never approve of a system that might place in the hands of foreign central bankers such power over Federal Reserve policy as had been wielded by the Bank of France over the Bank of England. His conclusion was[25]

> that every one of the nations should reestablish the gold standard, restore its gold reserve or create a new one where needed, making special arrangements for doing so where necessary, and reestablish its own domestic autonomy in monetary matters without any such dependence upon other markets as implied by the gold exchange standard. Important balances in London or New York of course may be highly desirable, but the most desirable thing is autonomy and self-reliance and good conduct on sound monetary principles at home.

As Strong's interest in the other Genoa proposals cooled, so did his willingness to attend the proposed conference of central bankers. Almost from the beginning he had been concerned about the direction that a large meeting of central bankers would take and particularly about the possibility—indeed the probability—that, as the representative of the only powerful creditor country, he would be placed in the difficult position of having to disappoint the hopes for financial assistance that might be entertained by the various European central bankers who would attend the conference.[26] As time went on, Strong found additional reasons to resist Norman's repeated attempts to convene a formal meeting of central bankers. As he explained them to Sir Arthur Salter in the spring of 1928, some of Strong's reasons were strikingly similar to those expressed by Norman three years later when he testified to the Macmillan Committee on the periodic meetings of the

---

[23] *An account of these difficulties and how they were resolved is given on pages 116-30.*

[24] *Strong letter to John J. Mitchell, October 4, 1927, pages 1-2.*

[25] *Strong letter to Owen D. Young, June 11, 1928, pages 6-7.*

[26] *Strong letter to Norman, July 27, 1922.*

BIS governors.[27] According to a memorandum written by a member of the Federal Reserve staff who attended the meeting with Sir Arthur:[28]

> Governor Strong stated that he had always been opposed to any sort of a formal conference or meeting between the world's central banks, as contemplated at Genoa, for several reasons. In his opinion, it was expecting entirely too much of human nature to think that representatives of the central banks of a great many nations having differences of language, customs, beliefs and financial and political needs could sit down together and agree on anything at all. Moreover, in the course of his travels he had had occasion to meet a great many of the central bankers, as well as governmental and political representatives, and to learn considerable about the relations between the various banks and their governments, and he was not at all convinced that at a general meeting or in any common organization of central banks the policies of certain banks would not be dictated by the interests of their respective governments rather than by purely monetary considerations. Another point was that in any formal meeting of the central banks, the Federal Reserve Bank would represent the only lending market, while the others would all be borrowers, and he would never consent to go to such a conference with the prospect of being outvoted on every issue of any importance which affected the Federal Reserve System. He would have to be sure of having one more vote than all the borrowers combined.

A PRAGMATIC APPROACH TO CENTRAL BANK COOPERATION

Strong's misgivings about the Genoa proposals did not prevent him from developing a distinctive approach to central bank cooperation that, largely because it was consistent with his and his colleagues' responsibilities as national central bankers, was the approach that was generally followed during the 1920's and early 1930's. Briefly, he would encourage the Federal Reserve to cooperate with foreign central banks so long as the assistance contributed to the welfare of the United States or at the least was consistent with United States interests.[29] Apart from his 1922 flirtation with the idea of attending the proposed central bankers' meeting, he consistently favored what John H. Williams later called the "key currency" approach to cooperation. Early in 1919, he wrote Norman that, if currency stabilization could be worked out between the British, French, and United States central banks, he doubted that "anything further would be required or desirable

---

[27] Supra, *page 32.*

[28] *O. Ernest Moore, memorandum of conversation between Governor Strong and Sir Arthur Salter, May 25, 1928, pages 4-5.*

[29] *Strong letter to Norman, March 21, 1921, cited in Chandler, op. cit., page 247.*

40

for many years to come".[30] As things turned out, Strong participated with other central bankers in the work of monetary reform in numerous countries, but his major efforts were indeed directed successively to the stabilization of the British and French currencies. In all these efforts, his approach was selective and pragmatic. Discussing his monetary stabilization experiences before a Congressional committee in the spring of 1926, he declared that the best chances for success lay in dealing with the problems in detail, taking one situation at a time, rather than to attempt to deal with all countries at once.[31]

It was within this framework that cooperation between central banks developed. The first steps involved the performance of services that are now considered routine but that had not ordinarily been performed prior to World War I: the earmarking of gold, the investment of deposits, and the regular exchange of information on current developments in the financial markets. As the friendship between Strong and Norman grew in the early 1920's, it was entirely natural for them to exchange views on the economic outlook and on prospective changes in monetary policy and to offer each other advice on how to deal with the problems with which they were confronted. Such exchanges grew with the widening of Strong's circle of acquaintances among central bankers although none attained the intimacy of the exchanges with Norman. After Strong's death in October 1928, George L. Harrison continued these exchanges of information and opinions and was aided in this by the development of the transatlantic telephone which provided the central bankers with a means of daily and even hourly communication.

Financial cooperation between central banks arose in the 1920's as one of the ingredients normally required for currency stabilization. In these stabilization efforts, Strong and Norman (the latter often working in cooperation with the Economic and Financial Organization of the League of Nations) took the lead in formulating the conditions that, in their views, would facilitate an early return to gold payments and fixed exchange rates. Governments, which had dominated the central bankers during the war and early postwar years, should resume the role in which they were cast under the gold standard conception.[32] Above all,

---

[30] *Strong letter to Norman, February 5, 1919, page 3.*

[31] *House Committee on Banking and Currency,* Stabilization, *Hearings on H.R. 7895, April 12, 1926, page 504.*

[32] Supra, *page 29.*

they should put their finances in order. Budgets should be balanced; large-scale borrowing from the banking system should stop; excessive amounts of floating debt should be funded so that the need to refinance large and frequent short-term maturities would not impede the central banks' monetary control. Beyond this, central banks should be legally independent of governments and the continuity of central bank managements should be assured. On the external side, each country's prices should be brought into alignment with those of its major competitors at the exchange rate chosen for stabilization; its merchandise trade should be in balance or at least approaching balance; and the central bank should have accumulated international reserves adequate to convince the market that it could defend its chosen exchange rate against the payments pressures to which its currency was likely to be exposed in the ordinary course of events.[33] When a country had met these conditions and had thus covered most if not all of the road toward its goal, the central bank of the stabilizing country would obtain from one or more other central banks a credit calculated to insure market confidence in the stabilization plan. Sometimes the central bank credit would be supplemented by a commercial bank, or market loan, to the government of the stabilizing country. In either case, the arrangements normally would be of no more than two years' maturity and would be considered most successful if the funds made available under them were never drawn. Indeed, such loans and credits were most easily obtained when they were least needed.

In the areas of routine services, information exchange, and stabilization, central bank cooperation by and large was quite successful in 1924-31, but the main challenge lay elsewhere. It involved the question whether, once stabilization had been completed, cooperation could be continued to the extent required to maintain stable exchange rates. In meeting this challenge, the central bankers were subject to serious constraints. Monetary policy could be brought into play only when the central bank's international aims happened to coincide, or at least not conflict, with its domestic ones. In the efforts of the Federal Reserve to support sterling, for example, these aims happened to coincide in 1924 and again in 1927 when the United States economy was in recession. But when sterling came under severe pressure during the 1928-29 American boom, the conflict that arose in the

---

[33] *Chandler, op. cit., pages 261-62 and 281; Brown, op. cit., pages 343-44; and Strong letter to Herbert Hoover, April 22, 1922.*

internal and external aims of Federal Reserve policy was resolved in favor of the central bank's domestic economic objectives.

The same constraints applied to inter-central-bank credits because, whatever form they took, their use for support operations acted to expand the cash base of the creditor country's banking system. In a period during which the Federal Open Market portfolio was never much over $500 million, the addition of as much as $50-100 million to member bank reserves was always a matter to be taken seriously into account. Such an addition to the cash base was acceptable if the Federal Reserve was in any case aiming to ease money market conditions. It might even be acceptable if the Federal Reserve aimed at no change, provided that the holdings of the open market account were sufficiently large to permit offsetting sales. But when, as happened in the early months of 1929, the ammunition in the open market portfolio was virtually exhausted and when the Federal Reserve was struggling to keep a tight rein on the cash base, the scope for currency support operations was drastically restricted. Limitations such as these were even more severe in the cases of the Reichsbank and the Bank of France, neither of which had adequate authority to conduct meaningful open market operations.[34]

In addition to these problems, there were other more fundamental limitations on central bank cooperation that stemmed from the conceptual confusion about the nature of the international financial system. The authorities perceived only dimly, if at all, that in a system managed by national central banks the process of international adjustment was likely to be far slower and more difficult than it was supposed to be under the gold standard conception. Guided in their thinking by this vision, the authorities tended to demand too much from the adjustment process and to allow too little in the way of financing to support weak currencies while needed adjustments were taking place. Paradoxically, the British authorities, who presumably favored the managed currency proposals of Genoa, frequently took the sternest line—as did one economic adviser to the Bank of England in December 1930 when he said that Federal Reserve operations in support of sterling should not go above £10 million because of the danger that additional support would encourage England to postpone the making of funda-

[34] M. G. Myers, Paris as a Financial Centre (New York: Columbia University Press, 1936), pages 29-30; M. H. deKock, Central Banking (3rd ed.; London: Staples Press, 1954), pages 206-8.

mental adjustments. Norman was just as stern toward the end of August 1931 when he intimated that his government should adopt a retrenchment program sufficiently drastic to eliminate entirely the need for Britain to seek credit from abroad.[35] Presumably, attitudes such as these explain, at least in part, why on several occasions the British authorities declined financial assistance offers that were made by the Federal Reserve.

In these circumstances, it is hardly surprising that inter-central-bank currency support operations were on a relatively small scale and for relatively short periods—although certainly considerably larger in amount and longer in maturity than any that had been granted before 1914. Apart from the 1927-28 Bank of France swaps—which in any event were undertaken only to facilitate the achievement of French domestic monetary aims—the largest market operations of which we have any record were those conducted by the Federal Reserve in support of sterling. These rose to a peak of $60 million equivalent during the British-French difficulties of May-June 1927 but did not again exceed $35 million even in the difficult days of 1929-31. Larger amounts were granted under the more formal inter-central-bank credits, but even these credits tended to be too little and too late and—despite all the emphasis on the need for adjustment—were often uncoordinated with any convincing program to correct the underlying difficulties. The suggestion for a credit sufficiently large to stop a liquidity crisis and restore market confidence was made only once—by Hans Luther—at the height of the flight from the reichsmark in July 1931 but in such unpropitious circumstances that it was brushed aside as completely impractical.[36]

---

[35] *See Chapters 7 and 8;* Report of the Committee on the Currency and Bank of England Note Issues *(London: H. M. Stationery Office, February 1925), cited in Chapter 5.*

[36] Infra, *page 194.*

44

4. The Bankers' Role in the Stabilization of the German Mark: 1924

INTRODUCTION

The great international effort to stabilize the German currency surmounted many of the problems of the early 1920's reviewed in the preceding chapters. International political conflicts and financial rivalries were muted. The work that had previously been done both by the central bankers and by the League of Nations on the formulation of the conditions for currency stabilization bore fruit. Although the stabilization was heavily influenced by orthodox gold standard conceptions, the bankers' pragmatism also found expression in the adoption of management techniques that afforded a degree of protection to the German currency against external pressures.

Judged by its immediate outcome the stabilization was undoubtedly a great success. It marked the turning point of Europe from the political and economic upheavals of the early postwar years toward the short-lived normalcy of the later 1920's. It set the stage for the return to gold by Britain and several other countries and for the great outflow of United States capital that was to play such a crucial role in the developments of the next four years.

These achievements grew out of earlier disillusionments. By 1924 it was clear that the recovery of Europe was inseparable from that of Germany[1] and that a reparation settlement was a prerequisite for the reestablishment of international monetary order. Bitter experience had shown that attempts to collect reparations —regardless of the impact on the mark—led to extreme instability in the foreign exchange markets for the major Allied currencies.[2] As the mark depreciated, Germany's economic difficulties rubbed off on its major creditors and particularly on France, whose budgetary and reconstruction plans were based to a significant extent on the collection of reparations. Eventually, economic breakdown in Germany led to default on reparations and to the occupation of the Ruhr by French and Belgian troops. Germans retaliated with passive resistance,

---

[1] See, for example, the address of Charles E. Hughes before the annual meeting of the American Historical Association at New Haven, Connecticut, December 29, 1922. The relevant parts of the address are reprinted in H. G. Moulton and Leo Pasvolsky, World War Debt Settlements (Washington, D. C.: The Brookings Institution, 1929), pages 168-74.

[2] W. A. Brown, Jr., England and the New Gold Standard, 1919-1926 (New Haven: Yale University Press, 1929), page 119.

and the resulting stalemate led to further depreciation not only in the mark but also in the French and Belgian currencies. With the collapse of the mark in 1923 and the strangulation of the German economy, it became unmistakably clear that a dead end had been reached.

The incentive for Germany to cooperate in a stabilization program was certainly as strong as that of her former enemies. Such a program raised hopes that the Allied occupation could be terminated, that Germany's currency, precariously stabilized since the introduction of the rentenmark in the autumn of 1923, could be given a firmer foundation, that foreign exchange would become available to finance a revival in German foreign trade, and that this revival would in turn facilitate a recovery of the domestic economy.

The potential for recovery was at hand. To protect their financial assets against inflation, German industrialists had used their resources to modernize and expand plant and equipment.[3] The labor force was highly skilled. Germans held large foreign assets that could be mobilized if confidence in Germany's currency and in its economic and political future could be restored.[4] On the other hand, the inflationary process had destroyed the domestic financial assets of many families and had reduced the Reichsbank's holdings of gold to a mere $111 million, of which all but $48 million was pledged against credits from abroad.[5]

Thus, a catalyst was required that would release the existing potential of the German economy and attract foreign financial support. Conflicts over reparations had to be settled or at least suspended; Germany's territorial integrity had to be restored; and reparations could be extracted only to an extent compatible both with German economic recovery and with the stability of the German currency on the foreign exchange markets.

In the attainment of these conditions, central and commercial bankers from both sides of the Atlantic played a vital role about which little is to be found in the literature on the 1920's. History has of course recorded that prominent bankers served on the two Experts' Committees that were appointed in Novem-

[3] *Committees of Experts, Report to the Reparation Commission, reprinted in* Federal Reserve Bulletin, *May 1924, page 356 (hereafter referred to as* Experts' Report); *Carl Bergmann,* The History of Reparations *(Boston: Houghton Mifflin Company, 1927), page 255.*

[4] Experts' Report, *pages 371-72; Bergmann, op. cit., page 255.*

[5] *Hjalmar Schacht, testimony before a subcommittee of the Experts' Committees, January 19, 1924, page 8 (Young Papers).*

46

ber 1923 by the Reparation Commission. Charles G. Dawes, the American financier, who was soon to become Vice President of the United States, served as chairman of one of these committees while Reginald McKenna, formerly British Chancellor of the Exchequer and head of one of London's large clearing banks, chaired the other. Among other notable members were Owen D. Young and Sir Robert Kindersley, directors respectively of the Federal Reserve Bank of New York and of the Bank of England. Much has also been written about the conference of July 16-August 16, 1924, at which the major European governments, using the *Experts' Report* as a basis, negotiated the London protocol which laid the foundation for the stabilization.[6] But while this much is well known to historians, little has been published on the private discussions that lay behind the Dawes Plan, as the report of the Experts' Committees came to be known, or on the influential part that the bankers played during the London Conference and the frantic negotiations that preceded the flotation of the Dawes Loan.

Throughout this effort, central and commercial bankers cooperated closely. Although neither Schacht, who had been appointed President of the Reichsbank in December 1923, nor Norman were members of the Experts' Committees, both were at the center of the stabilization effort. American commercial bankers came on the stage largely because the Federal Reserve, like the Bank of France, played no major role. The French authorities of course were desperately preoccupied with their own financial difficulties and in any event were unsympathetic with Germany. The Federal Reserve's attitude reflected the ambivalent position of the United States Government. The doctrine that there was no connection between Germany's reparation obligation to the European Allies and the Allied war debt to the United States kept the Washington administration officially aloof, although—as we shall see— Secretary of State Hughes maintained a strong, informal interest in the stabilization effort.[7]

The vacuum left by the United States authorities was filled by J. P. Morgan & Co. This firm of investment bankers had vigorous and informed leadership,

---

[6] *Bergmann,* op. cit., *pages 260-65; J. W. Angell,* The Recovery of Germany *(New Haven: Yale University Press, 1929), page 62.*

[7] *Address by the Secretary of State before the annual meeting of the American Historical Association at New Haven, Connecticut, December 29, 1922. cited above. See also Bergmann,* op. cit., *page 191, and F. L. Benns,* Europe Since 1914 *(5th ed.; New York: F. S. Crofts & Co., 1944), page 244.*

was the fiscal agent in the United States of the British and French governments, and had close working relations with the banking houses of Morgan Grenfell in London and Morgan, Harjes in Paris. J. P. Morgan was on almost as close terms with Norman as Strong himself. For several years before the Dawes Loan was floated, Morgan had, together with Norman, been considering the possibility of an international loan to deal with the reparation problem.[8] When the question of securing American capital to support German stabilization arose in 1924, it was therefore natural for Morgan's to play a major role. In these negotiations the firm was represented by one of its partners, Thomas W. Lamont, who was in Europe almost continuously from January 1924, when the work of the Experts began, until the Dawes Loan was floated in mid-October. Indeed, Lamont, together with Owen D. Young, played the role that Strong might have played had his government's policy permitted him actively to participate.

COOPERATIVE ASPECTS

The provisions of the Dawes Plan in which the bankers were particularly interested were those relating to the annual amounts of reparation payments, the transfer of these payments across the exchanges, and of course the international loan.

The thorny question of Germany's total reparation obligation, on which earlier negotiations between Germany and the European Allies had broken down, was sidestepped. The Experts' Committees recommended an interim arrangement under which the annual payment would be geared to the changing strength of the German economy. Accordingly, the Committees established a rising scale of payments for the first five years of the plan and provided that payments thereafter should be determined by a "prosperity index" whose details they specified. Under this system, as the *Experts' Report* stated:[9]

> Germany will retain her incentive to develop, as she retains the major part of the advantage of any increase in prosperity, while the Allies obtain a reasonable share in this increase and avoid the risk of losing through a premature estimate of future capacity.

---

[8] *Bergmann, op. cit., pages 125, 135, and 137.*

[9] Experts' Report, *page 359.*

48

The Experts' second crucial recommendation was that reparations should be made in German currency to the Agent General for Reparation Payments who was to represent the Reparation Commission in Germany. Once such payments had been made, Germany's obligation to the Allies was fulfilled. Here the Experts introduced a significant degree of currency management into their proposals. For it was the responsibility of the Agent General, acting under the direction of a Transfer Committee, to determine how these funds were to be employed: to pay for reparation deliveries in kind, to meet Allied expenditures in Germany, or to be transferred across the exchanges. But in all cases this power was to be exercised only to the extent permitted by the exchange markets "without threatening the stability of the German currency".[10] Commenting on this provision, the *Experts' Report* said:[11]

> We are convinced that some kind of coordinated policy, *with continuous expert administration in regard to the exchange,* lies at the root of the reparation problem and is essential to any practicable scheme in obtaining the maximum sums from Germany for the benefit of the Allies.

Having safeguarded the stability of the German currency against excess pressure from reparations, the Experts also proposed that the currency be supported through the flotation by the German government of a foreign loan of 800 million gold marks ($191 million), equivalent to 8 per cent of Germany's imports in 1924. In the Experts' view, the loan would serve a variety of needs. It would facilitate the stabilization of the currency by financing the bulk of reparation deliveries during the preliminary stages of Germany's recovery and thus help to balance the government's budget and reduce government borrowing from the banking system. It was also regarded as essential to the successful establishment of the reformed Reichsbank. In particular, the loan would reconstitute the central bank's depleted gold reserve and would provide the basis on which the bank could at least partially satisfy the German economy's tremendous credit needs. It would thus serve as a catalyst that would facilitate the revival of the German economy and in so doing would help Germany, in the longer run, to meet its reparation obligation out of its own expanding resources.[12]

---

[10] Ibid., *page 404.*

[11] Ibid., *page 367. Italics added.*

[12] Ibid., *page 368.*

POLITICAL AND ECONOMIC CONDITIONS FOR THE DAWES LOAN. The bankers played a prominent part in formulating the political and economic conditions for the Dawes Loan, both while the Experts' plan was being drawn up and later during and following the London Conference.

Our information on the early stages of the negotiations comes primarily from the papers of Owen D. Young whose voluminous cable correspondence with members of the New York banking community during March and early April 1924 foreshadowed virtually all the principal features of the loan that was floated the following October. There was agreement that the loan should be a long-term one and that service of the loan should have a claim on Germany's resources prior both to reparations and to the service of any subsequent foreign loans to Germany. It was expected that half of the loan would be taken in New York, half in Europe, and of the latter part three quarters would be underwritten in London. Since seven eighths of the whole operation was to be done between New York and London, special emphasis was placed on the need for close Anglo-American cooperation. On the broader political and economic issues, Young was advised that American support for the proposed loan could be obtained only if the Experts' recommendations had the "hearty" approval of Germany, France, and England. The New York bankers did not object to the continued occupation of the Ruhr *per se,* but pointed out that, if the occupation led to German passive resistance or to a lukewarm British attitude toward the Experts' plan, the sale of the bonds in the United States "would be most seriously affected . . . if not made entirely impossible".[13] Perhaps most significant was an unsigned cable Young received, quite possibly from Morgan's, which emphasized that the flotation of the loan depended heavily on the adoption of a plan that would insure the stability of the German currency and which employed arguments and language especially designed to influence the French:[14]

> it goes almost without saying that the ability of the American market to absorb say $100,000,000 of the loan to the German Government would depend in part upon the bankers' ability to convince the American market that reparations [*sic*] payments in cash or in kind were not to be exacted from Germany in excess

---

[13] *Gerard Swope to Young, February 29, 1924. See also message transmitted to Young by Swope on March 29, 1924; Swope to Young, March 22, 1924; and unsigned messages March 25 and 26, 1924 (Young Papers).*

[14] *Unsigned message of April 2, 1924 to Owen D. Young (Young Papers).*

of her ability to meet them. (Stop) It would of course be a mistake for any members of the Experts Committee to infer that since the proposed currency loan was to constitute a first lien on Germany's assets and revenues (having priority to all reparations payments) our markets would not therefore be concerned with this question of the time when and the amount in which reparations payments were to be required. (Stop) That is not the case. (Stop) Our markets will need to be assured not only that the loan is a first lien on Germany's assets and revenues, but also that it is the obligation of a solvent Government and a solvent country. (Stop) The Experts who have studied cause and effect as they have operated for the last five years undoubtedly realize even better than we that if reparations payments in cash or in kind are to be exacted sooner or in amounts greater than Germany's international balance of trade and payments permits, then renewed depreciation of Germany's currency is bound to take place and the market position of bonds issued to provide Germany with a sound currency is bound to become impaired . . . .

There is no one here who would not like to see the German Reparations payments made just as large and just as soon as possible and no one who does not realize the great importance to France that this should be so. (Stop) Our sympathies are all for making Germany pay to the last drop. (Stop) Even friendly judgment however is rather against killing the goose which should someday lay the golden egg for France. (Stop) The immediate point however is that no operation of the kind now contemplated appears to us to be feasible at all unless France has come to the conclusion that the time has come when her interest will be best served by aiding Germany establish a sound currency, something which seems to us to be impossible until France is willing to defer her claim for reparations, not only in lien, but also in time and amount so far as may be necessary to insure preservation of a sound currency system in Germany.

The spirit of this message harmonized almost completely with that of the *Experts' Report,* and from the date of the report's publication on April 9 until the Dawes Loan was floated six months later, Morgan's worked in close collaboration with Young and Norman to persuade the Allied governments, particularly that of France, to bring their policies toward Germany into conformity.

Hope for success rose and fell like the tide. Within a few days of its publication the *Experts' Report* had been approved by the Reparation Commission and by the governments of Belgium, Britain, and Italy. In France, however, the government of Raymond Poincaré reserved its position. Then toward the middle of May, Poincaré was defeated in the Chamber of Deputies on another issue and was replaced by Edouard Herriot, whose government announced its approval of the report early in June and joined with the British government to call a conference to meet in London on July 16. But before the conference could convene a minor crisis blew up that made it clear that even the conciliatory Herriot government would be most reluctant to modify France's right to take independent action in case Germany was found to be in default on reparations, or to give any body other than the Reparation Commission the authority to decide whether such a default had in fact taken place.[15]

Opposing the French position on both points, the British government sought the views of the bankers. On July 12, Thomas W. Lamont wrote Prime Minister MacDonald a letter that was expected to strengthen Britain's hand in the forthcoming negotiations and whose purport was made known to the French delegation before the conference assembled.[16] Alluding to the first point at issue, Lamont stressed that the only basis on which the proposed loan could be successfully floated in the United States would be that it have a first claim on all Germany's resources. If this "fundamental condition" were to be qualified by an agreement authorizing the Allied governments to take any action that would weaken this prior claim or render service of the loan doubtful, then, he wrote, "I am confident that American investors would reject the Loan". On the second point at issue Lamont was equally categorical:[17]

> I may say that in our opinion no Loan issued under the Dawes plan, one of the conditions of which shall be that the Reparations [sic] Commission shall have power to declare default on the part of Germany will be acceptable to the American markets. It is not necessary to consider whether the attitude of the American public towards the operations of the Reparations Commission is or is not justified: the fact remains that, if the power to declare default is given over to the Commission, America will not in our belief subscribe to the Loan.

A preferred procedure, Lamont suggested, would be to vest the sole power to declare a default in the Transfer Committee, whose advantages from Lamont's viewpoint were that it was expected to be independent of the Reparation Commission and to be composed of bankers and foreign exchange experts in whose appointment Morgan's expected to have a say.

After the conference began, the bankers raised additional questions. During one long meeting that Lamont and Norman had with MacDonald,[18] the Prime Minister was told that New York not only was unsatisfied on the questions of default and independent action but wished, in addition, to have information re-

---

[15] *Sir Henry Clay, Lord Norman (London: Macmillan & Co., Ltd., 1957), page 212;* The Economist, *July 12, 1924, pages 43-44.*

[16] *Lamont cable to MacDonald, July 25, 1924 (Lamont Papers).*

[17] *Lamont letter to MacDonald, July 12, 1924, pages 1-2 (Lamont Papers).*

[18] *Memorandum of August 5, 1924 (Lamont Papers). This memorandum is unsigned but was clearly written by Norman.*

garding (a) the withdrawal of French and Belgian railwaymen from the German railways, (b) the military evacuation of the Ruhr, (c) the future means of interpreting the Versailles Treaty, (d) the date for the eventual evacuation of the Rhineland, and (e) the role, in the period before evacuation, of the Rhineland Commission which had been established under the Versailles Treaty to represent the authority of the Allies in the occupied territory. MacDonald for his part replied frankly that he saw little prospect of an early and satisfactory understanding with the French on any of these points. On the following day Norman gave a detailed report of this discussion to the Chancellor of the Exchequer, Philip Snowden, who indicated (according to Norman's report) that he was entirely in agreement with the bankers' attitude. Norman also noted that he was to inform Schacht that, in the circumstances, Morgan's was unwilling to open negotiations for the loan with any representative of Germany.[19]

Gradually the conference hammered out compromises on these difficult issues. The deciding of a default on reparations was left with the Reparation Commission, but a United States citizen would participate, and if any such decision were not unanimous, it could be taken to arbitration by any dissenting member of the Commission. Furthermore, the Allied governments agreed that, in case sanctions were imposed on Germany for a default, the servicing of the loan would be accorded priority over all other claims on the Germany economy.[20] But still no date was agreed upon for the military evacuation of Cologne and the Ruhr. On August 16 Norman wrote to Lamont that he had a long talk with Snowden, who "was a good deal distressed at the way things had shaped themselves". Snowden, Norman wrote,[21] had asked whether

> under the conclusions now contemplated, the money required by the Dawes Report would be forthcoming, but I could give him no definite answer whatever, nor did I pretend to do so. He said, too, that so much pressure had been brought to bear on the Germans in order to obtain their agreement that they were almost acting under compulsion and, indeed, they might represent that they had done so . . . .
>
> I also had a talk with the Prime Minister [MacDonald] and found that he had no definite ideas about the Loan and not much interest in it. He wanted a political

---

[19] *Memorandum of August 5, 1924 (Lamont Papers).*

[20] *Final protocol of the London Conference and Annex IV, Inter-Allied Agreement of August 30, 1924.*

[21] *Clay, op. cit., page 215.*

agreement without delay, however it might have to be reached. Too much, he said, had been heard of the Bankers' needs which continually antagonised the French and some of his own friends (the Socialists). He was sure that no one in his position could reach a better settlement than was being reached and even if not perfect or so good as had been hoped, it would produce a new spirit in Europe.

Thereafter Norman left London on a much needed holiday,[22] and discussions on the loan seem to have abated until mid-September. Then, on September 17, J. P. Morgan arrived in London. Preparing for his arrival, Lamont reviewed the position with Norman. The latter reported that Schacht, whom the German government had designated to conduct the loan negotiations, had already been in touch with the Continental bankers about their tranches of the loan, and had obtained indications that he might raise $10 million equivalent each in Holland and Switzerland and an additional $2 million equivalent in Italy. Another hopeful development was that the French Finance Minister, Clementel, had indicated that his government would inform the bankers of its unequivocal intention to complete the evacuation of the Ruhr within a year unless Germany willfully defaulted on reparations.[23] Nevertheless the bankers still hesitated. When J. P. Morgan and Lamont saw Norman on September 17, they told him that they had not yet decided on the principle of issuing the loan, let alone the details, and Norman himself told the Bank of England's Committee of Treasury that he (in conjunction with Morgan's) intended to conclude the negotiations with Germany only after a satisfactory statement had been made regarding the Ruhr and Cologne.[24]

Despite these hesitations, it seems clear that by this time Norman at least was convinced that the loan must be issued. Indeed, Norman is depicted as a strong advocate of the loan in a message that Lamont and Morgan sent to their New York office after the September 17 meeting. The New York bankers voiced

---

[22] Loc. cit.

[23] *T. W. Lamont cable to J. P. Morgan & Co., September 16, 1924 (Lamont Papers). In fact, the Allied military evacuation of the Ruhr was completed in 1925.*

[24] *Clay, op. cit., pages 215-16. The Committee of Treasury is a committee of the Bank of England's Court of Directors. In the 1920's it consisted of the Governor, Deputy Governor, and seven other members of the Court and acted as a special body with which the Governors could consult on all the more important business of the bank.*

doubts about political pressures in Germany but they reported that[25]

> Norman is quite certain (and he has seen Schacht quite a little) that apart from the Communists on one side and the Nationalists on the other, in Germany the great masses of the people want peace and are ready to make the necessary sacrifices to get . . . .

> Montagu Norman advances many other arguments; most of them may be summed up in the statement that he has honest belief that the Germans intend to meet this loan and the conditions of the Dawes Report honourably. Further that the Germans will want a great deal more money than the contemplated loan all of which will be subsequent [i.e., subordinate in lien] to that loan and to the total reparations payments. But our loan will be a first charge on everything the country has and the country is subjected to foreign control to an extent that has never yet been accomplished in dealing with any nation; in fact he believes there is no foreign loan at present in existence which offers as good security as this one.

> Montagu Norman was perfectly clear that in his opinion unless the loan is made Europe will break. If on the contrary it is made he believes that the results will be as favourable as those of similar operations for Austria and Hungary have turned out but on an even larger scale.

This message was included by Dwight Morrow, then a partner of J. P. Morgan & Co., in a letter of September 18 to Secretary of State Hughes. After telling the Secretary that the "German Loan proposed in the Dawes Plan now seems imminent", Morrow made a prescient comment:[26]

> What really impresses us favourably in Governor Norman's opinion is not the extent of the foreign control upon Germany but the disposition of the German people at the present time. We have some fear however that that disposition may not continue. However desirous Germany is of getting the loan at the moment in order to free the hold which France has upon the industries of the Ruhr it is almost inevitable that this loan will be unpopular in Germany after a few years. The people of Germany in our opinion are almost certain after sufficient time has elapsed to think not of the release of the Ruhr but of the extent to which what was once a first class power has been subject to foreign control.

> The opinion of Governor Norman that unless the loan is made Europe will break is also of great importance to us. Our main reason for going on with the business would be the heavy responsibility that would rest upon us if our failure to proceed caused a breakdown.

---

[25] *J. P. Morgan, New York, to Morgan Grenfell, London, September 22, 1924 (Lamont Papers), pages 2-3. The original of the message sent after the September 17 meeting has not been found. However, the message was repeated in the September 22 message from New York.*

[26] Ibid., *pages 4-5.*

Replying on September 19 to Morrow's request for his views, the Secretary of State went about as far as he could to support the loan, while at the same time he explicitly avoided any obligation to the bankers on the part of the Government. He saw no reason to question the correctness of Norman's views; indeed he supported them. The failure of the plan would, the Secretary felt, lead not only to "chaotic conditions abroad" but to "a feeling of deep despair". He emphasized that the United States Government could give no pledge or guarantee, either legal or moral, but he nevertheless expressed the hope that the "American financiers would see their way clear to undertake the participation [in the loan] which the world expects and which is believed to be essential to the success of the Plan".[27] In forwarding Hughes' reply to Morgan and Lamont in London, Morrow commented on September 22: "We think on the whole that this is as good as we can expect."

The substance of this exchange was apparently made known to Norman, who in the meantime had had further discussions with MacDonald. These developments Norman reported on September 24 to the Committee of Treasury, which decided that their remaining doubts and uncertainties should be suspended, that the Bank of England should proceed with the loan negotiations and, if necessary, commit itself to a considerable subscription on its own account.[28]

THE TRANSFER COMMITTEE AND THE AGENT GENERAL. Although much of the bankers' energy was directed toward establishing the general economic and political conditions that they felt were prerequisite to the success of the loan, they were also anxious that the administrative machinery established under the Experts' plan should be staffed with individuals in whom they had confidence. Particularly was this true of the Transfer Committee, which, as already noted, was to receive reparation payments from Germany and to transfer them to the Allies to the extent that the exchanges allowed. The committee was to consist of the Agent General for Reparation Payments, who was to be its chairman, and five additional persons, qualified to deal with foreign exchange problems— one each from Belgium, Britain, France, Italy, and the United States.[29] Appoint-

---

[27] Ibid., *pages 8-9.*

[28] *Clay,* op. cit., *page 216.*

[29] Experts' Report, *Annex No. 6, page 404.*

ments to the committee were to be made formally by the Reparation Commission and, at one remove, by the governments represented on the commission. As it turned out, the bankers were to play—and insisted on playing—a major role in choosing the committee members and particularly the Agent General. Even before the *Experts' Report* had reached the United States, Morgan's took the position that the members "should meet the commendation of the investment community and should be such as to insure autonomous and sound decisions and action in the interest of the preservation of the integrity of the new currency and such as to resist all political pressure from Germany or abroad".[30]

At an early stage, London bankers apparently had hopes that an Englishman would be appointed Agent General, but this hope faded as it became clear that the largest tranche of the loan would be raised in New York. Early in June, Strong wrote to James A. Logan, the United States unofficial representative on the Reparation Commission and an aspirant to the post of Agent General:[31]

> I learn that the English have probably accepted the notion that an American will be necessary in that position. On the other hand, I have heard the view expressed that it is the key to the success of the plan as well as the insurance of the security for the loan, and on that account there may be a desire among the bankers to have some internationally known and outstanding figure, especially some one very well known in this country, appointed to the job.

After difficult negotiations, the choice of candidates narrowed to two. MacDonald, Herriot, and Coolidge favored Young while Norman and Lamont put forward the name of S. Parker Gilbert, who had been Under Secretary of the United States Treasury in 1921-23, having been appointed to that post when he was twenty-eight years old, and who had recently become a member of a New York law firm. As it turned out, Young was reluctant to accept the post for personal and business reasons and was persuaded to become Agent General only *ad interim*. He served for the first two crucial months when the Dawes Plan was coming into operation, that is, until October 31, 1924, when Gilbert took over as Agent General on a permanent basis.[32]

---

[30] *J. P. Morgan & Co., New York, to Morgan, Harjes and Co., Paris, April 18, 1924, page 4 (Young Papers).*

[31] *Strong letter to Logan, June 10, 1924, pages 1-2.*

[32] *Reparation Commission,* The Execution of the Experts' Plan: Reports of the Agent General for Reparation Payments *(Berlin: The Office for Reparation Payments, September 1, 1924 to August 31, 1925), page 9 (hereafter referred to as* Reports of the Agent General).

THE GOLD DISCOUNT BANK. The negotiations to implement the *Experts' Report* were conducted to the accompaniment of a competitive byplay that reflected the fundamentally changed international economic positions of Britain and the United States, and more particularly New York's challenge to London's traditional role as the world's major financial center. It is not difficult to understand how this conflict arose. In the winter of 1923-24, the German currency had been stabilized only precariously and the outcome of the Experts' work was still most uncertain. Schacht was in urgent need of external help. For this it was natural that he should turn to London, the traditional financial center, from which many of the proposals for the reconstruction of Germany's finances had emanated since the end of the war. Schacht arrived in London on New Year's Eve in 1923, with proposals that appealed to Norman. His aim was to employ sterling to stimulate a revival of German foreign trade and of the German economy generally. He would do this through the establishment of a Gold Discount Bank whose capital would be subscribed in sterling by the Reichsbank and by German private interests, and which would be managed by the Reichsbank and would extend short-term sterling credits to finance German foreign trade.

Before he left London on January 3, 1924, Schacht had obtained Norman's full support. The Bank of England would extend a £5 million credit to the Reichsbank for two or three years. The proceeds of this loan, together with an additional £5 million in sterling that would be raised in the German market, would provide the bank's capital. Additional arrangements were made under which bills of exchange, endorsed by the Gold Discount Bank, could be discounted in the London market up to a total of £10 million, it being understood that such bills would be eligible for rediscount at the Bank of England. Beyond this, Schacht obtained Norman's support on another important front, i.e., in opposing a Franco-Belgian scheme to establish an independent central bank in the Rhineland.[33]

In their contemporary comments on the Gold Discount Bank proposal, both Norman and Schacht emphasized that Germany's economic difficulties required prompt attention and could not wait upon the outcome of the Experts' deliberations. Writing to Strong a few days after Schacht had left London, Norman

---

[33] *Norman to Strong, January 7, 1924, and attached memorandum; Hjalmar Schacht,* My First Seventy-Six Years *(London: Allan Wingate, 1955), pages 195-202; and Clay, op. cit., page 212.*

commented that the Gold Discount Bank proposal (about which he enclosed a detailed memorandum) probably represented the "last chance" of preventing a complete collapse and that, if the proposal bore fruit, "it would be a *grand thing from every point* of view if you could co-operate".[34] Strong was probably embarrassed by this invitation because he was unwilling to bypass the Experts. When he did reply, almost a month later, he avoided any commitment to cooperate.[35] Nevertheless, Norman was determined to go ahead with the proposal for the Note Bank as he then called it. He wrote gloomily about the Experts:[36]

I have been twice in Paris within the last couple of weeks and from my talks with Kindersley and others it is clear that there are as many different angles of vision as there are members on that Committee. As I wrote to you on the 7th January, our wish here is to enable Germany at once to stabilise her position; that is, to provide her at once with some sort of a currency which will take care of her foreign transactions and provide foreign valuta for her trade, thus taking the strain off the Reichsmark and the Rentenmark. If something of this kind is not done pretty soon, I am afraid the Rentenmark will start to depreciate. This we believe can be avoided by the setting up of a Note Bank and we are prepared to enable the Reichsbank to start such a Note Bank; so, in principle, is Vissering and one or two other Central Banks I expect. The Committee, on the other hand, have so far refused their blessing or moral support to a scheme of this nature which was put before them by the new President of the Reichsbank. Your people on the Committee I fancy wanted to keep the whole German position fluid until they have dealt with it comprehensively, and if it worsens between now and then, that perhaps won't prevent their dealing with it. The Belgians have a plan of their own by which they want to combine the functions of a Note Bank and of a Caisse de la Dette, and nothing but that will please them. The French are entirely unwilling that any Note Bank should be started which would tend to mobilize the remaining liquid assets of Germany outside of Germany and therefore beyond the reach of the Reparation Commission and yet would make them available for German Trade. So there is a very confused "kettle of fish" and when the Committee come to leave Berlin— about the time this letter should reach you—I think we may have to go ahead with the Reichsbank in spite of the Committee, if we cannot obtain their goodwill, to the immediate establishment of a Note Bank.

Indeed it was only with some difficulty that Schacht persuaded the Experts not to block his proposal. Understandably, the Experts were concerned lest Schacht's scheme prejudice their own as yet unformulated proposals. At the same time, however, they wished to avoid responsibility for putting a new strain

---

[34] *Norman letter to Strong, January 7, 1924, page 2.*

[35] *Strong cable to Norman, No. 2, February 5, 1924.*

[36] *Norman letter to Strong, January 30, 1924, pages 3-5.*

on the German currency by killing the Gold Discount Bank plan.[37] Hence, they resolved their dilemma temporarily by issuing on January 23 a qualified public endorsement of Schacht's proposal, but in private they continued to haggle. Finally, Schacht publicized the difficulties in a speech in Koenigsberg on February 8. The Experts, he said, had generally approved his scheme, but they had admonished him that[38]

> it would not suffice to create a gold-bank which would answer to present circumstances, but that a definite gold-currency should be created in Germany. I replied to these gentlemen as follows: in principle I agree with you in recognising that we should create this gold-currency in Germany. I should gladly hear that you were willing to help us to achieve this result. I am also willing to believe that in the course of the next few weeks, you will come to a unanimous agreement on this point in the report you will submit to the Reparation Commission. But it remains to be seen what results will be obtained from your report. According to our experience up to the present with regard to nearly all the reparation negotiations, I am authorised to believe that not only weeks, but months will elapse before your report will result in a unanimous decision being adopted by the Allied and Associated Governments. We cannot afford to wait so long.**** I hope they (the Experts) will be reasonable enough not to thwart our efforts to create a gold-note bank, which will provide us with an instrument making it possible for us to recover and to work.

Thereafter, a compromise was reached under which the Gold Discount Bank was established subject to the condition that, if the Experts' proposals were implemented, the new institution would be absorbed by the Reichsbank.[39] In fact, the Gold Discount Bank did become a fully owned subsidiary of the German central bank in 1925 and, as such, continued throughout the interwar years to carry on a variety of functions in connection with German foreign exchange operations.

THE REICHSBANK'S INTERNATIONAL RESERVES. With the settlement of the problem of the Gold Discount Bank, the basic question of how the reformed Reichsbank should be required to hold its international reserves came to the fore. Here

---

[37] *Hjalmar Schacht,* The Stabilization of the Mark *(London: George Allen & Unwin, Ltd., 1927), translated by Ralph Butler, page 142.*

[38] *Leon Fraser's memorandum on the origin of the Gold Discount Bank, April 22, 1927, pages 3-4.*

[39] Ibid., *page 4. See also letter of July 7, 1924, to the Organization Committee for the Bank (Kindersley and Schacht), in which the Reichsbank-Direktorium (Schacht and Bocke) stated their intention not only to acquire all the shares of the Gold Discount Bank by exchanging them against new Reichsbank shares but also "to liquidate all transactions of the Gold-Discount Bank".*

strict logic—if not the economic realities—favored the Americans. Virtually everyone in authority in both Europe and the United States upheld the theoretical merits of the gold standard and agreed at least in principle that its rules should be applied to the German central bank. The implications were clear. The reformed Reichsbank's international reserves should be held either in gold or in balances that were freely convertible into gold at a fixed price. Since the United States was at the time the only major country where balances were thus convertible, Germany would be required to keep in New York any foreign exchange reserves that it might choose to hold. This logic implied in particular that, insofar as the Dawes Loan was raised outside the United States, its proceeds would have to be converted into either gold or dollars.

The logic of gold standard principles combined sometimes with self-interest to give various influential Americans a rather doctrinaire attitude about how the Reichsbank's international reserves should be composed. The Americans on the Experts' Committees, and those like Professor Edwin Kemmerer who were attached to the Committees' staff, took the view that the establishment of the reformed Reichsbank on a strict gold basis was essential for the maintenance of Germany's monetary stability and would exert powerful leverage on other European countries to return to gold.[40] Others looked at the question from a more frankly business viewpoint. Equating dollars with gold, they wanted Germany to hold at least part of the foreign exchange component of its international reserves in New York. Thus Paul M. Warburg, President of the International Acceptance Bank, sent Young a cable that applied both to the Gold Discount Bank (of which Warburg seemed primarily to have been thinking) but also to the Reichsbank:[41]

> I understand Dr. Schacht is in Paris. Is it not advisable to point out to him importance of resting his credit bank on stable gold instead of fluctuating sterling? Incidentally, it would be invaluable advantage for American discount market if as a result of America's entering the field now substantial portion future German gold reserve were invested in dollar acceptances. England realizes that and makes sacrifice to preserve predominance sterling market. Could not America be brought

---

[40] *E. W. Kemmerer* et al., *memorandum, "On the Necessity of a Gold Basis for Germany's Currency", March 19, 1924 (Young Papers). See also R. C. Dawes,* The Dawes Plan in the Making *(Indianapolis: Bobbs Merrill, 1925), page 262.*

[41] *Warburg cable to Young, March 14, 1924 (Young Papers).*

into the first line right now pari-passu with British banks. Pardon this cable but I am frankly alarmed at the thought that we may miss this unique opportunity for putting America's discount market on the map and complete our position as world bankers.

Among the Europeans, whose currencies were still a long way from the desired return to gold, there was vigorous opposition to views such as those of Kemmerer and Warburg. To some extent the opposition stemmed from considerations of national prestige: the French authorities in particular were far from enthusiastic about any proposal that the United States and the Allies should help Germany return to gold while the franc continued to fluctuate on a depreciated basis.[42]

No doubt such prestige considerations were influential also in the British opposition but, in London, international banking needs and aspirations played a preponderant role. Despite its difficulties, sterling remained, as Norman reminded Strong, "very much the exchange of Europe".[43] Of the capital that had fled Germany during the inflation, the bulk was probably held in sterling. London played a major role in the Austrian and Hungarian stabilizations and in establishing the Gold Discount Bank, and it was expected that sterling would play almost as large a role in the Dawes Loan as the dollar. In the City of London, and particularly in the Bank of England, any proposal that would oblige Germany to transfer a significant part of its London balances to New York was quite unacceptable. Such transfers would not only reduce the City's banking business; far more important, they would push the sterling-dollar rate still farther away from the $4.867 parity. Britain's international financial aims thus required—as a minimum—that nothing should be contained in the statutes of the reformed Reichsbank that would prevent Germany from holding part of its international reserves in London, even in the period prior to sterling's return to gold. A more ambitious aim would have been to draw the bank's statutes so that the new German currency could be based entirely on sterling; there is strong evidence that this was the aim that Norman actually sought to achieve.[44]

---

[42] *Hamlin Diary, account of talk with Professor Kemmerer, June 9, 1924; S. M. Crocker, interview with Kemmerer, May 9, 1925, pages 4 and 12 (Young Papers); and Dawes, op. cit., page 262.*

[43] *Norman letter to Strong, January 30, 1924.*

[44] *In his letter to Strong of June 16, 1924, Norman expressed his feeling, with reference to the German stabilization, that the European currencies were "better stabilised on Sterling than on Gold . . . ." See also the excerpt from this letter quoted below, pages 65-66, and Hamlin Diary, June 9, 1924.*

Schacht's views on this issue are unclear. It is true that Schacht, like his central banker colleagues, professed devotion to gold standard principles, but he also held that Germany could not be expected to apply these principles while convalescing from inflation and while other major European countries still did not apply them.[45] As to how he believed the Reichsbank should hold its reserves in the interim, the evidence is contradictory and he may indeed have been quite opportunistic, taking full advantage of the divergence of opinion between the European and American experts. Young believed in mid-March 1924 that Schacht wanted a dollar basis.[46] In contrast, Kemmerer told Governor Hamlin early in June that Schacht strongly favored sterling.[47] The truth seems to have been someplace between these two extremes, and this view is supported by Schacht's statement at the end of May in a letter to Paul Warburg that "it is our desire not to base ourselves entirely on the Pound Sterling".[48]

The *Experts' Report* reflected these conflicting pressures. In its main body, it clung to the principle that the Reichsbank note issue should be convertible into gold but averred that conditions were not yet such that this principle could be put into practice.[49] Hence it recommended only that the Reichsbank's reserve, which was to be equal to at least one third of its note liabilities and to 12 per cent of its deposit liabilities, "be held largely in the form of deposits in foreign banks".[50] However, the report's annex on the organization of the bank reflected the more orthodox views of the American members of the committees. It recommended that the reserves[51]

> be kept in gold bars or gold coin at any office of the bank, and or in the form of demand deposits made payable in gold or its equivalent at the rates at which the deposits were made in banks of high standing located in foreign financial centers.

Plainly the Experts had left the issue unresolved. In effect, they passed the

---

[45] *Hjalmar Schacht, The Stabilization of the Mark, pages 175-76.*

[46] *Young cable to Warburg, March 14, 1924 (Young Papers).*

[47] *Hamlin Diary, June 9, 1924.*

[48] *Schacht to Warburg, May 31, 1924, page 3.*

[49] Experts' Report, *page 357.*

[50] Loc. cit.

[51] Ibid., *page 386.*

question along to Schacht and Kindersley, to whom had been assigned the task of drafting the central bank's statutes. And so the debate continued. Five weeks after the *Experts' Report* was published, the Federal Advisory Council (FAC) of the Federal Reserve System, of which Paul Warburg was chairman at the time, issued a statement that could not fail to raise hackles in the City of London. After discussing various other aspects of the *Experts' Report,* the FAC launched, somewhat sententiously, into the question of whether the German currency would be best stabilized on sterling or dollars: [52]

> It is the question of whether the world is more likely to regain the blessings of economic stability under the sway of several fluctuating standards of exchange or by a general return, as speedy as circumstances may permit, to definite relations of exchanges to gold as the ultimate measure and regulator.
>
> The Dawes Report leads the world to the crossroads in this regard. It provides for a German note-issuing bank on a gold basis, but leaves the door open to place it on a sterling basis, and it cannot be denied that there is no small probability of the latter basis being chosen. In the opinion of the council the sooner Germany can be placed on a gold or gold exchange basis, the sooner can England, and other countries also, return to an unrestricted gold standard, while if Germany were placed on a sterling basis, England—in returning to an unrestricted gold basis—would have to pull not only her own weight, but that of Germany also. It is obvious, therefore, that, if the new German bank is placed on the sterling-exchange basis, the world must prepare itself to remain on a basis of exchange instability for a prolonged period, the end of which can not be foreseen, while the adoption of the gold (that is, the dollar) basis would accelerate the return to world-wide stability.

The FAC's pronouncement gave rise to an exchange in which Strong and Norman set forth their contrasting positions on this issue. Strong seems to have been somewhat embarrassed; he wrote Norman on June 3 that, on returning from his European trip, [53]

> One of the first things I encountered was the report of the Federal Advisory Council on the Dawes plan, in which were interjected certain remarks in regard to dollars and sterling! It sometimes strikes me that we are unduly burdened with people in this world who believe that human ingenuity and efforts of imagination can perform miracles.

---

[52] *Federal Reserve Board,* Eleventh Annual Report, 1924 *(Washington, D. C.: Government Printing Office, 1925), page 281.*

[53] *Strong letter to Norman, June 3, 1924.*

On the substance of the question Strong took a balanced view. He recognized that, even though sterling was still detached from gold, London had sound claims as an international financial center because of the "better organization" of its money market and also because of its "better knowledge of German conditions". It was therefore natural that Germany should turn to London to satisfy part of its credit requirements; certainly "no discrimination should be directed against the London market" in the plans to raise the Dawes Loan. On the other hand, Strong felt that, if Germany was to have a gold-valued currency, it was to Germany's advantage "to obtain all possible credits" in New York because "it is the gold market". Heavy German reliance on New York would also be to Britain's advantage[54]

> because the credit burden on the London market is one of the present difficulties in the way of a return of sterling to par. Our interests in this subject are mutual and interdependent and should not be the subject of any controversy or dispute.

Strong made a third point that was only partly valid. He argued that it was to Germany's advantage "to borrow in the market where the currency is not at a discount with gold so as to escape the loss which might arise through the enhancement of the value of sterling vis-à-vis a German currency at par with gold".[55] However, Strong's point would have been valid only if the Reichsbank expected to spend the London tranche of the Dawes Loan (e.g., to acquire gold or dollars) at a time when sterling was still at a discount from its gold parity and was then obliged to service the London tranche in terms of sterling that was at par with gold.

Norman saw another possibility. Germany could *hold* the sterling portion of the loan in the expectation that the British currency would soon rise to par. He illustrated his point by referring to the Hungarian stabilization which was then being carried out largely on the basis of borrowing in London:[56]

> Is it necessary under those conditions that Hungary should start off with a Gold currency? If so she must transfer the proceeds of her foreign loan to New York in order to avoid the risk of exchange. Is she not justified in basing her currency

---

[54] *Strong letter to Norman, July 9, 1924, page 12.*

[55] Ibid., *page 1.*

[56] *Norman letter to Strong, June 16, 1924, pages 2-3.*

on Sterling and hoping, as I confidently do, that over a few months or years Sterling will attain parity with Gold and her currency at the same time will become a Gold valued currency?

But even while Strong and Norman were debating, the question of the composition of the Reichsbank's reserves was being settled by Kindersley and Schacht. Their draft of the bank's statutes made significant departures from, and tightened up, the rather loose recommendations of the *Experts' Report* and, despite Norman's efforts to the contrary, did so in a manner more favorable to the American view than to the British. The proposal to require 12 per cent cover for the Reichsbank's deposit liabilities was dropped because such liabilities (which would include deposits held for the account of the Agent General for Reparation Payments) were expected to show large fluctuations.[57] Instead, the required cover against the bank's note liabilities was raised to 40 per cent from the recommended 33⅓ per cent. In addition, no more than one quarter of this cover could be held in foreign exchange while no less than three fourths was required to be held in gold.[58]

These provisions, which were incorporated unchanged into the bank's statute as it was adopted on August 30, 1924, were clearly disappointing from Norman's point of view, but there is no record that he continued to struggle for a sterling basis after mid-June. A variety of considerations may have led him into acquiescence. He may have been concerned lest insistence on his view jeopardize the success of the Dawes Loan in the United States, where sentiment was so strongly in favor of a gold basis. Beyond this, he had two sound reasons for expecting that the Reichsbank would hold its outstanding and accruing sterling balances at least in the near term. To do so was clearly in Germany's interest, provided Schacht could assume that Britain was determined to bring the sterling-dollar rate—which averaged $4.32 in June 1924—back up to the $4.867 parity as soon as possible. In fact, it is clear that Germany's imminent stabilization had put Norman under great pressure to commit himself to an early "return", and it is not inconceivable that he had indicated as much to Schacht. Secondly, it was equally clear that Schacht would feel no immediate need to employ his sterling

---

[57] *Kemmerer told Crocker on May 9, 1925 that the recommended 12 per cent ratio was too low; he had wanted it set at 40 per cent (Young Papers).*

[58] *Kindersley and Schacht, memorandum to the Reparation Commission, July 11, 1924, and Draft Bank Law of July 28, 1924, page 11.*

balances to acquire gold. With half of the Dawes Loan scheduled to be floated in New York, the Reichsbank, initially at least, would be in a position to buy any gold that it might require for note cover in the United States where authorities would welcome a reduction in what they considered to be their excessive holdings of the metal.

FINAL NEGOTIATIONS FOR THE DAWES LOAN

During the week beginning Monday, September 22, 1924, as has already been seen, Norman and J. P. Morgan reached the decision to begin negotiations for the German loan. They talked first with Schacht, who came to London, and then with commercial bankers from other European countries in which tranches of the loan were to be placed, and also with Dr. Luther, the German Finance Minister.[59] By all accounts these negotiations, in which Young also played a major part, proceeded smoothly. According to Lamont, they were "neither prolonged nor difficult"; both Schacht and Luther were "quite evidently prepared to accept any fair terms which the investment markets deem necessary".[60] Of his part in the negotiations, Schacht wrote in 1927 that he had made "no attempt to haggle", that he had emphasized the desirability of making the loan "a big success", and that he considered terms offered to be in line with the prevailing market conditions.[61]

While negotiations with Schacht and Luther gave little trouble, the raising of the European tranches was difficult. A relatively minor problem was that most of the Continental bankers preferred to have their tranches issued in sterling; to this the British authorities were agreeable, subject to the understanding that for two years such sterling bonds would be offered on the British market only with the consent of the Bank of England.[62] The main problem, of course, was that there was much public opposition to lending money to Germany. In one of his letters Lamont noted the steady campaign against the loan in several British newspapers, and commented that British coal miners had protested to the Prime

---

[59] *Jay letter to Crissinger, October 17, 1924, page 4.*

[60] *Lamont draft of letter to Clementel, October 6, 1924, pages 1-2 (Lamont Papers).*

[61] *Hjalmar Schacht,* The Stabilization of the Mark, *page 185.*

[62] *Lamont letter to Herman Harjes, September 24, 1924 (Lamont Papers);* The Economist, *October 18, 1924, page 600.*

Minister against the entire Dawes Plan. On the Continent, Lamont reported, only in Sweden and Switzerland was the arranging of the loan going more or less smoothly. In Paris the bankers were especially balky. To overcome this resistance, Morgan's told the French Minister of Finance in firm but diplomatic terms that a $100 million long-term loan, which the French government had asked Morgan's to arrange in New York, would not be floated unless the French bankers cooperated.[63] Elsewhere, too, the flotation of the loan required strong leadership. In Britain, Norman summoned together representatives of the banks and issuing houses and allocated to each the amount necessary in order to underwrite the total London tranche. Similar procedures were apparently followed by the Belgian, Dutch, and Swiss authorities.[64]

The arranging of the loan became more hectic as time went on. J. P. Morgan and Lamont sent a telegram to their firm in New York that is illustrative:[65]

> For the last two weeks aside from the constant work of drafting, etc. our heaviest efforts have been directed towards getting the Continental shares into line (stop) If we had taken towards the Banking representatives or the Governments themselves a take it or leave it attitude we believe that we should have gotten nowhere and the whole operation would have broken down an outcome far worse to be sure for Europe than for us yet nevertheless at this stage not to be contemplated (stop) Each Continental share has had its own particular difficulties due to public sentiment against Germany as in the case of France and Belgium and exceeding difficult currency situations as applied to those two countries and Italy (stop) Holland has had its own financial trouble and heavy difficulties of personnel as well (stop) Switzerland has had a particular egg of her own to try to hatch out (stop) Sweden is literally the only country that we have not had to bleed and die for (stop) In France Italy and Belgium it has not as you suggest been a question of how much the Governments wanted them to take but rather how much the Governments could force the reluctant and short-sighted Bankers to take (stop) It has taken a long time to get the Governments in the right frame of mind (stop) At first Theunis [Prime Minister of Belgium] and then Herriot at last called the Bankers together and read the Riot Act to them (stop) The Governments having thus come up to the scratch and having forced their Bankers to do likewise it became of vital importance to seize this psychological moment and not to let it escape probably never to return (stop)

After three weeks of negotiations in London, Young returned to Paris with an agreement on the loan and with a set of stipulations that he was to present

---

[63] *Lamont draft of letter to Clementel, October 6, 1924, pages 4-5 (Lamont Papers).*

[64] Ibid., *page 3.*

[65] *Morgan and Lamont cable to J. P. Morgan & Co., New York, October 8, 1924 (Lamont Papers).*

to the Reparation Commission for adoption; these made it absolutely clear that the loan would be a first charge on Germany's resources, ahead of reparations and all other payments. Pierre Jay related[66] how on October 10 Young presented these stipulations:

> The Reparation Commission which, as I wrote you before, had not heretofore been very prompt, to say the least, in making its decisions has during the past month been called upon by Mr. Young to make promptly a large number of decisions on very important matters. The one they were called upon to make on the 10th without much previous opportunity for discussion, declaring for the absolute priority of the loan and dealing with a lot of other details, with the bankers at the other end of the telephone wire waiting to send cables that evening to the members of the underwriting syndicate in America was an especially large order . . . . Mr. Young's handling of the situation was masterful and the evening wound up with a complete decision on the part of the Commission, a telephone message to the London bankers, and their dispatches of the necessary cables to the underwriting syndicate.

Then one last hurdle had to be surmounted. The bankers required a resolution by the Transfer Committee to the effect that service of the loan would be given priority and absolute right of remittance irrespective of the effect on the German exchange rate. On October 13, Young contacted as many of the members of the committee as he could reach and obtained their informal approval.[67] In due course the committee, at its first meeting on October 31, formally adopted a resolution to this effect.[68]

With this final question settled, the loan was issued in New York on October 14 and in London and other European centers the following day (see table). It was underwritten at 87 in New York and 87½ in Europe. The issue price was 92, its maturity was twenty-five years, final redemption being scheduled for October 15, 1949 at par in European markets and at 105 in the United States. It carried a 7 per cent coupon, thus yielding approximately 7¾ per cent to maturity.[69] The loan was rapidly oversubscribed in New York, London, and most of the Continental markets and quickly rose to a premium in early trading.[70]

Much has already been written about the economic recovery of Germany after

---

[66] *Jay letter to Crissinger, October 17, 1924, page 4.*

[67] *Young cable to Crocker for Sterrett, October 13, 1924 (Young Papers).*

[68] Reports of the Agent General, *September 1, 1924 to August 31, 1925, page 10.*

[69] *Bergmann, op. cit., page 280;* an *"Official Statement"* dated October 10, 1924 (Lamont Papers).

[70] The Economist, *October 18, 1924, page 600, and October 25, 1924, page 638.*

THE DAWES LOAN

Market	Currency of tranche	Nominal amount of tranche* (in millions of specified currencies)	Net proceeds In millions of tranche currency*	In millions of gold marks †
United States........Dollars	Dollars	110.0	95.6	400.6
Britain..............Sterling	Sterling	12.0	10.3	192.9
Belgium.............Sterling	Sterling	1.5	1.3	24.4
Holland.............Sterling	Sterling	2.5	2.2	40.6
France..............Sterling	Sterling	3.0	2.6	48.2
Italy................Lire	Lire	100.0	86.3	15.7
Sweden.............Kronor	Kronor	25.2	21.8	24.3
Switzerland.........Sterling	Sterling	2.36	2.1	38.9
	Swiss francs	15.0	11.9	9.5
Germany............Sterling	Sterling	0.36	0.3	5.9
Total..............				801.0

---

* *The difference between the nominal amount of each tranche and the net proceeds reflects commission charges and the discount at which the bonds were issued.*

† *The exchange rate at which the net proceeds of the New York tranche were converted into reichsmarks was 4.1896 marks to the dollar, the noon buying rate for cable transfers in New York on October 14. Parity for the gold mark was 4.198 marks to the dollar. The sterling tranches were converted at 18.8138 marks to the pound. This rate reflects the 8 per cent discount from sterling's gold parity at which the British currency was being quoted in the London market at the time the loan was floated.*

Source: Reports of the Agent General, September 1, 1924 to August 31, 1925, page 11.

the flotation of the Dawes Loan,[71] and part of that story enters into the account that follows of central bank cooperation during the later 1920's. Here it suffices to add that the immediate outcome of the Dawes Plan realized, and perhaps even surpassed, the highest hopes of the bankers who negotiated the loan. Confidence in the economic future of Europe revived and political tensions eased. The despair of 1923 gave way in 1925 to hopes that a new era had begun.

---

[71] *See, for example, J. W. Angell, op. cit., Chapters III-IX; Hjalmar Schacht,* The Stabilization of the Mark *(London: George Allen & Unwin, Ltd., 1927), Chapters VII-IX; Horst Mendershausen,* Two Postwar Recoveries of the German Economy *(Amsterdam: North-Holland Publishing Company, 1955); and C. T. Schmidt,* German Business Cycles 1924-1933 *(New York: National Bureau of Economic Research, Inc., 1934).*

5. Britain's Return to Gold

INTRODUCTION

The stabilization of the German currency was followed in the spring of 1925 by the long awaited return of sterling to its prewar gold parity. The conditions were unique and compelling. The temporary reparation settlement had brought Europe a surge of renewed optimism. This, combined with the mild 1924 recession in the United States, led to a greatly enlarged outflow of American capital. The United States balance of payments, which had been in surplus during the three previous years, swung into deficit during the latter part of 1924, when the capital outflow was heaviest, and this helped to buoy the European exchanges. In these circumstances sterling might have climbed back to its prewar parity under its own power, but the climb was accelerated by the known desire of the authorities in Britain, the United States, and elsewhere for an early return to gold. Speculative balances that had fled Europe in the troubled years before the German stabilization now left New York and, encouraged by the prospect for sterling appreciation and by relatively high British interest rates, settled in London.

Strong and Norman showed a high order of statesmanship in grasping this favorable opportunity to achieve their international financial objectives. Their subsequent difficulties arose from a failure fully to understand that the return was only the beginning of their tasks and that the maintenance of sterling's link with gold would involve problems far more complicated than those encountered in bringing about the return. The complex reasons for this failure are discussed in other chapters[1] and need only be summarized here. Among them were (1) the illusion that once the major countries had stabilized their currencies in terms of gold, the functioning of the international economy would be regulated automatically, as was thought to have been the case under the nineteenth century gold standard; (2) the related faith that national economies were best regulated by the free play of market forces, a belief that discouraged the search for policy instruments to hasten the international adjustment process and to foster steady economic growth; (3) the priority accorded by the monetary authorities to national policy objectives, a priority that restricted the extent to which the

---

[1] *See especially Chapters 3 and 9.*

authorities put into practice the gold standard-free market principles they professed and that resulted in the shifting of most of the burden of international adjustment on to the economies of the deficit countries; (4) the primitive state of balance-of-payments statistics and analysis, which left the authorities and the public badly informed about major imbalances in the international economy, about the slow pace of adjustment, and about the extent to which such imbalances were being financed by short-term borrowing; and (5) the failure to develop international cooperative techniques to cope with severe financial strains between major countries; central bank cooperation remained merely a fair weather instrument. But these were lessons that became clear only after the tragic events of the twenties and thirties had run their course.

THE OBJECTIVES OF ANGLO-AMERICAN COOPERATION

In working together to restore sterling to its 1914 gold parity, Strong and Norman were fostering national objectives about which they were quite clear. In Strong's view, the stabilization of sterling was the key to the elimination of fluctuating exchange rates which had been a "withering influence" on international trade ever since 1914.[2] Expanding world trade, he felt, would bring with it a growing demand for United States products, particularly agricultural output, and thus help to alleviate the chronic difficulties of the American farmer. He also saw in sterling's return to gold an opportunity for New York to gain in stature as an international financial center since, under the cooperative arrangements to facilitate the return, New York would for a time maintain its interest rates below London's and so become the more attractive center in which foreigners could borrow.[3] Finally he hoped that the return would reduce the threat of inflation in the United States by reversing the inflow of gold that had proved so troublesome to the Federal Reserve during the early twenties.[4]

For his part, Norman saw the return to gold as the culmination of Britain's

---

[2] *United States Congress, House Committee on Banking and Currency*, Stabilization, *Hearings, 69th Congress, 1st Session, on H.R. 7895 (Washington, D. C., 1927), Strong testimony, April 12, 1926, page 507.*

[3] *Hamlin Diary, May 22, 1924.*

[4] *Strong letter to Mellon, May 27, 1924, page 6; Norman cable to Bank of England, No. 16, paragraph 6, January 6, 1925.*

postwar efforts to restore its position as a major center of international trade and finance. In this view, he was supported by the influential report published in 1918 by the Cunliffe Committee (so called because it was headed by the then Governor of the Bank of England, Lord Cunliffe), by the overwhelming weight of informed British opinion, and by the country's three major political parties. There was little dissent from the view that the long-term economic advantages to Britain would greatly offset the temporary adjustment difficulties that might arise. And this view was echoed both by the Committee on the Currency and Bank of England Note Issues,[5] whose report was presented to the government some weeks before the decision to return was announced, and by the press after the announcement.[6]

In their private discussions, the British authorities were more specific about the aims they hoped to achieve by the return to gold and about the costs. Sir James Grigg, who was Winston Churchill's private secretary at the time, recalls a dinner at which some of the major proponents and opponents of the return presented their arguments to the Chancellor.[7] Keynes and McKenna, who represented the opponents, argued that sterling would be seriously overvalued in terms of the dollar, that the achievement of external equilibrium would consequently entail a deflation of British wages and prices, and that such a deflation would bring prolonged strikes and a permanent contraction in some of the country's heavy industries. To avoid these difficulties Keynes, at least, favored the maintenance of domestic wages and prices at the existing level and the continuation of a fluctuating exchange rate for sterling.

The proponents' case was argued by Lord Bradbury, chairman of the Committee on the Currency and Bank of England Note Issues. He held, according to Grigg's account, that the return to gold would save Britain from living in a fool's paradise of false prosperity and would force the export industries to become competitive. Bradbury rejected the suggestion that the return could be at a lower rate than the prewar parity, contending that this would cause a shock to confidence and thus endanger Britain's international reputation merely for an ease-

---

[5] *This committee, which was appointed by the government in June 1924 to explore the problems surrounding Britain's return to gold, included Austen Chamberlain, a former Chancellor of the Exchequer, Sir (later Lord) John Bradbury, then a member of the Reparation Commission, Gaspard Farrer of Barings, Sir Otto Niemeyer of the Treasury, and Professor A. C. Pigou of Cambridge University.*

[6] *R. S. Sayers, "The Return to Gold, 1925",* Studies in the Industrial Revolution *(London: Athlone Press, 1960), page 315.*

[7] *Sir James Grigg,* Prejudice and Judgment *(London: Jonathan Cape, Ltd., 1948), pages 182-84.*

ment that would be small and ephemeral. The old export industries, he held, would probably need to contract in any event, and the country's best course was to develop its newer and more sophisticated manufacturing industries and its international banking, insurance, and shipping services.[8]

Bradbury's view faithfully reflected the weight of opinion in the City of London and particularly at the Bank of England in the early months of 1925, and to a considerable extent this view continued to prevail during the difficult years ahead. Norman testified in this same spirit before the Macmillan Committee in March 1930. With reference to maintaining the gold value of sterling, he declared that[9]

> the disadvantages to the internal position are relatively small compared with advantages to the external position .... the whole international position has preserved for us in this country the wonderful position which we have inherited, which was for a while thought perhaps to be in jeopardy, which to a large extent, though not to the full extent, has been re-established. We are still to a large extent international bankers. We have great international trade and commerce out of which I believe considerable profit accrues to the country; we do maintain huge international markets, a free gold market, a free exchange market—perhaps the freest almost in the world—and all of those things, and the confidence and credit which go with them are in the long run greatly to the interest of industry as well as to the interest of finance and commerce.

The central bankers were motivated, not only by expectations of the advantages that would be derived from the return to gold, but also by their fears about what the course of developments might be if sterling were not stabilized at the old parity. Bradbury's belief that any other course would jeopardize London's future as an international financial center has already been noted. Norman and Strong were even more apprehensive. They felt, according to a memorandum that Strong wrote early in January 1925, that the consequences of a failure of Britain to resume gold payments would be "too serious really to contemplate". Such a failure, Strong continued,[10]

> would mean violent fluctuations in the exchanges, with probably progressive deterioration of the values of foreign currencies vis-à-vis the dollar; it would prove an incentive to all of those who were advancing novel ideas for nostrums and expedients other than the gold standard to sell their wares; an incentive to Govern-

---

[8] Ibid., *page 183.*

[9] Macmillan Evidence, *Vol. I, questions 3332-33, pages 212-13.*

[10] *Strong memorandum of January 11, 1925, page 4.*

74

ments at times to undertake various types of paper money expedients and inflation; it might, indeed, result in the United States draining the world of gold with the effect that, after some attempt at some other mechanism for the regulation of credit and prices, some kind of a monetary crisis would finally result in ultimate restoration of gold to its former position, but only after a period of hardship and suffering, and possibly some social and political disorder.

THE STRATEGY OF COOPERATION

As it became clear that the circumstances of 1924-25 would be propitious, Strong and Norman facilitated sterling's return to gold by adopting a strategy of cooperation that dealt with relative prices and interest rates and with stabilization credits. Regarding the first, the central bankers understood the limited extent to which monetary policy could influence prices. Nevertheless, they stressed the need to realign British and American prices from the distortions induced by the war and postwar inflations. Strong himself estimated that the prices of internationally traded commodities in Britain in the spring of 1924 were on the average still about 10 per cent higher than those in the United States, calculated from a common 1913 base, and he held that this gap would need to be more or less eliminated before Britain could return to gold.[11]

That spring, after he had spent some weeks with Norman in London, Strong wavered from the position that he had previously adhered to so firmly,[12] and was to reassert thereafter, on the question whether the United States authorities might condone or even facilitate a rise in American prices in order to help Britain return to gold. He wrote to Mellon at the end of May 1924 that, since Britain was suffering from poor trade and heavy unemployment, it would "be difficult politically and socially for the British government and the Bank of England to force a price liquidation in England beyond what they have already experienced". Hence, he argued, the burden of the readjustment of prices "must fall more largely upon us than upon them". More specifically, there would need to be "some small advance in prices here and possibly some small decline in their prices".[13]

As events developed, Strong does not seem to have persuaded his Federal Reserve colleagues that the United States should accept the larger part of the

---

[11] *Strong letter to Mellon, May 27, 1924, pages 11-12.*

[12] Supra, *page 31.*

[13] *Strong letter to Mellon, May 27, 1924, pages 11-12.*

adjustment burden, and he soon reverted to his earlier views, perhaps partly because of talk among his colleagues suggesting that he was too much under Norman's influence.[14] In any case, the record of the Strong-Norman discussions in New York early in January 1925 contains no reference to the desirability of higher American prices. Strong was extremely cautious. He told Norman:[15]

> it was my belief, and I thought it was shared by all others in the Federal Reserve System, that our whole policy in the future, as in the past, would be directed towards stability of prices so far as it was possible for us to influence prices, but that it was a matter on which no engagements could be made, as we must be free at all times to reduce or increase discount rates and to establish our open market policy so as to adequately meet domestic developments.

For his part, Norman was content to stress that the maintenance of the gold standard in Britain would depend on "a certain degree of stability" in the United States and that, in returning to gold, the British authorities were working on the assumption that the United States intended neither "to embark upon a deliberate policy of deflation" nor to "permit the development of any considerable inflation of prices".[16]

The second major element in the strategy involved cooperation between the Federal Reserve and the Bank of England to maintain lower interest rates in the United States than in Britain.[17] Both Norman and Strong hoped that a significant interest rate differential between London and New York would help to close the gap between British and American prices but, recognizing the multitude of other influences that act on prices, they placed their main reliance on the hoped-for effects of interest rate differentials upon international capital flows. Strong felt, to be sure, that so long as sterling was not stabilized, exchange risks would minimize the movement of United States short-term capital to London, but he hoped that foreign long-term borrowing might be diverted from London to New York. Even here, however, Strong was not overly optimistic because he questioned how

---

[14] *On May 5, 1924, Charles Hamlin noted in his diary that Governor Harding of the Boston Reserve Bank had commented to him that he was "certain that the movement for lower rates at N.Y. was inspired by Gov. Strong, now sick in Gov. Norman's house in London; that Norman wanted inflation in United States to put us more nearly on a parity w. Gt. Britain".*

[15] *Strong memorandum of January 11, 1925, page 5.*

[16] Loc. cit.

[17] *Strong letter to Jay, April 23, 1924, page 7; Hamlin Diary, May 7, 1924; and Strong letter to Mellon, May 27, 1924, pages 11-12.*

far Americans would place their capital abroad when there were safe and profitable investment opportunities in the United States. He also questioned how far the City of London would be willing to forego long-term lending business that traditionally had been theirs.[18] On the latter point Strong was close to the truth. Despite a change in interest rate relationships that made New York the cheaper center in which to borrow, the British authorities found it necessary in November 1924 to impose an informal control over the flotation of new foreign issues in the London capital market.[19]

The third part of the strategy of cooperation would come into play—as Strong wrote in his May 27, 1924 letter to Mellon—when the basic conditions for the return to gold had been achieved or were at least within reach: the United States would need to provide credits to Britain. At this early stage, Strong had two types of credit in mind. At first, he wrote:[20]

> large private credits must be opened in this country for use by the Bank of England or by the British Government or British banks in order to steady the rate of exchange and gradually work it to a higher level corresponding to the international price parity, and hold it there, until the time arrives to actually announce a plan of resumption based upon such adequate credits in this country as will insure the final recovery of sterling to par.

Although Strong was not explicit, it seems clear that he expected the Federal Reserve to participate only in the credits that would be granted upon the announcement of the plan to return to gold.

While Norman certainly agreed with Strong about the need for American credits to support the return to gold, others in Britain were opposed or at least doubtful. When Norman was in New York in January 1925, he received cables indicating that several Bank of England directors felt that, if Britain was to return to gold, it should do so solely on the basis of its own resources. They felt that the acceptance of foreign credits would cast doubt upon the determination and capacity of the country to establish sterling at its prewar parity and to

---

[18] *Strong letter to Norman, July 9, 1924, pages 3-4.*

[19] *W. A. Brown, Jr.,* England and the New Gold Standard, 1919-1926 *(New Haven: Yale University Press, 1929), page 224; Royal Institute of International Affairs,* The Problems of International Investment *(London, 1937), page 134.*

[20] *Strong letter to Mellon, May 27, 1924, page 12.*

maintain it there "at all costs".[21] The Report of the Committee on the Currency and Bank of England Note Issues also expressed concern lest the proposed credits be employed to soften the economic disciplines that Britain was expected to accept when it returned to gold. The report agreed that the credits would help to discourage speculation against sterling and would contribute to the creation of confidence, but it warned that, if the authorities felt it was necessary to arrange for credit in the United States,[22]

> we feel strongly that recourse should not be made to it unless and until substantial gold exports have taken place and are already producing their normal effects on the monetary situation at home, and in the event of the credit being actually drawn upon, the amount drawn should, until it has been repaid, be treated from the point of view of the Bank of England's monetary policy as equivalent to a corresponding loss from its own reserves.

> Unless these precautions are taken, borrowing abroad will, as has again and again happened when it has been resorted to as a remedy for exchange difficulties, merely aggravate the mischief which it has been applied to cure.

TIMING

The timing of sterling's return to gold was inherent neither in the objective itself nor in the strategy that was adopted. Rather it was set by the same sweep of events that made it possible to discuss the return as a practical objective. Indeed, given the favorable circumstances of 1924-25 and the intensity with which the return was desired by the British authorities—to say nothing of Strong and central bankers elsewhere—the task of resisting the pressures that were pushing sterling back to gold would have been difficult indeed.

It is true that Norman himself took a cautious line in his discussions with foreign central bankers, but within his own councils he advocated a prompt return. As early as May 1924, he expressed his view[23] that the wartime power under, which the government had embargoed gold should not be renewed when it expired at the end of 1925—which was tantamount to recommending that the

---

[21] *Lubbock cable to Norman, No. 54, January 10, 1925.*

[22] Report of the Committee on the Currency and Bank of England Note Issues *(London: H. M. Stationery Office, February 1925), page 7, paragraphs 30 and 31.*

[23] *Sir Henry Clay,* Lord Norman *(London: Macmillan & Co., Ltd., 1957), page 149.*

78

return should be during that year. On the other hand, his 1924 correspondence with Strong reads as if he were in no hurry at all.[24] As late as October 16, 1924, Norman wrote that attempts to stimulate market support for sterling through official proclamations of confidence in a return to gold "would have been difficult, and perhaps dangerous". It was his feeling that "however wearisome the pace has been, we have been wise so far to hurry slowly" and that, in view of the unexpected change in government from Labor to Conservative, "we must 'wait and see' " what course would now be taken. Purely as a guess, he suggested that the return might come "either at the end of 1925 or at the end of a somewhat later year, say 1927".

Norman's display of caution seems in part to have been merely a reaction to pressure from Strong, who did not conceal his wish that Britain should return to gold as quickly as possible. Indeed it was natural that Norman should take such a line with Strong, because he could not commit himself until his government had made the needful decisions and because his bargaining position was improved if he let Strong be the one to urge him to do what he wanted to do anyway.

However, his caution probably also reflected the attitude of some of his colleagues at the Bank of England. When he was in New York in January 1925, Norman received a long cable from Lubbock, his Deputy Governor, who urged that even after sterling had reached parity the authorities should delay any final commitment to the gold standard until they had had an opportunity to test whether sterling could be maintained at that level "by the natural play of the market force of supply and demand without resort to any artificial aids", by which he presumably meant the restrictions on the flotation of new foreign issues in London and the use of the proposed credits from the Federal Reserve and J. P. Morgan. He warned that it would be a mistake to fix a date for the return "before conditions warrant it", for the risk "would be too great and the consequences of failure too grave for us to recommend it".[25] In subsequent cables,[26] Lubbock indicated that three influential members of the Bank of England's Court of Directors agreed with the substance of this cable and that Sir Otto Niemeyer

---

[24] *See especially Norman letter to Strong, June 16, 1924.*

[25] *Lubbock cable to Norman, No. 54, January 10, 1925.*

[26] *Lubbock cables to Norman, Nos. 55, 57, and 59, January 10, 12, and 13, 1925.*

of the Treasury had similar reservations.

But such counsels of caution were overwhelmed by the pace of events. Sterling was pushed back to parity in the spring of 1925, partly by the movement of speculative balances in markets dominated by the conviction that the return was imminent and partly by fear among Britain's financial leaders lest the opportunity to restore sterling to a preeminent place in international finance might never return. Prestige plainly played a large role. Sweden, whose central bank governor had urged Norman to lead the way back to gold, had grown tired of waiting and in March 1924 returned alone.[27] When the acceptance of the Dawes Plan in the spring of 1924 made it seem likely that the German currency would be stabilized in terms of gold before sterling, the British authorities were struck with consternation.[28] Strong was quite aware of British sensitivity on this score and, when the Hungarian currency was stabilized during the summer of 1924, he twitted Norman by writing that "the question uppermost in my mind is whether sterling is not now rather far behind in the procession".[29] Subsequently, in early December, Strong warned Norman of the rapidly changing monetary conditions in the United States and of upward pressures on our interest rates. Norman did not need to read between the lines to know that conditions in the United States favoring sterling's return could not be expected to last indefinitely.

As time went on, the pressure grew. In January, while Norman was still negotiating in New York, the South African government announced that its currency would return to gold effective July 1, 1925.[30] Similar action was urged by the monetary authorities in Australia whose currency had moved to a premium in terms of sterling during the winter of 1924-25.[31] Then during the spring word came that a return to gold was also being planned by Holland, Switzerland, and perhaps other Continental countries.[32] Noting this when he announced Britain's

---

[27] *Clay, op. cit., page 142; W. A. Brown, Jr.,* The International Gold Standard Reinterpreted, 1914-1934 *(New York: National Bureau of Economic Research, Inc., 1940), Vol. I, page 323.*

[28] *Strong letters to Jay, April 23-28, 1924.*

[29] *Strong letter to Norman, July 9, 1924, page 4.*

[30] *Lubbock cable to Norman, No. 59, paragraph 7, January 13, 1925.*

[31] *L. F. Giblin,* The Growth of a Central Bank: The Development of the Commonwealth Bank of Australia *(Melbourne: Melbourne University Press, 1951), pages 11, 24-26.*

[32] Report of the Committee on the Currency and Bank of England Note Issues, *page 6, paragraph 21.*

return at the end of April, Churchill commented that "we could not have afforded to have remained stationary while so many others moved".[33] Subsequently, Churchill was more explicit about the reasons behind the timing of the return. After mentioning the seasonal strength of sterling during the spring and the expiration at the year-end of the authority to embargo gold, he noted that[34]

> if we had not taken this action the whole of the rest of the British Empire would have taken it without us, and it would have come to a gold standard, not on the basis of the pound sterling, but a gold standard of the dollar.

IMPLEMENTING THE STRATEGY

The favorable circumstances of 1924-25 and the compatibility of the objectives of Strong and Norman combined to simplify the task of cooperation between the Federal Reserve and the Bank of England. In this respect, the discussions on sterling's stabilization contrasted sharply with the difficult German negotiations of 1924.[35] Before the Dawes Loan could be floated, the recuperative strength and economic potential of Germany had to be assessed, distrust among the participating countries alleviated, and conflicting objectives reconciled. In the end, it was agreed that the stabilization of the German currency called for long-term and large-scale financing and that means must be provided whereby future pressures on the exchange rate could be relieved if necessary. Thus recognition of the difficulty of the German problem brought international agreement on means that were appropriate for its solution. But the very success of this international effort helped to make sterling's problem appear simpler than it really was; it encouraged the British authorities to adopt policies from which they could not turn back without precipitating a major international crisis, and to adopt them with only limited and rather short-term assistance from the United States.

THE FEDERAL RESERVE AND MORGAN CREDITS.   The lines of credit from the Federal Reserve and a syndicate headed by J. P. Morgan & Co. which supported the stabilization of sterling were negotiated with very little difficulty. The

---

[33] Parliamentary Debates (*Great Britain, House of Commons*), *Vol. 183, April 28, 1925, column 57.*

[34] The Economist, *August 8, 1925, page 222.*

[35] *Cf. Chapter 4.*

principal negotiators were Strong and Norman themselves, their major tasks being to ensure that the use of the credits should conform to their need to maintain control over their respective money markets and that official press releases on the credits should stress that neither party had made any commitment that would limit the conduct of his monetary policy.[36]

The course and outcome of these negotiations have been detailed elsewhere[37] and need not be repeated here. Suffice it to say that the improvement in the international economic balance during the second half of 1924 made it unnecessary to consider such private credits to Britain as Strong had originally envisaged.[38] The purpose of the credits that were in fact negotiated was not to help push sterling up to parity but rather to strengthen confidence that sterling would be maintained at parity once that level had been attained and Britain had again committed itself to the free export of gold. For its part, the Federal Reserve Bank of New York arranged to grant the Bank of England a $200 million line of credit that could be drawn upon at any time during the two years beginning May 14, 1925, either in gold or in dollars. Interest was to be charged only on amounts actually drawn, the rate being set at 1 per cent above the New York Reserve Bank's rate of discount on ninety-day bills, with a minimum of 4 per cent and a maximum of 6 per cent, except that a rate equivalent to the discount rate would be charged if the latter should be raised above 6 per cent. The terms on the Morgan line of credit to the British government were identical except that Morgan's charged an additional commitment fee of 1¼ per cent on the full amount of the credit during the first year and, if no drawing were made, half that rate in the second year.[39] Reluctant to bear this fee, the British Treasury cut down the amount of the line from the $300 million originally desired by Norman and Strong to only $100 million.[40]

The central bankers' concern to ensure that the use of the credits should not impair their monetary control is fully understandable. Each wanted to be free

---

[36] *Strong letter to Norman, April 15, 1925, page 2.*

[37] *L. V. Chandler,* Benjamin Strong, Central Banker *(Washington, D. C.: The Brookings Institution, 1958), pages 308-21.*

[38] *Supra, page 77.*

[39] *Strong cable to Norman, No. 60, April 4, 1925;* Parliamentary Debates *(Great Britain, House of Commons), May 4, 1925, column 623, and May 5, 1925, column 815.*

[40] *Chandler, op. cit., pages 316-17.*

to adjust monetary policy in accordance with his assessment of his money market's changing needs, and both were concerned because the credits were large relative to the central banks' holdings of marketable securities. In the United States the total of Federal Reserve "bills bought" and government securities averaged a little less than $650 million in April 1925, while the holdings of the Open Market Investment Account averaged only $248 million, compared with maximum possible drawings on the credits of $300 million, or $500 million under the original plans. Clearly, a Federal Reserve policy that aimed to keep a tight rein on member banks' reserves could have been seriously complicated, or even vitiated, if the Bank of England could draw on its Federal Reserve credit to make payments to the Street; or, to take the opposite extreme, a policy that aimed to pump reserves into the banking system could be checked if the Bank of England were to use the Morgan credit to buy gold at the Federal Reserve. By the same token, the credits could clearly be so employed as to reinforce Federal Reserve policy or have a neutral effect on the money market. From the beginning of the negotiations for the credits, it was therefore understood that the Bank of England would consult with the Federal Reserve both about the amounts to be drawn and about which of the credits was to be used.[41] By the time the negotiations were complete, Strong had obtained a large measure of control, it being agreed by the Bank of England and the British Treasury that[42]

> In the event of recourse being desired to either of the Credits established in America, the Treasury or the Bank of England shall use the particular Credit which the Governor of the Federal Reserve Bank shall from time to time select.

For the Bank of England the problem and its solution were similar, at least so far as the Federal Reserve credit was concerned.[43] It was agreed that, upon making a drawing, the Bank of England would credit the account of the New York Reserve Bank with the sterling equivalent, the amount so credited to be adjusted daily to reflect fluctuations in the cable rate of exchange.[44] However,

---

[41] *Strong memorandum of January 11, 1925, page 7.*

[42] *Norman letter to Strong, April 22, 1925.*

[43] *No relevant information is available regarding the Morgan credit.*

[44] *Norman letter to Strong, April 8, 1925; Minutes of the Board of Directors of the Federal Reserve Bank of New York, April 23, 1925; Strong and Moreau conversation, August 23, 1926.*

in the event that the full amount were drawn, the total so deposited would come to some £41 million, equivalent to two fifths of the average government and other securities holdings of the Bank of England's Banking Department in April 1925 and to almost three fifths of average bankers' balances at the bank.[45] In order to reconcile the management of such Federal Reserve balances with Bank of England monetary policy, it was agreed that these balances could be invested by the Federal Reserve only in specified types of sterling commercial bills, and that the timing and magnitude of any bill purchases would be arranged in a mutually satisfactory manner between the two central banks. It was also agreed that earnings from such commercial bills would be credited at the current rate of exchange against any interest payable in dollars by the Bank of England on its drawings.[46]

Such was the harmony between Strong and Norman at this time that these were the only significant conditions on the credits. Other conditions were minor. Drawings could be in gold or dollars and were similarly repayable; service was guaranteed by the British Treasury.[47] Strong asked for and received assurance that Norman would remain governor at least for the next year and probably for the next two years.[48] With a view to strengthening monetary control, he also asked assurance that no increase in the British Treasury currency note issue be allowed without the approval of the Bank of England, but Norman wrote that formal compliance with this request would provoke a serious public controversy, and Strong was content to let the matter drop on receiving Norman's assurance that he would attempt to persuade the Committee on the Currency and Bank of England Note Issues to include in its report a recommendation that would meet the request.[49] Actually no such recommendation was included in the committee's report which was not made available to Parliament and the public until April 28, the day Churchill announced the return to gold. At this point, when it would have been futile to press the matter, Strong agreed with as good grace

---

[45] Macmillan Report, *page 302.*

[46] *Norman letter to Strong, April 8, 1925. pages 2-3; Strong letter to Norman, April 20, 1925; and resolution passed at the Board of Directors' meeting, Federal Reserve Bank of New York, April 23, 1925.*

[47] *United Kingdom Treasury Minute, May 14, 1925, signed by Sir Otto Niemeyer.*

[48] *Strong letter to Norman, January 15, 1925; Norman letter to Strong, February 10, 1925.*

[49] *Norman letter to Strong, April 20, 1925.*

as possible to postpone discussion of control of the Treasury note issue until a more opportune time.[50]

As events developed, neither of the credits was drawn upon. How far they contributed to the confidence in sterling that developed immediately after the return is a moot point, but there is firm evidence that foreign balances that had moved to London before the end of April 1925 remained for several months thereafter. On the other hand, Strong's hope that the credits might be employed to reduce the Federal Reserve's "excessive" gold holdings was never realized, despite at least one hint to Norman that the purchase of gold in New York would be welcome.[51] In the end, no efforts were made to renew the credits and they expired on schedule, May 14, 1927, a few weeks before another major cooperative effort of a different character was launched.[52]

COORDINATION OF MONETARY POLICY.   The monetary policies of the United States and Britain went through several phases between May 1924, when the cooperative effort for sterling's return to gold began in earnest, and the latter part of 1926, when the return appeared to have been firmly consolidated.

May-November 1924. The first phase extended over the six months ended November 1924, a period during which the United States economy reached the trough of, and started to recover from, a mild recession and when United States monetary policy gave more support to sterling than it was able to give at any time thereafter. During the winter of 1923-24, the Federal Reserve had begun to ease monetary conditions but, as late as April, New York money rates were still well above the corresponding London rates, as they had been during the two preceding years. That spring the Federal Reserve embarked on a further major easing of monetary conditions. The New York Reserve Bank's discount rate was reduced in three ½ percentage point steps—on May 1, June 12, and August 8, 1924—from 4½ per cent to 3 per cent, where it was held until February 1925 (Chart 2). At the same time Federal Reserve credit was pumped into the banking system. The Open Market Investment Committee (OMIC), at its meetings between April 22 and July 16, authorized Government securities purchases totaling

---

[50] *Strong letter to Norman, April 30, 1925.*

[51] *Strong letter to Norman, May 21, 1925.*

[52] Infra, *page 119 f.*

$300 million, and the Federal Reserve average holdings of such securities actually increased $264 million in the six months ended November 1924. Over the same period, the Federal Reserve bought some $188 million in bills and $84 million in gold. These purchases, along with those of Government securities, swamped the effect on member bank reserves of a moderate outflow of currency into circulation, and permitted further reductions in member bank borrowings at the Federal Reserve, a significant expansion in member bank reserves, and a 14.5 per cent increase in net demand deposits of weekly reporting member banks— the most rapid deposit expansion to occur over any six-month period in the years 1924-31.[53]

While United States monetary conditions were becoming easier, the Bank of England maintained firmness in the London money market. The total of London clearing banks' cash and balances at the Bank of England was permitted to expand only slowly in the six months ended November 1924, and total clearing bank deposits remained virtually unchanged. However, with unemployment in Britain continuing high, Norman was unable, as he wrote Strong in mid-June, to find a satisfactory excuse to raise the discount rate above the 4 per cent at which it had been held since mid-1923,[54] but he was able to help widen the spread of London money market rates above New York through Bank of England operations that were reflected in a ½ percentage point rise during July 1924 in the London rate for three-month bankers' bills.[55] The rise in the London market rates continued in August and subsequent months, three-month bankers' bills fluctuating in the 3.72-3.79 per cent range for the remainder of the year, about 0.70 point above their April-June level.

These changes brought a major shift in the interest rate relationships between New York and London. Market discounts on bankers' bills in New York, which had been about 1 percentage point above London in April 1924, fell to 1½ points below London in July and were still more than 1 point below in November. For other money market rates the relationship changed correspondingly, although

---

[53] *For the sake of complete accuracy, it may be noted that the percentage increases in net demand deposits in the two overlapping six-month periods ended in October and November 1924 were virtually the same.*

[54] *Norman letter to Strong, June 16, 1924.*

[55] *Norman cable to Strong, No. 95, July 19, 1924.*

CHART 2

SHORT-TERM INTEREST RATES
NEW YORK AND LONDON, 1924-26

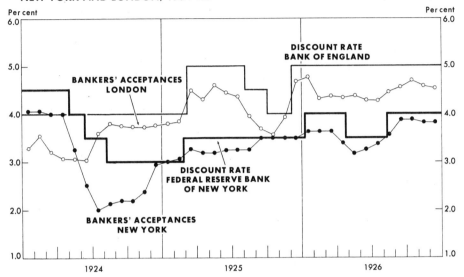

Note: Bankers' acceptances are monthly averages of rates on three-month bankers' acceptances.

Sources: Board of Governors of the Federal Reserve System, Banking and Monetary Statistics (Washington, D. C., November 1943); R. G. Hawtrey, A Century of Bank Rate (London, 1932).

the change in call loan rates involved only a narrowing of New York's spread above London.[56] In the capital markets, yields on United States long-term Government bonds, which had been only 0.17 point below corresponding yields in Britain in April 1924, declined to 0.46 point below them by July and, contrary to the movements in the two money markets, this spread did not narrow significantly during the rest of the year. Even more important, long-term funds became increasingly available in New York, whereas in London, as already

[56] *Paul Einzig,* The Theory of Forward Exchange *(London: Macmillan & Co., Ltd., 1937), chart opposite page 276.*

87

noted, informal controls were adopted to curtail the outflow of long-term capital.

November 1924-May 1925. In the second major phase, which extended from November 1924 to May 1925, United States monetary policy changed from ease to moderate restraint and, in order to maintain the interest rate relationship with New York that had been established during the previous half year, Bank of England policy was further tightened. The initial change in Federal Reserve policy was made at the October 24, 1924 meeting of the OMIC, which moved away from the buying of Government securities toward a more neutral posture under which either purchases or sales of Governments were authorized, depending on market conditions. In the event, the recovery from the 1924 recession proceeded apace, and the Federal Reserve's holdings of Government securities were reduced $227 million in the six months ended May 1925. Changes in other factors—primarily money in circulation and the gold stock—were largely offsetting during the six months. Thus, the overall effect of Federal Reserve operations was a withdrawal of $212 million from member bank reserves, all but $32 million of which was recouped, however, through increased member bank borrowings from the central bank. At the same time, United States interest rates were again moving upward. The upturn in money market rates had begun as early as August 1924, but not until February 27, 1925 was the discount rate of the Federal Reserve Bank of New York increased—by ½ point to 3½ per cent, at which level it was to remain for almost a year.

Strong gave Norman full advance warning of these changes in United States monetary policy.[57] Early in December 1924 he cabled Norman about the possibility of a ½ point increase in the New York Reserve Bank's discount rate, and inquired whether, if such an increase became necessary, Norman would prefer to advance his discount rate first.[58] Norman's reply was that the Bank of England would increase its rate by 1 point if New York went up ½ point and that he would prefer to follow New York "and so appear to have our hands forced by you".[59] Later, after Strong had cabled that the increase in the New York rate was imminent, Norman confirmed his intention and added that he expected that a further increase in the Bank of England discount rate to 6 per

---

[57] *Strong letter to Norman, November 4, 1924; Strong letter to Norman, December 2, 1924.*

[58] *Strong cable to Norman, No. 4, December 5, 1924.*

[59] *Norman cable to Strong, No. 39, December 8, 1924.*

cent would be required if free gold payments were resumed in April.[60] As events developed, the Bank of England did raise its discount rate to 5 per cent on March 5, just a week after the New York Reserve Bank's increase, but the further increase to 6 per cent was made unnecessary by the unexpected strength of sterling in the spring and summer following the return.

The tightening of Bank of England policy was also reflected in its market operations. In the first phase, the cash base had been allowed to expand, albeit at a much slower rate than in the United States, but now that the expansion of the United States cash base had been stopped, the British cash base had to be contracted. Bank of England holdings of government and other securities declined 10 per cent in January-May 1925 and, along with a modest contraction in discounts and advances, far more than offset various expansionary factors, leading to a 7 per cent decline in the central bank's deposit liabilities.

Monetary developments in the two countries reflected these shifts in policy. In the United States, the sharp expansion of May-November 1924 was halted. Weekly reporting member banks' reserves declined slightly in the six months ended May 1925, and their total deposits dropped ½ per cent. In Britain the contraction was sharper, London clearing banks' cash and balances at the Bank of England and total deposits each declining 2 per cent in the six-month period. The greater degree of stringency in Britain kept market rates of interest there well above those in the United States. On both three-month bankers' bills and long-term government bonds, the spread of the London rates above the corresponding New York rates was wider in May 1925 than the previous November. Even in the call loan market, in which London rates were normally relatively low, the sharp rise in London rates reduced the margin in favor of New York to only 0.28 point in May 1925, compared with 1.71 points in November 1924.

The achievements of the year ended May 1925. The changes in United States and British monetary conditions in the year ended May 1925 were accompanied by the achievement of the international financial goals sought by Norman and Strong. The sterling-dollar rate, which had fluctuated in the $4.30's during May 1924, moved in late July into the $4.40-$4.50 range, where it continued through October, after which it pushed on, sometimes falteringly, until at the end of April 1925 it had reached the lower part of the $4.84-$4.90 range within which

---

[60] *Norman cable to Strong, No. 71, February 24, 1925.*

the rate could fluctuate under the old gold parity. Throughout the month following the return to gold, the rate continued to strengthen and averaged just over $4.85. The appreciation of sterling appears the more remarkable when it is remembered that the British authorities were building up dollar balances with which to meet war debt payments to the United States, some $92 million having been accumulated during the fall and early winter of 1924 to meet the payment due in mid-December[61] and an additional $166 million in the early months of the following year to meet the payments due in June and December 1925.[62]

Gold flows also shifted significantly. The United States continued to be a net importer of gold through most of 1924, as it had been during most of the postwar period, but the net inflow slackened markedly after midyear. Reflecting the change, the average monthly increase in the United States gold stock fell from $42 million in January-May 1924 to only $12 million in June-November. Beginning in December the gold stock itself dropped sharply for the first time in four years, the decrease averaging $28 million monthly in the six months ended May 1925.[63]

No corresponding movements are reflected in the Bank of England gold holdings, because until the end of April 1925 its statutory buying and selling prices for gold remained out of touch with the market. Its holdings of gold coin and bullion did increase by £27.6 million in the year ended April 29, 1925, but £27 million of this was attributable to the transfer to the bank of gold held by the British Treasury as backing for its currency note issue.[64] In the months that followed, the bank did begin to gain a considerable volume of gold which, as we shall see, caused Norman no little difficulty and embarrassment.

In the price field, the central bankers' goals were also achieved, although the process was a slow one. The spread of British wholesale prices above those in the United States which had been 11.5 per cent in April 1924, remained

---

[61] *Brown,* England and the New Gold Standard, 1919-1926, *page 220.*

[62] Parliamentary Debates *(Great Britain, House of Commons), April 28, 1925, column 56.*

[63] *Board of Governors of the Federal Reserve System,* Banking and Monetary Statistics *(Washington, D. C., 1943), pages 536-37.*

[64] Parliamentary Debates *(Great Britain, House of Commons), April 28, 1925, column 56.*

obstinately wide throughout the remainder of the year but thereafter narrowed to only 2½ per cent by May 1925 (see Chart 3). The realignment of export prices in the two countries was also elusive until March 1925, the problem during 1924 being that British export prices tended to move in sympathy with those of the United States. Indeed, the spread of British export prices above those of the United States (Federal Reserve indexes, 1913 = 100) was only 2 per cent in April 1924, but widened to 5 per cent by the autumn of that year. Not until January 1925 did this spread begin to narrow, but then the change came rapidly because of a sharp but temporary upturn in United States export prices and a sharp downturn in those of Britain. By March 1925 British export prices were 3 per cent below those of the United States and, despite the subsequent sharp downturn in United States export prices, the margin in favor of Britain

CHART 3

**WHOLESALE PRICE INDEXES
UNITED STATES AND UNITED KINGDOM, 1924-26**
1913=100

Note: Data on wholesale price indexes for the United States were compiled by the Bureau of Labor Statistics, and those for the United Kingdom by the Board of Trade.

Source: Federal Reserve Bulletin.

had widened slightly by May.[65]

Analysis of the achievement. It is already clear that the attainment of sterling parity, the reversal of the gold flow to the United States, and the realignment of United States and British prices resulted from a host of forces. Strong and Norman were aware of the complexity of the conditions in which they were operating, and at least in 1924, when the outcome of their efforts was still uncertain, they were little inclined to exaggerate the power of central bank policy to achieve their objectives. As already noted, their greatest hopes lay in the employment of monetary policy to shift long-term foreign borrowing from London to New York. In this they were highly successful, and there can be little doubt that this shift contributed significantly both to the strengthening of sterling and, to a lesser degree, to the reversal of the gold flows to the United States. New capital issues in London on behalf of foreign countries (excluding British dominions and colonies) dropped to a monthly average of only £2.8 million in the seven months ended May 1925, about half the rate in the first ten months of 1924.[66] At the same time the outflow of capital from the United States was greatly enlarged. Although the United States current account surplus was considerably larger in both 1924 and 1925 than it had been in 1923, the change was far more than offset by a rise in long-term capital outflows to $700 million in 1924 and $570 million in 1925 from only $45 million in 1923.[67] The nominal value of new capital issues in the United States on behalf of foreign countries was four times larger in the year ended June 1925 than in the year before.[68] The available balance-of-payments data also support Strong's expectation that little United States short-term capital would move to London, but since no figures are available to show changes in short-term capital movements within the halves of the year, the evidence is not conclusive. In any case, the enlargement of capital outflows was sufficient to change the United States overall balance of payments from a $266 million surplus in 1923 to a surplus of

---

[65] *Various issues of the* Federal Reserve Bulletin. *The data for the period up to March 1925 are collected in E. V. Morgan,* Studies in British Financial Policy, 1914-25 *(London: Macmillan & Co., Ltd., 1952), page 363.*

[66] *Midland Bank,* New Capital Issues, *1926.*

[67] *United States Department of Commerce,* United States in the World Economy *(Washington, D. C.: United States Government Printing Office, 1943), Appendix Table 1.*

[68] *Midland Bank,* Monthly Review, *August-September 1927.*

only $28 million in 1924 and to a deficit of $40 million in 1925.

This change in the outflow of United States long-term capital and in the United States balance of payments stemmed from shifts: (1) in the relative attractiveness of Europe and the United States as investment outlets, (2) in the availablity of funds in the London and New York capital markets, and (3) in relative interest rates. The first element was clearly of overriding importance. The huge rise in long-term capital outflow from the United States could hardly have developed without the simultaneous brightening of European investment prospects and the dampening of those in the United States. And the very recession that was associated with this dampening contributed to a slackening in the demand for funds in the United States and—along with Federal Reserve policy—to the greater availability and reduced cost of credit here.

Apart from the shift in long-term borrowing from London to New York, other factors also supported the strengthening of sterling. Speculation on the appreciation of sterling was almost certainly a major influence; it was widely noted by contemporary observers[69] and seems to have involved primarily foreign balances that had fled to New York in the uncertain months and years before the spring of 1924 and thereafter moved back to Europe, and especially to London, as the prospects on the other side of the Atlantic improved. The speculative movement seems to have developed in both the spot and forward markets. At a time when forward sterling should theoretically have been at a discount, the speculation was reflected in the disappearance of the discount on three-month forward sterling during the late autumn and the appearance thereafter of a premium; this premium was maintained almost until sterling's return to gold[70] and, combined with the differential in short-term money rates, it gave a substantial covered incentive to move funds from New York to London (Chart 4).

A partly fortuitous influence that helped support sterling during the autumn and winter of 1924-25 was the exceptionally heavy demand from continental European countries for sterling commodities. Much of the Continent's demand, which originated in the need to make up the deficiencies of a bad harvest in

---

[69] *See especially* Report of the Committee on the Currency and Bank of England Note Issues, *page 7, paragraph 28; Reginald McKenna in the* Monthly Review *of the Midland Bank, February-March 1925, page 3; and J. A. Schumpeter,* Business Cycles *(New York: McGraw-Hill, Inc., 1939),* Vol. II, pages 725-26.

[70] *Einzig, op. cit., page 256 and chart opposite page 276.*

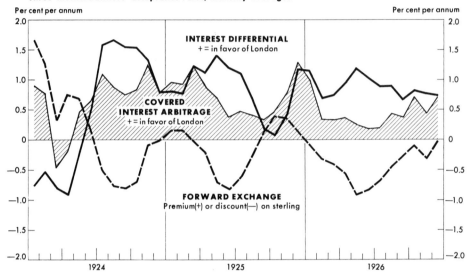

CHART 4

ARBITRAGE OPPORTUNITIES BETWEEN
NEW YORK AND LONDON, 1924-26
Three-month bankers' acceptance rates; monthly averages

Per cent per annum

INTEREST DIFFERENTIAL
+ = in favor of London

COVERED
INTEREST ARBITRAGE
+ = in favor of London

FORWARD EXCHANGE
Premium(+) or discount(—) on sterling

1924   1925   1926

Sources: Board of Governors of the Federal Reserve System, Banking and Monetary Statistics (Washington, D. C., November 1943). Data on forward exchange calculated from figures in Paul Einzig, The Theory of Forward Exchange (London, 1937), Appendix 1.

1924 and to rebuild inventories depleted during the war and early postwar years, was of course directed to the United States. However, a large share also went to such British dominions as Australia, New Zealand, and South Africa. The magnitude of the expansion in demand is indicated by the 275 per cent increase in the physical volume of wheat imports from Australia by five major Continental countries[71] in the year ended June 1925. The volume of Continental imports of wool, jute, and rubber from sterling countries also expanded significantly.[72]

---

[71] *Italy, France, Belgium, Germany, and the Netherlands.* Official Yearbook of the Commonwealth of Australia *(Melbourne, 1927), page 648.*

[72] *Brown,* England and the New Gold Standard, 1919-1926, *page 194.*

94

At their peak in the early months of 1925, prices of these commodities had about doubled from a year earlier.[73]

The reversal of the flow of gold to the United States was also the result both of international financial cooperation (and the accompanying large outflow of long-term capital from the United States) and of fortuitous developments. Most clearly the result of the former was the large export of gold from the United States to Europe in the six months ended May 1925, particularly $87 million sold to Germany during that period. Some $50 million of this was acquired by the Reichsbank, using part of the proceeds of the New York tranche of the Dawes Loan and United States currency that had been circulating in Germany and was turned over to the bank after the stabilization of the mark began to take hold during 1924.[74]

However, the larger part of the reversal of the gold movement to the United States is attributable to factors that were connected only remotely, if at all, with the efforts of Strong and Norman. The export of $27 million in gold by the United States to Australia in January-April 1925 occurred because booming sales abroad of Australian wheat and wool had pushed the Australian pound to a substantial premium over sterling. The constellation of exchange rates made it advantageous, as a pure arbitrage transaction, to acquire gold in the United States, ship it to Australia, and sell the Australian pound proceeds in London.[75] Similarly, the export of some $67 million of gold from the United States to India in the ten months ended May 1925 is attributable to a favorable monsoon that brought bumper crops in 1924, a strengthening of India's balance of payments, and speculation that the rupee might appreciate in terms of gold.[76]

Increased Indian demand for gold led, not only to imports directly from the United States, but to a cessation of British gold exports to the United States. Indian demand was of course normally a major element in the London gold market, but its expansion in 1924 and early 1925—combined with some rise in the off-take of continental Europe—was so great as to absorb fully the residual supply that had previously been sold to the United States.

---

[73] *"Commercial History and Review"*, The Economist, *1924 and 1925.*

[74] *G. L. Harrison letter to G. B. Winston, December 4, 1924; Crissinger letter to Strong, December 26, 1924.*

[75] *Brown,* England and the New Gold Standard, 1919-1926, *page 194, and* The International Gold Standard, Reinterpreted, 1914-1934, *Vol. I, pages 369-70; Giblin,* op. cit., *pages 24-26.*

[76] *Brown,* England and the New Gold Standard, 1919-1926, *pages 186-90.*

The movements of United States and British export prices during the year ended May 1925 were the product of complex forces in which monetary policy, as both Strong and Norman recognized, played only a relatively small part.[77] In the fluctuations of United States export prices, the influence of Federal Reserve policy was swamped during the summer of 1924 by expectations that agricultural produce (which constituted about half of United States exports) would be moving into rather weak markets. It was swamped again by unexpectedly heavy European demand, which pushed up agricultural prices during the autumn and winter and which slumped thereafter, leading to an almost equally sharp price decline. It is true that, in facilitating the large expansion of United States long-term loans, Federal Reserve policy made it easier for Europe to buy American exports and thus acted to support United States export prices. However, even in the absence of increased American lending, Europe might have been forced to curtail spending in other countries, or to draw down its international reserves, in order to make good some part of its agricultural deficiency by importing from the United States. At least part of the rise in United States export prices that developed during the winter of 1924-25 might, therefore, have occurred even if there had been no easing of Federal Reserve policy.

Fluctuations in British and American export prices were closely associated. They declined together during the summer of 1924 and, as the central bankers noted with some dismay, they rose together during the following autumn and winter. Thus, the upsurge in international commodity prices more than offset the downward pressure on sterling prices that was being exerted both by monetary restraint in Britain and by the appreciation in the sterling exchange rate. Only when international commodity prices turned sharply downward in March 1925 did the deflationary pressures gain the upper hand to bring the export prices of Britain and the United States into alignment.

CONSOLIDATING STERLING'S POSITION

The consolidation of sterling's position on the basis of the $4.867 parity was a task at least as difficult as the return to gold. For the latter, the central bankers

---

[77] *Strong letters to Norman, July 9, 1924, page 2, and November 4, 1924, page 4; Norman letter to Strong, October 16, 1924, pages 2-3; and Strong letter to Lubbock, September 10, 1924.*

had chosen an occasion when economic conditions were highly favorable. Thereafter, the need was so to strengthen Britain's fundamental international economic position that sterling's link to gold could be sustained when the economic climate turned from fair to unsettled and even to foul.

As events developed, international economic conditions were to remain "fair" for some years after the return. In this, the American prosperity of the mid-twenties played a major part. The recovery from the 1924 recession was rapid and continued, after the initial surge, at a moderate pace and with only minor interruptions until the onset of another mild recession late in 1926. At the same time, United States imports soared, far outpacing the modest rise in exports. The outflow of long-term capital from the United States—attracted by high interest rates and continued favorable prospects abroad—remained large, and the overall balance of payments moved definitely into deficit which amounted to $362 million in 1926. However, foreigners chose to increase their short-term dollar assests by no less than $455 million in 1926. Consequently, the gold outflow that had developed during the winter of 1924-25 was again reversed, and by the end of 1926 the United States gold stock was only slightly lower than it had been before the outflow began in December 1924.

The combination of rising prosperity in the United States and the renewed inflow of gold confronted the Federal Reserve with a problem that was handled quite easily in 1925 and 1926 but became progressively more difficult toward the end of the decade. In mid-1925, as in later years, the authorities hoped to stretch out the country's prosperity, to prevent the development of undue speculation and other inflationary pressures that could lead to boom and bust. Lacking any fiscal policy instruments, they could only curb such domestic pressures by tightening monetary policy which would, however, tend to strengthen the dollar against foreign currencies, increase the gold inflow, and so complicate the Federal Reserve's control of member bank reserves. Strong anticipated this problem toward the end of the summer of 1925 during which a similar unwanted inflow of gold to Britain had led to pressure on the Bank of England to ease its monetary policy. Writing to J. H. Case, Deputy Governor of the Federal Reserve Bank of New York, Strong stated:[78]

[78] *Strong letter to Case, August 25, 1925.*

that up to a certain point we should make every effort to accommodate our policy to theirs [the Bank of England]. If they feel it necessary in meeting domestic conditions to reduce their rate, then, of course, they must do so, but should not necessarily expect us to go down with them if *our* domestic situation would render it perilous to do so. And, in fact, that is our situation at home. We cannot now afford a rate reduction, and the only question is whether we can afford to stay at our present level as the best we can do, or whether, notwithstanding a reduction in London say to 4%, it may be necessary for us to go up to 4%.

Of course you understand that the consequence of an increase in our rate, in the face of rate reductions among the gold standard countries of Europe, will be some transfers of funds to the United States by bankers generally, and by the banks of issue specifically; and that we cannot then escape further shipments of gold.

Our earning assets are now nearly $300,000,000 above what they were a year ago, and of our earning assets over $200,000,000 are Government holdings under the control of the [Open Market Investment] committee and about $100,000,000 are Governments not under committee control. If, therefore, we are now obliged to pursue a policy of higher rates and it does result in gold imports, the Federal Reserve System must definitely face a period of liquidation of earning assets at least equal to gold imports, and it may be that the sale of securities must be extended beyond the committee's holdings and take in some of the holdings of the individual banks.

I am hoping that there will be no important change in the situation prior to the date of the Governors Conference. At that time I shall be glad to explain to our colleagues everything that I know about the situation abroad and endeavor to induce them to a complacent state of mind about earnings during this temporary period of readjustment. If we are not successful in doing that, we are going to have a struggle with an inflation and a boom sooner or later, unless, indeed, they have an up-set in Europe which would act as a deterrent.

As events turned out, the inflationary pressures with which the Federal Reserve System had to deal in the one and one-half years beginning May 1925 were quite moderate and, despite the shortage of open market ammunition, the authorities were able to cope with them without undoing the achievements of 1924-25. Seasonal influences apart, the System kept member bank reserves under pressure. The expansionary effects of the gold inflows, of net purchases of commercial bills, and decreased currency circulation were more than offset by a net decline in Government securities holdings. About $100 million of reserves was thus withdrawn from the banking system in the eighteen months ended in November 1926 which marked the downturn into the 1926-27 recession. However, in meeting the credit demands of the expanding economy, member banks moderated the pressures on their reserves by borrowing more than $200 million from the Federal Reserve. Even so, the money supply grew less rapidly than the national product and interest rates tended to move upward.[79] Those Federal Reserve Banks whose discount rates were not already at 4 per cent moved to that level in November 1925 except for the New York Bank which made the ½ per cent increase in January 1926. All the Reserve Banks remained at the 4 per cent level throughout 1926, except New York whose rate was set at 3½ per cent for about four months ended mid-August when it was again increased to 4 per cent. By the end of 1926, rates in New York on ninety-day bankers' acceptances were close to 4 per cent and call money was above 5 per cent, these rates being 0.6-1.3 percentage points higher than they had averaged in May 1925.

The gradual tightening of monetary conditions in the United States was not Norman's major problem in the months immediately following the return. His problem was to enforce a monetary policy that would foster the economic adjustments that still had to be made by Britain if sterling was to be maintained on gold in the long run. This objective, as Norman indicated toward the end of May 1925, required a gradual contraction of credit and the continuation of interest rates in Britain at higher levels than in major centers abroad.[80] However, the relatively attractive London interest rates combined with optimism about the British outlook encouraged foreigners not only to maintain the sterling investments they had made during the winter of 1924-25 but to increase them. For this and other special reasons, the Bank of England gained between May and August 1925 almost £9 million in gold which acted to expand commercial bank reserves and, more importantly, also stimulated public demands that monetary policy be eased.[81]

Norman had a number of courses open to him in dealing with this perplexing problem. He could attempt to offset the expansionary effect of the gold inflow through open market sales, but here he faced the same dilemma as Strong. To the extent that such open market sales kept the money market taut, they only

---

[79] *Milton Friedman and Anna J. Schwartz,* A Monetary History of the United States, 1867-1960 *(Princeton: Princeton University Press, 1963), page 711; Harold Barger,* Outlay and Income in the United States, 1921-1938 *(New York: National Bureau of Economic Research, Inc., 1942), pages 114 and 179.*

[80] *Norman letter to Strong, May 26, 1925.*

[81] *Norman letter to Strong, May 26, 1925; Strong letter to Jay, August 1, 1925; Strong cable to Jay, No. 6, August 1, 1925; and "Commercial History and Review of 1925",* The Economist, *February 13, 1926, page 8.*

encouraged the flow of foreign balances to London and of gold to the Bank of England. The pressures for the relaxation of monetary policy would be increased. Other courses were suggested by Strong. One, which bore fruit in later years, was that the bank should take advantage of the demand for sterling to build up dollar balances that could be employed to meet the seasonal needs that were expected to develop in the autumn.[82] Another was that gold gains should be taken, not by the Bank of England, but by the Treasury which could employ them as backing for its note issue and so prepare for the day when the notes issued by the Treasury and the central bank would be amalgamated.[83] Both proposals had the advantage that they would prevent reserve gains from being reflected in the bank's published gold holdings and so might help reduce public pressure for easier money. However, neither proposal was taken up at the time—perhaps because the Treasury itself seems to have been exerting heavy pressure on the bank to relax its monetary policy.[84]

The upshot was that Norman took the more straightforward and—as it now appears—more daring course. He followed what were then believed to be the traditional rules of the game, and he did so with some vigor in order, in the end, to return to the tight money policy that he felt was necessary. He was of course aware that substantial foreign balances had been placed in London, and he anticipated that a good part of them would be withdrawn if his money market rates declined significantly relative to those offered in other centers, particularly New York. If the reduction in London money rates coincided with the normal autumn pressure against sterling, a substantial amount of gold would be lost, the Treasury and the public would become concerned, and the gold standard tradition would justify a sharp advance in the bank rate and the reimposition of a strict monetary discipline. Norman had employed the seasonal strength in the country's payments to foster the return to gold during the spring; he would now employ its seasonal weakness to enforce the tight monetary policy that he felt was necessary to support sterling in the long run.[85]

---

[82] *Strong cable to Norman, No. 91, May 23, 1925.*

[83] *Strong letter to Harrison, August 7, 1925.*

[84] *Grigg, op. cit., page 193; Clay, op. cit., page 293.*

[85] *Norman letters to Strong, May 26, August 21, and November 23, 1925; Strong letters to Case, August 1 and 5, 1925, and to Harrison, August 7, 1925. See also Strong cable to Jay, No. 6, August 1, 1925.*

The first phase of Norman's ease-squeeze tactics was executed during the summer of 1925. The expansionary effects of the gold inflow and of a moderate decline in note circulation was only partly offset by decreases in the bank's holdings of securities and in discounts and advances, with the consequence that bankers' and other deposits at the Bank of England rose 4.1 per cent in May-August. On August 6, the Bank of England's discount rate was reduced ½ per cent to 4½ per cent. The London rate for three-month bankers' bills averaged 3.94 per cent in August, 0.65 point below the May peak. With New York money rates rising, the margin of London bill rates above the corresponding rates in New York narrowed to an average of only 0.69 point in August from 1.40 points in May.

In September, the bank began to lose gold but the deflationary effect on the cash base was more than offset by an increase in the bank's holdings of securities and a modest increase in discounts and advances, so that bankers' and other deposits rose another 2.8 per cent. Rates on bankers' bills in London continued to decline, narrowing the margin above New York to only 0.18 point. On October 1, the bank rate was again reduced by ½ per cent to 4 per cent and, in the following two weeks, London rates on bankers' bills averaged 0.19 per cent *below* New York.[86] On a comparison of call money rates, London averaged 1.56 per cent *below* New York during October.[87]

Developments in the forward exchange market followed these changes in interest rate relationships with considerable faithfulness. The discount on three-month forward sterling which had been 0.82 per cent in June 1925, had disappeared during September and had changed to a premium of 0.49 per cent in early October. Although on a comparison of bankers' bills there remained a modest incentive to move covered funds from New York to London, on a comparison of call money rates there was a much stronger incentive in the opposite direction, particularly during September and October when the movement of a significant volume of balances from London to New York was in fact recorded.[88]

As these movements of funds gathered momentum, they added to the seasonal

---

[86] The Economist, *October 3 and 10, 1925;* Federal Reserve Bulletin, *October 1925.*

[87] *Einzig, op. cit., page 501.*

[88] Federal Reserve Bulletin, *June 1926, pages 377-78.*

weakness of spot sterling. In the early summer the rate had hovered at or only slightly below the $4.867 parity. It began to slip late in July. By mid-September it was at $4.84¾, approximately the gold export point to New York, and thereafter dipped still further to fluctuate at or a little above $4.84. In October some $40 million in gold was shipped from London to New York, and for October and November as a whole the Bank of England showed a £13 million decline in its holdings of gold.

This very substantial gold loss, which pushed the Bank of England's holdings below the £150 million minimum recommended by the Cunliffe Committee, set the stage for the second phase of Norman's tactics, i.e., the restoration of the 5 per cent bank rate. Particularly during October, the bank reduced its securities holdings and so reinforced the squeeze that the gold losses were putting on the market. Discounts and advances expanded, short-term interest rates rose sharply, and the market began to expect an early bank rate increase. In these circumstances, market tenders for Treasury bills declined and the Bank of England found it necessary to come to the rescue to cover the Treasury's short-term borrowing requirements. At the end of November, as the Deputy Governor told the Macmillan Committee,[89]

> the amount which the Bank had to provide in order to cover the required amount of tenders was very substantial . . . . finally we were compelled, simply in order to get the bills taken up, and to avoid our being driven into a very difficult position by reason of the large additions of credit that we were having to create, to raise the rate from four per cent to five per cent.

The bank's decision put a severe strain on its relations with the Treasury. In the late evening of Wednesday, December 2, Norman called at the Treasury to inform the Chancellor, as a matter of courtesy, of the impending bank rate increase. About 11:20 a.m. the next day, Churchill telephoned to protest vigorously against the increase. He threatened to tell the House of Commons that he had not been consulted and that the increase was against his wishes. Noting that such action on the part of a Chancellor was without precedent, Norman stood on his legal rights and for some time thereafter relations between the Governor and Churchill were decidedly cold.[90]

---

[89] Macmillan Evidence, *Vol. II, question 7596, pages 179-80.*

[90] *Grigg,* op. cit., *page 193; Clay,* op. cit., *page 293.*

102

Norman's tactics were vindicated by a decided strengthening of sterling. Immediately following the bank rate increase, the spot rate rose to $4.85 and from January through August 1926 it was, with a few exceptions, at or above $4.86. Even when the adverse seasonal pressures set in during the autumn, the rate did not fall to the gold export point. Early in 1926 the Bank of England ceased to lose gold, and during the entire second half of that year its holdings remained somewhat above £150 million.

Behind these superficially satisfactory figures was the beginning of the adjustment process. It was painful although perhaps not more so than the authorities had originally anticipated. The Bank of England enforced a strict monetary discipline. Reductions in its holdings of securities and in discounts and advances more than offset the expansionary effects of the rise in its gold holdings and of a continued reduction in note circulation, with the result that bankers' and other deposits at the Bank of England declined 6.2 per cent in the year ended November 1926. Although the London clearing banks partially offset the squeeze on their cash base by working to a lower cash ratio, the total of currency circulation plus clearing bank deposits was on the average virtually unchanged in 1926 from the year before and was slightly lower than in 1924.[91] Pressure to reduce wages and other costs was continued, leading to an especially long and embittered strike in the coal mines and a nine-day general strike in May 1926. Unemployment continued high. The overall gross national product was only slightly larger in 1926 than in 1924, but a beginning was made to changing its composition away from the old staple trades such as coal, steel, and shipbuilding where output declined toward such technically advanced and expanding industries as those producing rayon, motor vehicles, and electrical apparatus.[92] Equally significant, British export prices continued to decline in 1926 but—allowing for the difficulties of international price comparisons—not enough to eliminate more than a little of the competitive advantages held by Britain's major commercial rivals.[93]

While the adjustment process was moving slowly forward, the financing of the deficit in Britain's current and long-term capital accounts remained pressing. The problem was particularly serious in 1926. Although imports were somewhat

[91] London and Cambridge Economic Service, The British Economy: Key Statistics 1900-1964 (London, 1965), page 16.

[92] Ibid., page 6; G. C. Allen, British Industries and Their Organization (4th ed.; London: Longmans, Green and Co. Ltd., 1959), pages 24 and 31.

[93] League of Nations, Review of World Trade (1930), pages 63-65.

smaller in value than in the two previous years, exports dropped very much more sharply, not only because of reduced sales of coal abroad, but also because of smaller exports of textiles, iron, and steel.[94] Beyond this, the lifting of the controls in November 1925 had been followed by a spurt of new capital issues on foreign account which rose by 27 per cent in 1926 from the year before. All told, Britain's deficit on current and long-term capital account widened to almost £ 100 million in 1926, more than double the 1925 deficit.[95]

Bank of England policy certainly facilitated the financing of this deficit by maintaining attractive conditions in the London market. However, a renewed flight from the French franc was probably the main factor in the large positive errors and omissions item that balanced the accounts. While London rates for three-month bankers' bills remained well above the corresponding New York rate throughout 1926 and there was a significant incentive to move funds on a covered basis both at the beginning of the year and at the end, the actual flow of United States funds does not seem to have been significant. In relation to most Continental centers, on the other hand, London money market rates were relatively low, yet such was its attractiveness on other counts that London continued to be a preferred center in which to hold short-term balances. Overseas borrowers invested in London a considerable proportion of the proceeds of their loans, some of which were floated for the express purpose of acquiring sterling reserves.[96] Moreover, the proceeds of some of the loans raised in New York by Australian, German, and other foreign borrowers were transferred to London to be held there at least temporarily.[97] Other ordinary commercial transactions probably also contributed to the buildup of balances in London during 1926, but the single most important factor was almost certainly the renewed flight from the French franc. The flight began in October 1925 and reached its climax in July 1926, by which time the foreign exchange value of the franc had been reduced to half the level at which it had been stabilized

[94] Board of Trade, Accounts Relating to Trade and Navigation of the United Kingdom (London: H. M. Stationery Office, 1926), page 6.

[95] T. C. Chang, Cyclical Movements in the Balance of Payments (Cambridge: Cambridge University Press, 1951), table opposite page 144; A. E. Kahn, Great Britain in the World Economy (New York: Columbia University Press, 1946), page 126.

[96] Kahn, op. cit., page 166.

[97] Clay, op. cit., page 237; Strong letter to Bachmann, November 18, 1927, page 1; Strong letter to Norman, October 21, 1927; and Nadler memorandum to Goldenweiser, December 27, 1926, pages 2-3 (Federal Reserve Board Papers).

during the summer of 1924. No doubt some of the huge movement of funds out of France was reflected in the rise in foreign-owned dollar balances mentioned above, but the available—though admittedly skimpy—evidence suggests that the bulk of it found its way to London.[98]

The magnitude of the flow of funds to London and the resulting strength of sterling during most of the year following the December 3, 1925 bank rate increase once again confronted the authorities with the problem of avoiding an unwanted easing of monetary policy. Partly, the problem was to avoid gold gains so large as to arouse renewed public pressure for easier money. With this objective in view, the Bank of England followed one of the suggestions that had been made by Strong in 1925.[99] Even when it was still losing gold during October-December 1925, the Bank of England was increasing its dollar balances at the Federal Reserve Bank of New York. The process was continued during 1926. Of the $115 million increase in Bank of England holdings of dollars at the Federal Reserve and of gold, only the $38 million rise in gold was revealed in its weekly balance sheet. The $77 million gain in dollars was lumped with changes in the bank's "other securities" and was thus hidden from public view. Moreover, the bank fully offset the expansionary effect of these dollar gains on the domestic cash base by selling sterling securities, thus foreshadowing the operations of the Exchange Equalization Account that was to be established six years later.[100] Britain's need to maintain a tight monetary policy in order to foster adjustment was forcing Norman, like Strong, to ignore the gold standard tradition under which monetary policy was supposed to be automatically linked to movements in international reserves.

THE UNFINISHED TASK OF INTERNATIONAL ECONOMIC COOPERATION

By the end of 1926, the restoration of sterling to the prewar gold parity appeared to have been successfully accomplished. The British currency was relatively strong on the foreign exchange markets, and London was regaining its position as a major international financial center. Beyond this, eighteen other countries had

---

[98] *Institut National de la Statistique et des Études Economiques,* Annuaire Statistique de la France, *Rétrospectif Edition, 1961, page 211; J. M. Keynes, "The British Balance of Trade",* Economic Journal, *Vol. 37 (December 1927), page 556.*

[99] Supra, *page 100.*

[100] *Clay,* op. cit., *page 255.*

by then stabilized their currencies in terms of gold, and France, the only major country whose currency was not formally stabilized, was making rapid progress in that direction.

Compared with the chaos of the earlier postwar years, the relatively stable exchange conditions of the latter part of 1926 represented a major advance. Yet, despite all appearances, these conditions rested on shaky foundations. An appreciable part of the large foreign balances in London consisted of French flight capital that was likely to be repatriated as confidence in the franc strengthened. The heavy outflow of capital from the United States was continuing, but there could be no assurance of how long it would last. Nor was there any assurance that, if this outflow declined, the consequent difficulties could be handled through central bank cooperation. The United States economic conditions that had made it possible for the Federal Reserve to cooperate so successfully with the Bank of England in 1924-25 were bound to change, as the central bankers themselves clearly recognized. As early as January 1925, well before the British authorities had made the final decision to return to gold, Strong had warned Norman that,[101]

> in a new country such as ours, with an enthusiastic, energetic, and optimistic population, where enterprise at times was highly stimulated and the returns upon capital much greater than in other countries, there would be times when speculative tendencies would make it necessary for the Federal Reserve Banks to exercise restraint by increased discount rates, and possibly rather high money rates in the market. Should such times arise, *domestic considerations would likely outweigh foreign sympathies . . . .*

Looking back, it seems clear that Norman and Strong were confronted with urgent questions: Could the monetary contraction that was being pursued by the London authorities bring about an adequate strengthening of Britain's fundamental external position before the disappearance of the international conditions that favored sterling? Was it not necessary to develop more effective policy techniques to accelerate the adjustment process, or failing this, could new forms of international cooperation be arranged to support sterling in the interim? Confronting their day-to-day problems, Strong and Norman almost certainly sensed the long-term difficulties with which they were faced, but there is no evidence that they thought in terms of questions such as these. Such questions were foreign to the intellectual milieu in which they worked. They were influenced

---

[101] *Strong memorandum of January 11, 1925, page 3. Italics added.*

by the illusion that the stabilization of most currencies in terms of gold had brought about the realization of the gold standard conception to which they aspired. Consequently, they tended to deal with some of the knotty problems of the mid-1920's in terms of glib textbook formulas that were of doubtful validity even in the nineteenth century heyday of the gold standard. It is certainly true that, where their own pressing national problems were concerned, Strong, Norman, and their colleagues were tough, penetrating, and gave short shrift to orthodox preconceptions that ran counter to their views of the public interest. However, where the problems of others were concerned, they sometimes based their judgments on the pieties of the gold standard rules of the game. These were venerable, accepted, and were particularly convenient when they shifted to foreign shoulders the burden of dealing with the adjustment problem. But there was far more than an understandable orthodoxy behind the failure to develop and systematize central bank cooperation. The priority that the monetary authorities were expected to give to their respective domestic needs discouraged the discussion of how the burdens of adjustment should be distributed among deficit and surplus countries. In a period when financial probity was equated with budgetary balance and the virtue of government noninterference in the economy was almost beyond question, there was little disposition to ask whether monetary policy alone could be relied upon to foster required international adjustments in the time that was likely to be available, or whether policy-induced movements of capital might actually obscure the need to adjust.

Looking at the records of the midtwenties, one is forced to the conclusion that the authorities failed to develop any genuine understanding of the nature and magnitude of the international adjustment problem and of how and on what terms such adjustments should be financed. But one senses that, in his persistent efforts to convene a central bankers' conference, Norman was groping in his intuitive way toward such understanding and that a significant step forward was made when Strong agreed in November 1925 that "a quiet meeting of some of the heads of the central banks" might be useful.[102] Such a meeting was eventually held but not until July 1927. It was only with painful slowness that the central bankers reviewed and extended their cooperative techniques, far too slowly to cope effectively with the overwhelming international economic pressures that were soon to be upon them.

---

[102] *Strong letter to Norman, November 20, 1925, page 2.*

6. The Defense of a Key Currency: 1926-28

INTRODUCTION

The strains to which the international financial system was subject in the later 1920's arose from the sharply contrasting economic conditions of the major industrial countries, from divergences both in national aims and in official views about how the international financial system should operate, from inadequacies in monetary instruments and policies, and from peculiarities in the international market for gold.

It has already been noted how the rapid recoveries of Germany and France led to heavy movements of capital into those countries from the more slowly expanding United States and British economies. The German and French central banks consequently acquired substantial short-term claims on New York and London but, as they did so, they pumped cash into their own economies to an extent which caused official concern about the maintenance of monetary stability. Having inadequate instruments with which to enforce monetary control in their own markets, the German and French authorities attempted to shift the application of gold standard remedies abroad by converting foreign balances into gold. They hoped that, by so doing, they would force the gold-losing countries to raise interest rates and thereby to check the outflow of capital. In the United States, where the Federal Reserve felt its stock of gold to be excessive, such conversions presented no problem, but in Britain they soon gave rise to grave concern. Despite the flow into the London market of the gold output of South Africa and other British Empire countries, the addition of German and French conversions to existing demand exhausted market supplies and at times forced the Bank of England to meet the residual demand from its own holdings. Since all but a slim margin of these holdings served as note cover, the loss of only relatively modest amounts of Bank of England gold tended to force the authorities to intensify the deflationary pressures on the already depressed economy, and confronted them with the questions whether the accentuation of such pressure would be politically tolerable in Britain and whether sterling's link with gold could be maintained.

The Bank of England's problem was openly discussed by Norman, Strong, Moreau, and Schacht, who understood that the breaking of the link between sterling and gold would gravely threaten the newly restored international financial system and who therefore worked for a time to alleviate the pressures on sterling. But little was done either to correct the underlying difficulties or to develop more permanent international machinery by which the major countries could support each other's currencies. Indeed, the temporary rise in the Bank of England's gold holdings that was the immediate outcome of the cooperative efforts diverted attention from the fundamental economic difficulties, encouraged the authorities to adopt measures that eventually exposed sterling to renewed pressures, and complicated the problems of central bank cooperation.

PAYMENTS SURPLUSES COMPLICATE MONETARY POLICY

Cooperation among the major countries in 1926-28 was fundamentally different from that of 1924-25. In the earlier phase, Norman and Strong had worked to attain a mutually desired objective: the restoration of sterling to its 1914 parity. In the second phase, cooperation involved the reconciliation of the major countries' conflicting needs in order to maintain that parity. Of several sources of conflict, the one that is relevant here arose from the heavy flow of funds into Germany and France in 1926-28 and from the problems of currency management that grew out of these inflows. In both countries, these flows were considered by the authorities to threaten not only domestic monetary control but also the external stability of their currencies.

GERMANY. The trouble arose first in Germany, to which a particularly large volume of foreign long- and short-term capital flowed in 1926. So large was the inflow that, despite substantial outpayments on account of the country's merchandise trade deficit and reparations, the Reichsbank's international assets rose by one fourth during the year. However, the Reichsbank was not well equipped to deal with the domestic monetary effects of these reserve gains. It held no government debt that could be shifted to the market, and its holdings of bills and other marketable paper were small in relation to the value of the foreign balances that were coming into Germany. For a few months in the early part of 1926, the Reichsbank succeeded in offsetting its foreign exchange purchases by reducing its holdings of marketable securities but, as Schacht subsequently related to Norman, when this open market ammunition had been exhausted, "I lost totally control of the market".[1]

---

[1] *Schacht letter to Norman, May 21, 1927, page 1.*

At the same time, Schacht was gravely concerned about the threat to the external stability of the reichsmark. He never ceased to insist that heavy foreign borrowing was placing Germany in a completely false position. It was false because, under the Dawes Plan, reparation payments and the service of the Dawes Loan were given absolute priority over all other German obligations: Germany's private creditors abroad were being deluded about the security of their loans. Moreover, Germany itself, Schacht insisted, was living in a fool's paradise because the proceeds of a significant proportion of its foreign borrowings were not being employed in a manner that would increase the economy's ability to export and so meet its foreign obligations. As Schacht saw it, the time would inevitably come when the inflow from abroad would cease, bringing the threat of default not only on the private obligations incurred abroad but perhaps even on the Dawes Loan and reparations. Unsound and excessive foreign borrowing thus threatened to undermine the financial structure that had been so painfully built only two years before.[2]

FRANCE. At about the same time, parallel problems were developing in France. There they arose, not only from the huge influx of balances from abroad that followed the successful July 1926 effort of the newly formed Poincaré government to deal with France's chronic fiscal difficulties, but also from the inability of the French authorities to agree upon the exchange rate at which the franc should be legally stabilized. Indeed, this exchange rate debate continued with varying degrees of intensity until June 1928 when the franc was finally stabilized *de jure*.

In the intervening period, the exchange markets were swept by ever-changing rumors about the level at which the franc parity would be fixed. However, after August 7, 1926 when the Bank of France was authorized to acquire gold, silver coin, and foreign exchange at a premium over the rate at which it was empowered to operate under its prewar statutes, the authorities were in a position to choose whether to let these market pressures be reflected in movements of the exchange rate or of official reserves. Actually they operated at first to moderate the appreciation of the franc, as balances were repatriated during the fall of 1926.

---

[2] *Hjalmar Schacht*, The Stabilization of the Mark *(London: George Allen & Unwin, Ltd., 1927), Chapter 9, and* The End of Reparations *(New York: Jonathan Cape and Harrison Smith, 1931), Chapter 3.*

Subsequently, however, they pegged the currency at roughly 25 francs to the dollar, at which level the exchange rate was stablized *de facto* in December 1926.

During the first half of 1927, the French economy continued to attract balances from abroad. Frenchmen, whose confidence in their currency had revived, repatriated their funds. Yields on long-term government bonds were high. The country's economic prospects seemed promising. Equity prices on the Paris bourse seemed likely to rise. Above all, influential persons—including Poincaré and Doumergue, the President of the Republic—were working for a further substantial appreciation of the franc.[3] Indeed, certain directors of the Bank of France favored a return to the prewar parity and said as much in public.[4] When the Bank of France had the satisfaction of announcing in April 1927 that it had paid off a substantial loan from the Bank of England in a lump sum and well in advance of maturity and had thus regained custody of gold which had been pledged against the loan, speculation that the franc would be allowed to appreciate further was greatly intensified. Not only did Frenchmen hasten to repatriate their funds but the evidence suggests that other Europeans, and perhaps Americans too, joined the rush to get into the franc. The Bank of France's foreign exchange holdings, which totaled no more than $50 million at the end of November 1926, mounted to $770 million by the end of May.[5]

The heavy inflows of foreign balances caused problems for Moreau in the spring of 1927 similar to those that had confronted Schacht during 1926. On the domestic side, the threat was perhaps not so great in France as in Germany because close cooperation between the French central bank and Treasury enabled the authorities to maintain a degree of monetary control. In effect, much of the cash that was pumped into the market by the Bank of France's purchases of foreign exchange was mopped up by Treasury funding issues, the proceeds of which were employed to reduce the government's short-term debt to the central bank. The authorities thus shifted government debt from the central bank to the market and achieved the same results that would have been attained through central bank open market sales.[6] The drawback, of course, was that the central

---

[3] Moreau Diary, *April 29, 1927, January 9, 1928, and page 572.*

[4] *Strong letter to Harrison, May 15, 1926. Also* Moreau Diary, *April 29-May 12, 1927.*

[5] *Quesnay letter to Goldenweiser, November 29, 1928 (Federal Reserve Board Papers).*

[6] *League of Nations,* International Currency Experience *(Princeton, 1944), page 76.*

bank could maintain monetary control only so long as the cooperation with the Treasury continued, and despite the success of this cooperation there is evidence that Moreau believed the continuing inflow of foreign balances was leading to an excessive increase in the bank's note issue.[7]

It was the external threat posed by France's balance-of-payments surplus that caused the gravest concern to Moreau, because the inflow of funds was working on the side of those influential persons who wished to have the franc stabilized at, or at least nearer to, its 1914 gold parity. To Moreau and his closest colleagues any such appreciation of the currency was unthinkable, not only because it would bring severe losses on the Bank of France's existing exchange holdings, but also because it would involve the deflation of French wages and prices, an increase in the burden of debt on the domestic economy, and a serious weakening of France's international competitive position. They felt intensely that France should avoid the mistake that they believed Britain had made in 1925.[8]

THE SHIFT TOWARD GOLD

While the inflows of foreign funds led to problems that were broadly similar in Germany and France, the manner in which Schacht and Moreau attempted to deal with these problems in 1926 and 1927 showed marked contrasts, stemming in large part from the differences in the relations between their two countries and Britain and between themselves and Norman.

GERMANY. Throughout the early postwar years Britain, against French opposition, had generally supported a lenient Allied policy toward the defeated Central Powers and had worked actively for the political and economic rehabilitation of Germany, Austria, and Hungary. In this work, Norman, as we have seen, had taken a leading part. It was, therefore, to Norman that Schacht turned as soon as he had become President of the Reichsbank at the end of 1923, and he received a warm and helpful welcome during his visit to the Bank of England

---

[7] Moreau Diary, *April 28, 1927, February 28, 1928, March 22, 1928, and April 5, 1928; Strong's memorandum on discussion with the Bank of France, May 27, 1928; Rist letter to Strong, June 9, 1928.*

[8] *Strong memorandum, "Program of Stabilization of the Franc", August 19, 1926, pages 3-5;* Moreau Diary, *April 25 and May 12, 1927 and page 573; Moreau and Norman conversation, May 27, 1927, page 1.*

early in January 1924.[9] Norman's subsequent work to obtain acceptance of the Dawes Plan and to float the Dawes Loan further solidified his relations with Schacht. For all these reasons and because, in addition, the British government was the most likely one to lead a movement for the reduction of reparations and war debts, Schacht was inclined to look with sympathy and understanding on Britain's financial difficulties, to do what he could to relieve them, and thus to practice with moderation and restraint the gold standard principles which he professed.

Accordingly, Schacht's external policy in 1924-26 was designed to minimize the pressure on the London gold market and particularly on the Bank of England's gold reserve, and to transfer as much of this pressure as possible to New York, which was willing and able to take it. His policy thus served as the prototype for the broader cooperation among the central bankers that was to be arranged in the summer of 1927. It was, of course, to the Reichsbank's advantage to hold the sterling proceeds of the Dawes Loan until the British currency had returned to par and to obtain in New York the gold that it needed toward the end of 1924.[10] Nevertheless, there is evidence that for a year or more after April 1925 Schacht did not let his sterling balances fall much, if any, below the level to which they had been raised by the Dawes Loan and that he continued, though London was the cheapest market, to meet the bulk of his gold requirements elsewhere, primarily in New York.[11]

However, as Schacht's currency management problems mounted during 1926, his willingness to spare London declined. Measures to curb the heavy inflow of foreign funds became essential. Accordingly, the authorities unpegged the reichsmark from its fixed relation to the dollar and, by allowing the exchange rate to fluctuate within the gold points, introduced an element of exchange risks into the foreign exchange market. They also suspended the preferential tax treatment that had previously been accorded to income from German bonds floated in foreign markets.[12] More important from the viewpoint of this monograph, Schacht

[9] *Hjalmar Schacht,* My First Seventy-Six Years *(London: Allan Wingate, 1955), Chapters 24 and 25.*

[10] Supra, *page 65. Shepard Morgan letter to Strong, January 28, 1925.*

[11] *Schacht,* The Stabilization of the Mark, *page 208; W. A. Brown, Jr.,* The International Gold Standard Reinterpreted, *1914-1934 (New York: National Bureau of Economic Research, Inc., 1940), Vol. I, page 636.*

[12] *Brown,* The International Gold Standard Reinterpreted, 1914-1934, *Vol. I, pages 479-80.*

sought to treat his currency management problems with a gold standard remedy: he no longer operated quite so gently as before in the London gold market. Toward the end of October, Norman was writing to Strong that "Schacht had already sucked £6½ million in gold out of London".[13] A little later, the Reichsbank encouraged private interests to acquire gold from abroad by announcing that it would accept the metal in Bremen as well as in Berlin, thus saving private arbitragers the cost of shipping the gold to the bank's head office.[14] In the six months ended February 1927, British gold exports to Germany totaled almost $60 million, more than half the output of the South African mines during that period.[15]

How far Schacht expected his gold purchases to mitigate his monetary control problem is not clear. He probably expected them to have no effect on the Federal Reserve, whose strength and policy he understood, but he may have hoped to encourage a tightening of British monetary policy that would curb the flow of funds from London. If so, he was disappointed when he received a letter toward the end of December 1926 in which Norman said:[16]

> Your German concerns borrow money in America (of which I do not think they have need, but that is another question) and Dutch or German Bankers, seeing the strength of the Mark-Pound Exchange, withdrew the proceeds of these Loans from London in gold. There is nothing within reason which I could do to protect this market: it is not a question of interest rates against which a Central Bank may need to be defended but is rather a question of ½% or thereabouts on the charges for the shipment of gold from New York.
>
> I am not complaining but merely thinking aloud of the difficulties which nowadays arise owing to our international machine being so greatly out of gear .

Clearly Norman and Schacht were at cross-purposes. When he received a sympathetic reply from Schacht, Norman went on to encourage the German central banker to consider cooperative means by which to avoid gold movements that, in Norman's words, "are nowadays often fortuitous and irrelevant to the

---

[13] *Norman letter to Strong, October 29, 1926.*

[14] *W. A. Brown, Jr.,* England and the New Gold Standard, 1919-1926 *(New Haven: Yale University Press, 1929), pages 293 and 295.*

[15] The Economist, *January 14, 1928, page 61.*

[16] *Sir Henry Clay,* Lord Norman *(London: Macmillan & Co., Ltd., 1957), page 224.*

monetary situation in one country or another".[17] But before these discussions could proceed very far, Germany's balance-of-payments position turned around. By mid-1927, the Reichsbank's international assets had dropped $250 million.[18] The pressure on London was no longer coming from Berlin but from Paris.

FRANCE. The atmosphere in which Norman and Moreau attempted to deal with the flow of funds to Paris was hardly conducive to cooperation. They came to the task without the fund of mutual understanding and confidence that existed between Norman and Strong and Schacht. This lack stemmed in large part from the long history of rivalry between the two countries and particularly from conflict in their postwar policies relating to Germany.[19] It also grew out of Norman's unhelpful attitude toward France in the difficult years before July 1926. It is impossible to say how far Norman's attitude was determined by the broader political conflict and how far by the inability of successive French governments to deal firmly with the country's deteriorating finances and thus create conditions that would justify help from the Bank of England. The fact remains that there is nothing in the record of the years up to July 1926 to indicate that Norman went out of his way to help the French authorities, and several instances are known in which he opposed the granting of any financial assistance or, if assistance was given, insisted on terms that the French considered onerous.[20]

The early conflicts and humiliations were keenly remembered by the management of the Bank of France after the franc recovered its strength in mid-1926. Led by Émile Moreau, who became Governor in June 1926, the bank's management was intensely patriotic, as dedicated to the political objectives of the Poincaré government as to the strength of the franc, but isolated from the monetary authorities elsewhere in Europe and unfamiliar with the problems of the evolving international financial system. Indeed Strong, in the course of his protracted discussions with Moreau and his colleagues in August-September 1926, became convinced that the Bank of France management was suspicious and mistrustful of most European central bankers, and especially of Norman and

---

[17] Ibid., *page 225.*

[18] Reports of the Agent General, *September 1, 1926 to August 31, 1927, Vol. I, page 240.*

[19] *Arnold Wolfers,* Britain and France Between Two Wars *(1st ed.; New York: Harcourt Brace and Co., 1940). See also Chapter 2.*

[20] *Clay,* op. cit., *page 223; Moreau Diary, February 26, 1927; Norman cable to Strong, No. 43, December 13, 1924.*

Schacht, and would listen to advice only from the Federal Reserve authorities, whom the French considered to be uninvolved with Europe's perennial quarrels.[21]

An instance of the mutual suspicion that permeated the relations between the British and French central bankers arose in the early months of 1927 when Moreau approached Norman about modification of the terms of a loan that the Bank of England had made to the Bank of France in 1923, secured by the deposit of French gold in London. Writing to Harrison, Strong described the atmosphere in which these negotiations took place.[22]

> The Bank of France did not believe that the [$] 90 millions of gold due from the Bank of England was actually there, but feared that it had been used. The Bank of England did not believe that the Bank of France had the sterling available with which to repay the commercial debt, and feared the entry of the Bank of France into the exchange market. I think this mistrust continued despite assurances by both sides as to what the facts were. On the whole, it was a pitiful exhibition on both sides, not as to the character and intentions of the individuals, but as to the general atmosphere in which all of these matters are discussed and dealt with, and I admit that I was greatly impressed by the fact that they both [i.e., Siepmann and Quesnay, with whom Strong had been discussing the problem] accepted the point of view that individually any and all of them were willing to do the utmost to improve matters, but that collectively, because of the overshadowing influence of political considerations in Europe as a whole, they were almost helpless.

It was against this unpromising background that the difficulties arising from the flow of funds to Paris were handled. Holding large short-term balances in London, the Bank of France, after so many years of weakness, found itself in a powerful bargaining position, which it fully appreciated and employed to force the adoption abroad of measures to check the inflow. By the same token the position of the Bank of England was extremely weak, forcing Norman to fall back, after all else had failed, on the warning that, if pressed too far, Britain might have no alternative but to abandon the gold standard and thus jeopardize the reconstruction of the international financial system. In the end the impasse was broken not only by a degree of accommodation on the part of both the British and the French but also by the intervention of Strong, under whose leadership the Federal Reserve adopted policies that were to shift much of the burden of adjustment from the British economy to that of the United States.

---

[21] *Strong cable to Harrison, No. 46, July 31, 1926; Strong letter to Harrison, August 17, 1926, pages 3-4 (Harrison Papers).*

[22] *Strong letter to Harrison, July 27, 1928, page 6.*

In the struggle to deal with the inflow to Paris, the Bank of France made the first move. Its aim was to bring about a rise in the Bank of England discount rate, a tightening in the London money market, and a curtailment of British credit that the French authorities believed to have been extended to the major Continental centers and, by this means, to force a tightening of monetary conditions in Amsterdam and Berlin as well as in London.[23] To achieve these objectives the Bank of France began, apparently without prior notification to the Bank of England, to convert sterling balances both into dollars and into gold. On several days in mid-May 1927, Moreau noted in his dairy that, although the Bank of France was still taking in substantial amounts of sterling, it had sold even larger amounts for dollars.[24] At about the same time Moreau asked Strong to convert $100 million of the Bank of France's dollar balances into gold, which was done during the latter half of May. Similarly, he requested the Bank of England to acquire gold in the London market to the value of £1.5 million on May 18, another £1 million on May 21, and thereafter £3 million weekly until a total of £20 million had been acquired.[25] When Moreau learned of the alarm that this program had created at the Bank of England, he agreed to postpone further gold purchases in London, so that the British authorities might have an opportunity to suggest alternative means by which to curb the flow of funds to France. It was to discuss such means that Norman visited the Bank of France on May 27.

The record of this meeting brings sharply into focus the opposing position of the two central banks.[26] In a brilliant exposition Norman described Britain's domestic economic difficulties and argued that a tightening of Bank of England monetary policy would only aggravate these difficulties while failing to offset the overwhelming pull of the French economy on foreign balances. Norman concluded that the inflow could be effectively checked only if the French authorities themselves were to adopt corrective measures including the *de jure* stabilization of the franc or at least a firm declaration that speculative pressures would not force the abandonment of the existing exchange rate. Unfortunately, the disagree-

---

[23] Moreau Diary, *May 12, 1927; Norman and Moreau conversation, May 27, 1927, pages 1-3 and 13-17.*

[24] Moreau Diary, *May 13 and 16, 1927.*

[25] Moreau Diary, *May 18, 1927. See also Norman's cables to Strong, No. 38, May 24, 1927 and No. 40, May 25, 1927, in which Norman refers to Moreau's "capricious demands" and to his "fear" that Moreau's gold buying program would "menace the gold standard".*

[26] *The record is published in full in the* Moreau Diary, *May 27, 1927, and in an abbreviated English version in Clay, op. cit., pages 228-32.*

ment among the French authorities precluded any such declaration at the time—let alone *de jure* stablization. Consequently, Moreau and his associates, Rist and Quesnay, did not budge from their position that, since the flow was coming to France primarily in the form of sterling, the responsibility for checking the flow rested squarely on the Bank of England. They sympathized with Britain's domestic problems; they did not wish to impair sterling's link with gold; but they insisted that the Bank of England should tighten the London money market, if only to attract new funds from abroad to replace the balances that the Bank of France wished to convert into gold and dollars.

Although neither side gave any ground in these discussions, the May 27 meeting prepared the way for accommodation. The French authorities wanted to shift the burden of adjustment abroad but, in exerting pressure to achieve this aim, they did not wish to go as far as to push sterling off gold. Only a few days before the meeting, Poincaré had indicated to Moreau his opinion that Britain's financial position had greatly deteriorated in recent months and that, if a Labor government were to replace the Conservative one, the existing sterling parity could not be long maintained; he recommended that the Governor follow a cautious course in his dealing with the Bank of England.[27] At the May 27 meeting, Moreau may have been left unmoved by Norman's warnings that French pressure could undermine the gold standard, but subsequently he became convinced of Norman's desperation by a countermove that the British authorities threatened to make if the Bank of France pressure became too severe. In effect, the British would shift the dispute from one between central banks to one between governments. As Moreau understood it, the British authorities would say:[28]

> You have claims on us of £70 million. If you insist on repayment, if you wish to liquidate and thereby ruin us, the [British] Treasury will collect its £600 million claim on France [for war debts]. This debt is not yet consolidated. These notes, which until now have always been renewed and which represent the indebtedness of the French Government, we shall put on the market or present for collection. And, in the ensuing chaos, we shall see who gets the better of it.

By mid-June, Moreau had had an opportunity to size up Britain's countermove and had become convinced that his dominance over the Bank of England was counterbalanced by the dominance of the British Treasury over that of France:

---

[27] Moreau Diary, *May 23, 1927*.

[28] Moreau Diary, *May 30, 1927*.

118

"When we exert pressure upon the [Bank of England], M. Churchill threatens M. Poincaré."[29] The confrontation had ended in a draw.

BRITISH-FRENCH ACCOMMODATION

While this standoff was approaching, changes were occurring in the London market that enabled Moreau to modify his position in good grace. The Bank of England did not change its bank rate, but it did squeeze the market and thus encouraged modest increases in the rate for acceptances toward the end of May and again at the beginning of June. Simultaneously, the flow of funds to France slackened, although Norman attributed the change less to the interest rate increases than to the exhaustion of the speculative forces.[30] Whatever the causes, the pressures that were undermining Bank of France monetary policy were on the wane and Moreau could shift his aim to other targets. After the end of May, the Bank of France concentrated increasingly on the diversification and—as it believed—the improvement of the quality of its international assets. Some of its sterling balances were converted into gold, some into various other forms of foreign exchange, primarily dollars. Beyond this, Moreau indicated that he would continue to maintain balances in London equal to the amount of speculative funds which he estimated would leave Paris when the prospective *de jure* stabilization of the franc finally killed any remaining hopes for a further appreciation of the currency. However, he felt strongly that his London balances should not rise above this minimum.[31]

A program to rearrange the composition of the Bank of France's international assets was completed early in June 1927. Under the plan proposed to the Bank of England by Quesnay, the Bank of France would increase its gold holdings by £30 million. Of this, Strong offered to supply £12 million[32] against

---

[29] Moreau Diary, *June 13, 1927.*

[30] *Norman and Moreau conversation, May 27, 1927, page 9;* Moreau Diary, *May 27, June 13, and June 30, 1927; Moreau letter to Strong, June 2, 1927.*

[31] *Moreau cable to Strong, No. 23, June 8, 1927.*

[32] *The gold sold by the Federal Reserve to the Bank of France was originally part of the £18 million held by the Bank of England against its 1923 loan to the Bank of France. When this loan was repaid in April 1927, £6 million of the previously pledged gold was sold by the Bank of France to the Irving Trust Company of New York and the remainder to the Federal Reserve, which kept its £12 million earmarked in London in order to facilitate the disposal of the gold in Europe by avoiding the cost of shipping it to America and back again.*

sterling. Another £15 million was to be acquired in the London gold market within six months. The total was completed by the inclusion of £3 million that had already been acquired from the Bank of England before the negotiations were completed in the second week of June.[33] On the foreign exchange side, the Bank of France would attempt to discourage any renewed rise in its claims on London by discriminating against sterling in its market operations, i.e., by offering a better price for dollars and for the various continental European currencies than for sterling.[34]

On several counts these arrangements provided welcome relief to the Bank of England. Strong's willingness to sell his London gold holdings reduced the amount that Moreau planned to take from London to £18 million from the £20 million he had set as his target in mid-May.[35] At least for the time being, no more gold was likely to be taken from the Bank of England's reserve, and as events worked out only a relatively small amount seems to have been taken from the London market. By late July, when the balance of payments was turning temporarily against France and the Bank of France suspended its gold purchases in London, the Bank of England held no more than £18.4 million of gold earmarked for France,[36] of which the bulk was of course accounted for by the earlier purchases from the Federal Reserve and the Bank of England.[37] Thereafter, there are no indications that the Bank of France was an important factor in the London gold market until the end of 1928.[38]

Moreau's foreign exchange policy had certain obvious drawbacks for the Bank of England, but it had the advantage that it tended to shift sterling balances into more willing hands and, when France was gaining reserves, led to the buildup of Bank of France claims on markets other than London. As events worked out, France's claims accumulated largely in New York, where they were to complicate the problems of the United States monetary authorities in later years.[39]

---

[33] Moreau Diary, *June 7, 1927.*

[34] *Moreau cable to Strong, No. 23, June 8, 1927;* Moreau Diary, *June 9 and 14, 1927.*

[35] Supra, *page 117.*

[36] *Norman cable to Strong, No. 112, July 28, 1927; Rist cable to Strong, No. 51, August 4, 1927.*

[37] *These earmarks were shipped to France in February-March 1928 in connection with the preparation for the* de jure *stabilization of the franc.*

[38] *Clay, op. cit., pages 243-44.*

[39] Moreau Diary, *June 14, 1927.*

The June 1927 arrangements were not wholly satisfactory from the French viewpoint. A major aim of the French authorities at this stage was to curb the amount of cash pumped into the economy and, to do this, they wished to limit the Bank of France reserve gains not merely in sterling but in any form. Consequently, when France's balance-of-payments surplus reappeared about the middle of August 1927, the Bank of France changed its tactics and dealt with the surplus of the next ten months mainly through swap operations that made it advantageous for French private interests very substantially to increase their balances abroad.

The circumstances were particularly favorable for the use of the swap technique under which the Bank of France sold foreign exchange spot and repurchased it for future delivery. Although long-term interest rates in France were high relative to those in major financial centers abroad, the rate on three-month bankers' acceptances in Paris had fallen sharply during the early months of 1927, because the funding of government debt had led to an extreme scarcity of short-term paper in the Paris market; in the year beginning May 1927, it fluctuated between 1.82 per cent and 2.95 per cent.[40] On the other hand, the corresponding rate in New York moved in the 3.1-3.7 per cent range while in London, as already noted, acceptance rates had been pushed up to 4.3 per cent at the end of May and fluctuated within the 4.0-4.3 per cent range for most of the following year. With this pattern of interest rates there was a particularly strong incentive for commercial banks and others in Paris to hold balances in London, if forward cover could be obtained on favorable terms, and this the Bank of France proceeded to provide on an increasing scale beginning about the middle of August. Whereas the premium on forward francs had eliminated the incentive to move covered funds to London from Paris during the spring of 1927, the premium narrowed markedly thereafter, disappeared entirely in November, and fluctuated between 0.2 per cent and 0.7 per cent during January-June 1928. On a comparison of acceptance rates there was, under these conditions, a covered incentive to hold balances in London rather than in Paris of between 0.7 per cent and 1.9 per cent during the ten months ended June 1928 (see Chart 5).[41]

---

[40] R. G. Hawtrey, The Art of Central Banking (London: Longmans, Green and Co. Ltd., 1932), pages 12-21.

[41] Paul Einzig. The Theory of Forward Exchange (London: Macmillan & Co., Ltd., 1937), pages 352-53 and chart opposite page 286; Board of Governors of the Federal Reserve System, Banking and Monetary Statistics (Washington, D. C., November 1943), pages 656-57.

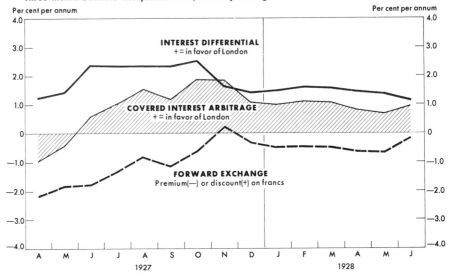

CHART 5

ARBITRAGE OPPORTUNITIES BETWEEN
PARIS AND LONDON, APRIL 1927-JUNE 1928
Three-month bankers' acceptance rates; monthly averages

Per cent per annum

INTEREST DIFFERENTIAL
+ = in favor of London

COVERED INTEREST ARBITRAGE
+ = in favor of London

FORWARD EXCHANGE
Premium(—) or discount(+) on francs

1927   1928

Sources: Board of Governors of the Federal Reserve System, Banking and
Monetary Statistics (Washington, D.C., November 1943). Data on forward
exchange calculated from figures in Paul Einzig, The Theory of Forward
Exchange(London, 1937), Appendix 1.

The Paris market was not slow to take advantage of this opportunity. Moreau's diary indicates that, by September 20, 1927, the Bank of France had entered into forward commitments to buy foreign exchange totaling almost $100 million equivalent. By the beginning of June 1928, when these commitments had reached their peak, the total was almost $600 million equivalent and was largely in sterling.[42] In effect, the French authorities had induced private

---

[42] *Strong memoranda on "Bank of England-Bank of France Relations", May 24, 1928, page 7, and on "Discussions with the Bank of France", May 27, 1928, pages 6-7. See also Einzig, op. cit.. page 353; and Bank of France,* Annual Report, *1928, published in* Federal Reserve Bulletin *(March 1929), page 203.*

banks and other firms to increase their foreign balances by an amount that was roughly equivalent to the surplus in France's balance of payments during August 1927-May 1928. They thus minimized the increase in official foreign exchange holdings and in Bank of France note circulation and facilitated the attainment of the central bank's monetary aims. They also greatly eased the pressure on sterling, although this result seems to have been merely incidental. There is nothing in the record to indicate either that the French authorities were aiming to help the Bank of England or that Norman and his colleagues realized that the Bank of France swap operations were a major factor contributing to the strength of sterling during the period.

THE CENTRAL BANKERS' MEETING OF JULY 1927

The respite enjoyed by sterling in the year beginning August 1927 stemmed from policy changes not only by the Bank of France but also by the Federal Reserve. Strong had, of course, been keenly aware of sterling's mounting difficulties. During the autumn of 1926 he had learned from Norman of the Reichsbank's purchases of gold in London. Later, frequent communications from both Norman and Moreau told him of the growing tensions between the British and French central banks. By the time he had read the record of the May 27 discussions, which Moreau had sent to him, Strong felt deeply concerned for the stability of sterling[43] and was convinced that the question of how to reduce the pressure on London should be topmost on the agenda of the informal meeting of central bankers that was scheduled to begin early in July.

For years Norman had been working for just such a meeting, and Strong, overcoming his earlier doubts, had issued invitations before the tensions between the British and French central banks became acute.[44] The meetings were held at the home of Ogden Mills on Long Island from July 1-6 and were attended by Norman, Schacht, Strong, and Rist, Moreau having been unable to come.[45] An attempt was made to keep the proceedings secret. No record of the discussions

---

[43] *Strong letter to Moreau, June 20, 1927, page 3.*

[44] *Strong letter to Moreau, May 19, 1927, and cable No. 24, June 7, 1927.*

[45] *L. V. Chandler,* Benjamin Strong, Central Banker *(Washington, D. C.: The Brookings Institution, 1958), page 375; Hamlin Diary, July 7, 1927.*

was kept, but enough was subsequently written by the participants to determine that they explored the questions: (1) Whether the pressures on the European authorities, especially in Britain and Germany, to tighten monetary policy could be relieved by an easing of United States monetary policy; (2) whether there was any connection between the monetary policies that were being followed by the gold standard countries and the declining tendency of commodity prices generally; and (3) how to deal with the Bank of France's huge short-term claims on London and New York and in particular (a) whether measures could be found to enable the Bank of France to shift its sterling into dollars without inconveniencing the Bank of England and (b) whether the gold requirements of the Bank of France, and indeed other central banks, could be met in New York rather than in London, which was normally the cheapest market.[46] The principal outcome of these discussions was Strong's second great effort in support of sterling.

THE EASING OF FEDERAL RESERVE POLICY

In this effort the basic instrument, as in 1924, was an easing of monetary policy which, in the light of the boom of the next two years and of the October 1929 crash, was to become one of the most controversial actions in the history of the Federal Reserve System. Actually the mid-1927 policy change was far less marked than that of 1924. In the earlier episode the discount rates of the Federal Reserve Banks had been reduced in successive steps from 4½ per cent to 3 per cent, whereas in 1927 they were cut by only ½ per cent to 3½ per cent over a period extending from July 29 to September 13. Similarly, the volume of reserves that was pumped into the banking system was far smaller in May-November 1927 than it was in the 1924 episode, which as it happens covered the same months of the year. System purchases of bills and Government securities totaled $391 million, $61 million less than in the 1924 period. On the other hand, the drain on member bank reserves from the outflow of currency into circulation and gold losses was $217 million larger. By the same token, both the decline in member bank discounts at the Federal Reserve and the rise in their reserve balances were significantly smaller in May-November 1927 than in the corresponding 1924 period. The rise in net demand deposits of weekly reporting member banks was less than half the 14.5 per cent increase attained

---

[46] Moreau Diary, *July 16, 1927. See also Strong letter to Jay, July 21, 1927.*

124

in May-November 1924.[47]

The controversy that was to develop over the 1927 easing of monetary policy turned largely on the question whether the Federal Reserve, in seeking its international objectives, had exposed the domestic economy to undue inflationary risks. The records of the meetings of the OMIC in early May and late July indicate that, although both sides of the question were discussed, external considerations probably weighed more heavily than domestic ones. Even so, there is nothing to indicate that Strong told what he knew of the seriousness of the Bank of England's position. The discussion was on a general plane; the note of urgency is absent. There was some feeling that the maintenance of the existing interest rate structure in the United States might attract additional gold to New York from Europe, force yet higher interest rates abroad, and thus lead to a weakening of European demand for United States exports, particularly of agricultural produce. If, on the other hand, monetary policy were eased, upward pressure on European interest rates would be reduced, European demand for United States exports would be better maintained, the financing of trade would tend to shift to New York from London, and America's pull on Europe's gold reserves would be lessened. An important technical advantage of a shift toward ease was that the System's open market portfolio could be replenished; open market sales to offset gold inflows during the early months of 1927 had reduced it to only $136 million on May 11.[48]

Apart from the stock market, the position and prospects of the United States economy were considered by the Federal Reserve authorities to justify a modest easing of monetary policy in mid-1927. Several of the participants at the joint meetings of the OMIC and the Federal Reserve Board on May 9, May 12, and July 27 felt that a recession was imminent or had already begun, slackness being particularly noted in the shoe, textile, and oil industries. Although the Governors of several of the interior Reserve Banks believed that conditions in their Districts did not call for a policy change, most of them favored a systemwide move toward ease because they felt that this would serve the national interest—by which they apparently referred to the external aims mentioned above and the desirability of

---

[47] *Board of Governors of the Federal Reserve System,* Banking and Monetary Statistics, *pages 137, 140, and 370. Supra, page 86.*

[48] *Minutes of OMIC, May 9 and 12, 1927 and July 27, 1927; memoranda prepared for those meetings; Hamlin Diary, July 27, 1927.*

acting promptly to check the recession. Only Governor MacDougal of the Chicago Bank refused to go along with a systemwide move, but his position was based primarily on what he took to be the special conditions of his District.[49]

Subsequent scholarly analysis confirms that the Federal Reserve authorities correctly diagnosed the conditions of the economy in the spring and early summer of 1927. If anything, they were late in recognizing the recession. The upper turning point, as subsequently determined by the National Bureau of Economic Research, came in October 1926.[50] Consumption turned downward in the fourth quarter of that year; investment in producers' durables declined moderately but steadily in each of the first three quarters of 1927 from a peak in the final quarter of 1926; the substantial 1926 accumulation of inventories changed to decumulation in January-June 1927, changing again to what looks like involuntary accumulation in the third quarter and again to decumulation in October-December, the quarter in which industrial production hit its cyclical low. Over all, however, the recession was considerably milder than that of 1924: from peak to trough the decline in industrial production had been 18 per cent in 1923-24, but it was only 6 per cent in 1926-27.[51]

If the mildness of the recession called for only a modest move toward easier money, so too did the continuation of speculative tendencies in the economy. The recession, even attended as it was by the collapse of several real estate and other speculative ventures, failed to dampen the exuberance of the New York stock market. It was widely believed in the market that the business slowdown was largely an outgrowth of the suspension of production at the Ford Motor Company, which was retooling for a major model change, and that the longer outlook was good. In this optimistic atmosphere, Standard and Poor's index of New York stock market prices rose by almost one third between January and December 1927.[52]

---

[49] *Minutes of OMIC, May 9 and 12, 1927, and July 27, 1927; memoranda prepared for these meetings; Hamlin Diary, July 27, 1927; and Harrison, notes taken at the May 9, May 12, and July 27 meetings.*

[50] *United States Department of Commerce, Bureau of the Census,* Business Cycle Developments *(November 1964), page 61 (data compiled by National Bureau of Economic Research, Inc.).*

[51] *Harold Barger,* Outlay and Income in the United States, 1921-1938 *(New York: National Bureau of Economic Research, Inc., 1942), pages 93, 114, and 326.*

[52] *Standard and Poor's Corporation,* Daily Stock Price Indexes, 1926-1957 *(New York, 1957), page 7.*

The question how the stock market would react to an easing of monetary policy was a major worry to the Federal Reserve authorities at the time. Fear that a speculative rampage would be encouraged led some to oppose any easing, and Strong himself felt that, if the heavy speculation in the stock market were all that had to be taken into account, some increase in discount rates might even be justified.[53] But, although Strong and most of his colleagues understood that a move toward easier money might invite further speculation, which could be dangerous,[54] they felt intensely that the behavior of the securities markets should not divert the System from the provision of an adequate supply of credit for what they considered to be the legitimate business of the economy.[55] Edmund Platt of the Federal Reserve Board put the OMIC majority view bluntly: "Lower [the discount rate] in New York first and to hell with the stock market."[56]

THE PAYMENTS BALANCE SHIFTS IN FAVOR OF EUROPE

While the United States economy was slipping into recession and Federal Reserve policy was being eased, in Europe economic activity was quickening and interest rates were on the rise. Investable funds were pulled eastward across the Atlantic, and, as in 1924-25, the United States payments position weakened and sterling appreciated on the exchange markets.

In Europe the volume of output expanded during 1927 everywhere except in France, whose postwar recovery had been interrupted by a short-lived "stabilization crisis". Economic performance was particularly impressive in Germany and Britain, where investment booms stimulated unusually rapid expansions in total output. The acceleration of economic activity was accompanied by a tightening of monetary conditions. In Germany, where sharply rising imports, together with a slackening capital inflow, had led to substantial reserve losses in the early months of the year, the Reichsbank discount rate was raised to 6 per cent early in June and to 7 per cent in early October, from the 5 per cent to which it had been reduced in January 1927. Throughout the second half of the year, short-

---

[53] *Strong letter to Moreau, June 20, 1927, page 5.*

[54] *Strong letter to Sprague, April 12, 1927, page 2.*

[55] *Minutes of OMIC, July 27, 1927.*

[56] *Harrison, notes on OMIC meeting with the Federal Reserve Board on July 27, 1927.*

and long-term interest rates in Germany were 3 to 4 percentage points higher than in New York. In France, too, long-term interest rates remained at levels well above New York, despite the sharp drop in short-term interest rates, and the stock market boom continued.[57]

In Britain the tightening of monetary conditions was rather gentle. Although the British economy was recovering rapidly from the 1926 coal strike, unemployment in 1927 still averaged 5½ per cent of the labor force,[58] and the bank rate remained unchanged. Nevertheless, the Bank of England so conducted its market operations that bankers' deposits at the central bank dropped 2.6 per cent in the six months ended November 1927 to the lowest level up to that time in the 1920's.[59] Under this squeeze the acceptance rate held firmly at the 4.32-4.34 per cent level to which it had been pushed at the end of May, and long-term rates hardened slightly. Since rates in the United States were declining, London's normal margin above New York widened. More important, the incentive to move covered funds from New York to London, which, on the comparison of acceptance rates, had narrowed during the spring, again widened and fluctuated between 0.49 per cent and 0.73 per cent during July-November (see Chart 6).

These various economic changes had a major impact on the United States balance of payments. Foreign long-term investment in the United States fell, and United States investments abroad (both short and long term) increased. Hence, despite a 6 per cent drop in imports, the deficit in the United States balance of payments rose to $1,047 million, almost $700 million larger than in 1926 and the highest for any year during the decade of the twenties.[60] All indications are that most of the increase in the deficit occurred during the second half of 1927 and that the net outflow of dollars continued at a very high rate in January-June 1928, when the volume of foreign capital issues publicly offered in the United States reached its peak for the 1920's.[61]

[57] Angus Maddison, "Growth and Fluctuation in the World Economy, 1870-1960", Quarterly Review (Banca Nazionale del Lavoro, June 1962), and Economic Growth in the West (New York: Twentieth Century Fund, 1964), pages 201-40; League of Nations, Statistical Year-book, 1930-31.

[58] Maddison, Economic Growth in the West, page 220.

[59] Brown, The International Gold Standard Reinterpreted, 1914-1934, Vol. II, Appendix Table 3A.

[60] United States Department of Commerce, Historical Statistics of the United States (Washington, D. C.: United States Government Printing Office, 1960), page 563.

[61] United States Department of Commerce, Handbook on American Underwriting of Foreign Securities (Washington, D. C.: United States Government Printing Office, 1930), pages 140-41.

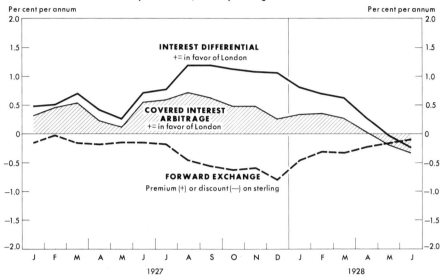

CHART 6

**ARBITRAGE OPPORTUNITIES BETWEEN NEW YORK
AND LONDON, JANUARY 1927–JUNE 1928**
Three-month bankers' acceptance rates; monthly averages

Sources: Board of Governors of the Federal Reserve System, Banking and Monetary Statistics (Washington, D.C., November 1943). Data on forward exchange calculated from figures in Paul Einzig, The Theory of Forward Exchange (London, 1937), Appendix 1.

It was through this enlargement of the United States payments deficit and the simultaneous strengthening of the major European exchange rates that the major objectives of the Long Island central bankers' conference were accomplished. The benefits to sterling of this payments shift were particularly great. Capital issues that would normally have been floated in London were raised in New York, the proceeds being sold for sterling and held in London.[62] And, as Strong had hoped, the financing of international trade was to some extent shifted to New York from London; the value of dollar acceptances outstanding at the end of December 1927

---

[62] *Strong letter to Deputy Governor, Commonwealth Bank of Australia, September 7, 1927.*

was almost $1.1 billion, 43 per cent higher than a year earlier.[63] Especially in the late summer and early autumn of 1927, when the United States economic outlook was particularly uncertain and the money market was particularly liquid, United States private short-term balances seem to have moved to London in considerable volume, taking advantage of both the covered incentive to move there and of certain speculative opportunities.[64] On one day in early October—a period when sterling normally would still have been weak for seasonal reasons—Norman cabled that he had bought $6 million in the market at rising rates.[65] In December and throughout the spring of 1928, sterling was only a little below the gold import point from New York. For the year ended June 1928 as a whole, the sterling-dollar rate averaged the highest for any of the years 1924-31.

THE LIQUIDATION OF THE FEDERAL RESERVE'S STERLING BALANCE AND THE SHIFTING OF THE DEMAND FOR GOLD TO NEW YORK

Sterling's exceptional strength facilitated both the speedy liquidation of the Federal Reserve's sterling balance and the rebuilding of the Bank of England's holdings of gold. Arrangements to liquidate the £12 million[66] that the Federal Reserve had acquired from the Bank of France in exchange for gold were worked out by Strong and Norman: the balance would be liquidated gradually at agreed rates, partly in London by the Bank of England and partly in New York by the Federal Reserve.[67] Operations began in mid-August when the sterling-dollar rate had climbed to parity and proceeded much more rapidly than Strong at least had anticipated.[68] The balance had been reduced to less than £5 million by the end of August, to £1.5 million a month later, and by October 5 it was down to the

---

[63] *Board of Governors of the Federal Reserve System,* Banking and Monetary Statistics, *page 465.*

[64] *Norman letter to Strong, October 11, 1927.*

[65] *Norman cable to Strong, No. 193, October 10, 1927.*

[66] *The bulk of these balances was invested in a special "money employed" account managed by the Bank of England and yielding the Federal Reserve 3⅞ per cent; the remainder was in sterling bills, yielding 4¼ per cent. Strong letter to Harding, September 6, 1927.* Daily Statements of Foreign Accounts, *June 16, 1927-October 5, 1927.*

[67] *Norman cable to Strong, No. 122, August 9, 1927; Strong cable to Norman, No. 47, August 18, 1927; and numerous other cables about this time.*

[68] *Strong letter to Norman, August 25, 1927;* Daily Statements of Foreign Accounts, *August 31, September 30, and October 5, 1927.*

£150,000 at which the Federal Reserve's London balance had stood in early June, before the gold was sold to the Bank of France.[69]

The rapidity and ease with which the Federal Reserve's sterling balance was liquidated did not relieve Norman and Strong from anxiety about longer term problems with which they were faced. Both realized that the strengthening of sterling was attributable primarily to temporary factors. Norman, fully aware that sterling might need support again in the future, was glad that the Federal Reserve's London balance could be reduced because, as he wrote Strong, "if we get near to Queer Street I may ask [you] to increase it".[70] For his part, Strong had been clear from the beginning that, while changes in interest rate relationships between Europe and America might provide temporary relief for sterling and other European currencies, such a change could hardly deal with fundamental difficulties.[71] He was also clear that the counterpart of the strengthening of sterling was a buildup of American private claims on London, that these new private claims were far larger than the original Federal Reserve claim which was being so rapidly reduced,[72] and that, if United States monetary conditions were to tighten relative to Europe, these private claims would doubtless be repatriated. Since he foresaw no fundamental improvements in Britain's position, he was driven to agree with Norman on the need to prepare the ground for further official support of sterling, although he made no specific commitments to Norman.[73] Therefore, once the sterling balance was back to normal, Strong asked for, and on November 2, 1927 the Federal Reserve Board approved, authority under which the System could act to prevent renewed physical movements of gold to the United States by acquiring up to $100 million in foreign balances or gold held under earmark abroad.[74] This authority was not employed during the

---

[69] *Strong letter to Governor Young, October 5, 1927; Strong letter to Harding, October 5, 1927.*

[70] *Norman letter to Strong, August 11, 1927.*

[71] *Strong letter to Jay, July 21, 1927.*

[72] *Strong letter to Norman, September 24, 1927.*

[73] *Strong cable to Norman, No. 95, September 24, 1927.*

[74] *Minutes of OMIC, November 1-2, 1927; memoranda prepared for the meetings; Young letter to Strong, November 2, 1927, in records of OMIC. The Board was asked to approve the proposed gold and foreign exchange operations apparently because Strong expected that they would be undertaken as a part of the System open market operations. On other occasions when it undertook similar, though smaller, operations, the New York Reserve Bank acted under the authority conferred on the Reserve Banks by Section 14 of the Federal Reserve Act, merely consulting or informing the Board of the action contemplated.*

remainder of Strong's lifetime, but it indicates the extent to which, despite his hankering after the gold standard, Strong and indeed the System generally were prepared to introduce flexibility and management into the operation of the international financial system.

Economic changes in the year ended mid-1928 also led to the shifting of a considerable proportion of the world's rising demand for gold from London to New York, an objective that clearly was sought by all the central bankers who participated in the Long Island meetings. They had hoped that new gold production could be channeled to those monetary authorities, especially in Europe and Latin America, who wished to increase their holdings of the metal in connection with the stabilization of their currencies, and that supplies from new production could be supplemented by sales from the Federal Reserve on terms at least as advantageous as in London.[75] Moreover, they had agreed to do their best to avoid gold sales to the United States. If such sales were unavoidable, the Federal Reserve would endeavor to take delivery in London, or elsewhere abroad, where the gold could be resold more cheaply because the cost of moving it across the Atlantic would not be included in its price.[76]

The key to the achievement of most of these objectives lay in the strengthening of sterling. As sterling rose during the second half of 1927, the cost of buying gold in London tended to rise in relation to the cost in New York. For certain monetary authorities, the cost in New York—which previously had been the highest of any major center—actually fell at times below the cost in London.[77] By the same token the rise in the sterling rate also made it increasingly advantageous to sell gold in London rather than in New York.

The change in the pattern of gold flows was fostered not only by these exchange market developments but also by administrative measures. In order to discourage gold arbitrage between London and Berlin, the Reichsbank in October 1927 reduced its buying price for the metal to its legal minimum.[78] A little later, when the French authorities resumed the buying of gold to prepare the way for the

---

[75] *Preliminary memorandum for the OMIC, October 18, 1927, page 11;* Moreau Diary, *July 16, 1927, page 372; Strong letter to Schacht, June 2, 1927.*

[76] *Norman cables to Lubbock, No. 11, July 13, 1927, and No. 14, July 19, 1927; Lubbock cable to Norman, No. 105, July 18, 1927.*

[77] *Preliminary memorandum for the OMIC, October 18, 1927.*

[78] Reports of the Agent General, *September 1, 1926 to August 31, 1927, Vol. I, pages 240-41.*

de jure stabilization of the franc, the Bank of France met its needs in New York, although at the time gold could apparently have been obtained somewhat more cheaply in London.[79] Moreover, with a view to bringing more of the supplies that were coming onto the London market into the Bank of England's reserve, the Committee of Treasury authorized Norman to offer as much as 77s. 10½ d. per standard ounce of gold, an amount that was equal to its legal maximum *selling* price.[80]

These changes in market conditions and in central bank policies brought about a major shift in the pattern of gold flows, and in so doing not only lightened but temporarily removed the pressure on London. This was accomplished despite a huge increase in official demand for gold, especially from countries that were stabilizing their currencies or were reducing—as was Germany—the foreign exchange component of their international reserves. Excluding the United States and Britain, the rise in official gold reserves was $458 million in 1927, more than quadruple the rise during the previous year, and the rate of increase accelerated substantially during January-June 1928. In meeting this enlarged demand the United States played the major role. Its gold stock, after increasing somewhat in the first half of 1927, dropped almost $500 million during the year ended June 1928, especially large sales being made to Argentina, Brazil, Britain, France, Germany, and Poland.[81] The meeting of official requirements was facilitated also by a major reduction in the "disappearance" of gold into industrial uses and hoards.

The consequence was that the amount of gold channeled into official reserves

---

[79] Moreau Diary, *April 24, 1928, page 546, and Strong letter to Governor Young, October 25, 1927. Referring to the eleven months immediately preceding* de jure *stabilization of the franc, Poincaré told the Chamber of Deputies on June 21, 1928 that in the interest of central bank cooperation the Bank of France had "voluntarily renounced buying gold on the London market".* Annales de la Chambre des Députés, 14me Legislature Débats Parlementaires, *Tome 135, June 21, 1928, pages 180-81.*

[80] *Clay, op. cit., page 237.*

[81] *The governments of Argentina, Brazil, and Poland floated loans in New York, where the proceeds were used in whole or in part for the acquisition of gold by their respective central banks. Initially the Bank Polski indicated that it wished to meet its gold requirements in London where, according to its calculation, the cost would be lowest. However, out of the total of $20 million in gold bought by the Bank Polski in October-December 1927, only $6 million was taken from the London market, the remainder being supplied by the Federal Reserve Bank of New York, partly out of its earmarks in London. G. E. Roberts, "Gold Movements Into and Out of the United States, 1914 to 1929, and the Effects", in* League of Nations, Selected Documents on the Distribution of Gold *(Geneva, 1931), page 48. The Bank Polski gold purchases were discussed in cables between Norman and Strong during the period October 27-November 6, 1927. Board of Governors of the Federal Reserve System,* Banking and Monetary Statistics, *pages 542-55.*

outside the United States in the eighteen months ended June 1928 was half again as large as the total of new gold production during the period. Most significant in view of sterling's key role was the fact that London attracted and retained some gold on its own account. Not all the regular inflow of new gold production from South Africa and other British Empire countries flowed out again. Moreover, in December 1927 and again in April-June 1928, when sterling was especially strong in relation to the dollar, gold flowed from New York to London. In these circumstances the Bank of England's reserve gains were the largest for any of the years 1924-31. In the year ended June 30, 1928, its holding of dollars rose about $70 million, and its gold holdings rose $93 million, which with a further $18 million gold gain in July 1928 brought its international reserves to their peak for the six years during which sterling was attached to gold.

THE INTERNATIONAL FINANCIAL SYSTEM BECOMES MORE RIGID

It is ironic that, although the central bank policies of 1927 and early 1928 succeeded in helping sterling, this very success was accompanied by a deterioration in the relations among the major central bankers and by yet other policy changes that were to make international financial cooperation more difficult in the future.

The cooling of relations among the major central bankers after the Long Island conference was complex in origin. In part, it arose because Strong and Norman were plagued by illnesses that made it difficult for them to keep in touch with the rapid change of events and with their counterparts abroad.[82] In part, it stemmed from the intense rivalry for financial leadership in Europe that developed between the British and French central banks as the strength and confidence of the latter increased. Perhaps most important, it arose from the disillusioning international monetary experiences of 1926-27 and from the rejection on the part of Strong, Moreau, and Schacht of the Genoa principles, which Norman had been so assiduously fostering, in favor of a rather strict and nationalistic version of the gold standard.

---

[82] *Harrison cables to Norman, January 1928; Strong letter to Norman, March 3, 1928; Chandler, op. cit., page 416. Early in July 1928 Schacht complained to Strong that he had lost contact with Norman, whom he had not seen for a year. Harry Siepmann of the Bank of England attributed the deterioration in relations between the British and German central banks to Norman's "illness, nervousness and preoccupations" (Strong letter to Harrison, July 27, 1928, page 12). Schacht himself, according to Strong, attributed the difficulties to Norman's personality; although Schacht was very fond of Norman, he sometimes found him impossible to deal with because of his reserve; he felt that he never knew what was in Norman's mind (Strong letter to Harrison, July 13, 1928, page 3).*

In this shift in sentiment, Strong played a significant role. As the years went by, his correspondence shows increasing skepticism about many of the ideas that had emanated from the Genoa Conference and especially about the gold exchange standard. His skepticism that any general gold shortage was impending, his feeling that national credit structures are less soundly based on foreign exchange than on gold, his concern lest his own monetary control problems be complicated by large movements of foreign-owned dollar balances, and his understanding of the problems that the buildup of foreign balances in London had brought on Norman and Moreau—all these considerations led Strong to sympathize with and encourage the movement toward the gold standard.

On the other hand, Strong remained convinced that sterling was a key to the maintenance of a stable international financial structure, and he was pragmatic enough to soften his orthodoxy with proposals that would protect the position of the British currency. With this object in mind, he urged the adoption abroad of monetary laws that would set relatively low minimum holdings of gold against note circulation.[83] The advantage would be, in the case of Britain, that the bulk of the Bank of England's gold would thus be available to defend sterling and, in the case of France, that Bank of France gold purchases from abroad in connection with the *de jure* stabilization would be minimized. If the French were to adopt a high and inflexible ratio, they would absorb a "mass of unusable metal" and would play into the hands of those who alleged the existence of a gold shortage and who were pressing for the extension of the gold exchange standard.[84]

Similarly Strong's opposition to the gold exchange standard in no way prevented him from feeling that central banks should be equipped to operate in the exchange markets and, if necessary, to hold foreign exchange on a short-term basis in the interests of cooperation. It was in this spirit that he obtained authority in November 1927 to enable the Federal Reserve to rebuild its foreign exchange balances and that, as the time for the French stabilization approached, he repeatedly urged Moreau to retain his authority to operate in the foreign exchange markets.[85] Otherwise, he warned, there would be the possibility that[86]

[83] *Strong memorandum on discussion with the Bank of France, May 27, 1928, page 12; Strong letter to Rist, June 12, 1928, page 1; and Strong letter to Norman, March 29, 1927.*

[84] *Strong letter to Rist, June 12, 1928.*

[85] *Minutes of OMIC, November 1-2, 1927; Strong memorandum on discussions with the Bank of France, May 27, 1928, page 7.*

[86] *Strong memorandum on discussions with the Bank of France, May 27, 1928, page 7.*

if the franc rose above the gold import point all French bankers who could import gold at a profit would do so and pump it into the Bank of France, and with the importation of gold for geographical reasons being cheaper from London than from any other market, there was danger of discord arising between the two institutions immediately stabilization was effective.

Strong's efforts to foster a shift to the gold standard, without at the same time undermining the position of sterling, had only limited success, and this success endured only as long as the heavy outflow of American capital continued. Indeed, the 1927-28 experience was strikingly similar to that of 1924-25, when the British authorities took advantage of the fleeting buoyancy of.sterling to fix their currency once more at its prewar parity. Now the removal of the immediate threat to sterling in the ten months ended June 1928 created a situation in which the German and French authorities in their turn, marching under the gold standard banner, adopted policy changes that were difficult to reverse and that increased the rigidity of the international financial system.

The shift in Reichsbank gold policy, which was already foreshadowed in the autumn of 1926,[87] became evident in the later part of 1927 and early 1928. In that period, the Reichsbank reconstituted only its working balances of foreign exchange, and then became a very conservative buyer in the exchange markets.[88] Under this policy the mark climbed gradually to the gold import point at which it became profitable for arbitragers to obtain gold abroad to sell to the central bank. The beauty of it was that, with sterling strong and the London gold price high in terms of foreign currencies, this major policy change was accomplished without putting pressure on London.[89] The United States and Russia supplied the bulk of the $54 million rise in the Reichsbank's gold holdings in the seven months ended June 1928, a period during which its published foreign exchange reserve actually declined $8 million.[90]

In France, too, the cessation of the virtually continuous official exchange operations of 1927 and early 1928 was accomplished with no immediate disturbances,

[87] Supra, *page 114.*

[88] Reports of the Agent General, *September 1, 1927 to August 31, 1928, Vol. I, page 86.*

[89] *Brown,* The International Gold Standard Reinterpreted, 1914-1934, *Vol. I, page 488.*

[90] Reports of the Agent General, *September 1, 1927 to August 31, 1928, Vol. I, page 86;* Annual Reports of the Reichsbank, *1927 and 1928.*

largely because the shift coincided with the June 25, 1928 *de jure* stabilization and with the consequent disappearance of hopes that the franc would appreciate. With the elimination of the speculative element in the exchange markets, both sterling and the dollar strengthened against the franc; indeed, it was not until nearly the end of 1928 that the effects of France's new policy began to be reflected in a renewed movement of gold from London to Paris.

While the change was initially painless, it was nevertheless irreversible. The experience with official management of the exchange market had not been a happy one for the French authorities. They had succeeded in preventing an appreciation of the franc but only—as they felt—at the cost of an intolerable threat to domestic monetary stability. The Bank of France had accumulated some $1.2 billion equivalent in spot and forward claims on foreign centers during the eighteen months prior to the *de jure* stabilization, equivalent to no less than half its total assets at the end of 1926. When the Bank had attempted to curb the inflow by converting part of its sterling claims into gold, Moreau had been told that he was jeopardizing the international financial structure. Although, as already noted, the Bank of France participated in the international cooperative arrangements to protect London during the year beginning July 1, 1927, the French authorities were determined by mid-1928 to abandon the policies which they associated with the embarrassments and difficulties of the pre-stabilization period.[91]

It must be emphasized, however, that the change was one in Bank of France policy and not, as many authors have written, in its legal power to operate in the foreign exchange markets.[92] To be sure, the law of August 7, 1926 which had authorized the Bank to buy gold, silver coin, and foreign exchange at a premium was abrogated when the franc was stabilized *de jure*. But the June 25, 1928 stabilization law itself made effective once again the authority under which the Bank of France had operated in the gold and foreign exchange markets before the war and which had been made inoperative as a result of the subsequent de-

---

[91] *Henri Cheron, Rapporteur Général de la Commission des Finances, Rapport au Sénat, June 24, 1928, Annales du Sénat, Débats Parlementaires, Session Ordinaire de 1928, Tome 58, page 1127.*

[92] *Virtually all publications on this subject hold erroneously that the June 25, 1928 monetary law deprived the Bank of France of authority to operate in the foreign market. See, for example, League of Nations,* International Currency Experience, *pages 36-38; Martin Wolfe,* The French Franc Between the Wars, 1919-1939 *(New York: Columbia University Press, 1951), page 98; and Hawtrey, op. cit., pages 20, 30, and 31.*

preciation of the franc in the foreign exchange markets.[93]

Hence even after the *de jure* stabilization, the Bank of France could have cooperated with the other central banks through exchange operations. Indeed, leaders of the Bank of France indicated that they expected to do so. To Strong's plea for the retention of power to conduct such operations, Moreau responded sympathetically, if somewhat equivocally, that the Bank of France would continue[94]

> to pursue the policy of the past, namely, freely buying valuta on the market in order to protect London from the drain, and he expected to continue that policy with courage so long as the Bank of England made it possible for him to do so.

Similarly, Rist wrote that, if gold inflows into France were to reach "disquieting proportions", the Bank of France was "quite determined . . . to intervene on the market by buying devisen, so as to prevent the gold import point being reached."[95]

However, these laudable intentions were carried into effect only on rare occasions. Indeed, the normally passive posture of the French authorities in the exchange markets in subsequent years seemed to confirm the general impression (shared by numerous distinguished scholars) that the Bank of France had in fact lost its legal power to operate in those markets, and the absence of any recorded effort by the French authorities to disabuse the public of its error suggests that the Bank of France was content to let the impression stand. It was of course close to the truth. For, although the bank retained power to conduct exchange operations, the French authorities felt that any further buildup of foreign exchange holdings by direct and systematic purchases in the open market would be contrary to the spirit (if not the letter) of the June 25, 1928 stabilization law.[96]

---

[93] *On this point, M. Robert Lacour-Gayet, Director of the Research Department of the Bank of France, wrote to E. A. Goldenweiser on December 3, 1930 that:*
> *the bank has the power under its statutes to discount bills payable abroad, drawn in foreign currencies; it likewise has the power to buy and sell gold, and by implication, to buy and sell foreign exchange representing gold.*
> *The abrogation [in June 1928] of the law of August 7, 1926, did not restrict the bank's freedom of action; it merely put an end to a temporary system which had grown out of the inconvertibility of the currency . . .*
This is confirmed by an examination of the statutes of the Bank of France. See Goldenweiser letter to Lacour-Gayet, October 15, 1930 (Federal Reserve Board Papers), and Galantière letter to Crane, December 29, 1930.

[94] *Strong memorandum on discussions with the Bank of France, May 27, 1928, page 7.*

[95] *Rist letter to Strong, June 18, 1928.*

[96] *Robert Lacour-Gayet letter to E. A. Goldenweiser, December 3, 1930 (Federal Reserve Board Papers).*

While Germany and France were moving toward a strict gold standard, the British authorities were taking advantage of the relatively favorable economic conditions of 1927-28 to push forward long-term plans aimed at the strengthening of sterling. Stimulated by the May 1927 crisis, the authorities intensified their efforts to improve Britain's international competitive position. Plans were formulated for the consolidation and modernization of industries, such as those producing textiles, whose small, high-cost firms were being squeezed out of international markets.[97] Efforts were made to transfer labor from redundant coal mines to more promising industries. On the financial side, the central bank was put in a better position to defend sterling in the exchange markets. Although the government did not go so far as to accept the view that the main purpose for which the central bank held international assets was to maintain the external value of the currency, it went some distance in this direction when it obtained the enactment of the Currency and Bank Notes Act of July 2, 1928.

Under this act, the Bank of England's fiduciary issue was set at a level that— had the law become effective in June—would have given the central bank a margin of "free" gold relatively large in terms of previous British experience: the bank could have allowed its gold to decline £54 million before it would have been obliged to enforce a contraction of note circulation.[98] Since at that time the bank also held £45 million in dollar balances, the total of its "free" international reserves would have been £99 million, a record for the period since April 1925 and of course many times larger than the small amount held before 1914.

The law also provided authority under which, in case of need, the amount of the fiduciary issue could be changed in order either to release additional gold for the defense of sterling without necessitating the adoption of deflationary measures or to absorb gold inflows that might unduly inflate the note issue. The government's intent was that this authority should be employed not only to deal with crises but in the ordinary course of events, for example, to prevent the credit stringencies that would arise if the existing note issue were insufficient to

---

[97] *Strong letter to Harrison, July 27, 1928, pages 1-2. See also Sproul letter to Harrison of March 31, 1934 and attached memorandum on "Bank of England and Industrial Credits".*

[98] Parliamentary Debates *(Great Britain, House of Commons), Vol. 217, May 22, 1928, column 1724;* Macmillan Report, *page 30.*

satisfy the needs of domestic economic expansion or, if gold were flowing out, to satisfy the stabilization requirements of foreign countries or because, for any other reason, foreigners decided to hold gold rather than sterling. This authority could be invoked only at the initiative of the governor of the bank, but its employment required the approval of the Chancellor of the Exchequer. Subject to his approval the fiduciary issue could be changed in any amount for periods up to six months, which could be extended up to two years. Changes for periods longer than two years required Parliamentary approval.[99]

Thus, the authorities were working to strengthen the British economy on both the real and financial sides, but progress was slow. Although those who knew the severity of the May 1927 crisis were keenly aware of the urgent need for economic adjustment, the general public was at best indifferent; when it was directly affected, it was often openly hostile to change. The difficulties involved in official attempts to improve the international competitive position of the textile industry provide a case in point. After discussing the problem with Harry Siepmann of the Bank of England, Strong wrote to Harrison late in July 1928:[100]

> There are some hundreds of mills, and Siepmann thinks the project will be large consolidations, but that it will fail because of the old family traditions in many of the mills, jealousy and inertia and inability to get together and cooperate. There are something over 1,500 directors in these concerns, and even that is a great obstacle, as all of them want to continue their positions and fees. He thinks the outlook in these industries is bad both industrially and financially, and that is especially true because the big banks which are carrying the financial load all say that they are indifferent. Credits that are good, they are glad to carry and even increase as needed. Those that are bad, they have entirely written off or reduced to a point where they are no factor and they do not care to be troubled.

The arrangements to put the Bank of England in a stronger position to defend sterling proved quite inadequate. In part, the failure was due to ignorance. The authorities were aware that foreigners held substantial balances in London, but apparently they were not aware of the huge magnitude of these liabilities. It was not until July 1931 that the Macmillan Committee published estimates of London's net short-term liabilities to foreigners[101] and even these large figures very

---

[99] Parliamentary Debates (Great Britain, House of Commons), May 14, 1928, columns 744-46; Macmillan Report, pages 139-40.

[100] Strong letter to Harrison, July 27, 1928, page 2.

[101] Macmillan Report, pages 112 and 301. The report estimates London's net short-term liabilities at £279 million at the end of 1927 and at £302 million a year later.

considerably underestimated the true total.[102] In mid-1928 these liabilities were probably three times or more the amount of the Bank of England's total "free" international reserves. Since in practice the Bank never allowed its free reserves to drop below the £20 million level before tightening credit policy, the effective ratio of short-term liabilities to the bank's free international assets was of course even higher.[103]

Another flaw in these arrangements was that the Bank of England was extremely reluctant to initiate action to change the fiduciary issue.[104] The hitch lay in the danger—foreseen by at least one member of Parliament during the debates on the Currency and Bank Notes Bill[105]—that any such action by the bank would be interpreted as a sign of weakness and would lead to nervousness in the exchange markets at a time when the authorities were seeking to encourage precisely the opposite sentiment. Summing up its criticism of the arrangement for changing the fiduciary issue, the Macmillan Committee noted in its report[106]

> we believe that it would be preferable that the Bank should have control over a much larger proportion of the total gold stock without calling in aid these provisions. If the object of the fixed fiduciary issue is to tie up the Bank of England, well and good. This may be inadvisable but it is intelligible. But if its object is not to fetter the Bank but merely to require it to make a public declaration of what will be interpreted as weakness, at the most inadvisable moment for creating such an impression, the disadvantages of liberty and of regulation are, it seems to us, heaped on one another.

CONCLUSION

By mid-1928, many of the individual problems that would combine to cause the September 1931 breakdown were already fairly clear and had indeed been recognized as sources of potential trouble. The decisive shift in German and French

---

[102] *David Williams, "London and the 1931 Financial Crisis",* The Economic History Review, *2nd Series, Vol. XV (April 1963), No. 3, page 528;* Royal Institute of International Affairs, The Problem of International Investment *(London, 1937), pages 339-40.*

[103] Macmillan Report, *page 302.*

[104] *It did so only once, in August 1931, when the fiduciary issue was increased by £15 million. The Macmillan Committee's critical report had been published in July.*

[105] Parliamentary Debates *(Great Britain, House of Commons), May 22, 1928, column 1724.*

[106] Macmillan Report, *page 141.*

gold policy was evident; their payments surpluses would in the future be settled very largely, if not wholly, in gold. Although the Bank of France was still holding a substantial part of the sterling it had accumulated during the early months of 1927, it was doing so with unmistakable reluctance. It was clear, moreover, that the demand for gold from Germany, France, and other sources would soon fall once again on London. The strength of sterling that had reduced the pressure on the London gold market during the ten months ended June 1928, depended on the greatly increased outflow of American capital, which was recognized as a temporary phenomenon. In addition, there was awareness that heavy short-term liabilities to foreigners had accumulated against Berlin and London, and also concern lest the international reserves of the Reichsbank and the Bank of England prove inadequate to deal with any substantial withdrawals.[107]

But, although each of the major danger spots was recognized individually, no one viewed them as parts of a single problem. None analyzed their interrelations or understood how they could act and react upon one another. Strong and Norman, who were in a position to see the whole problem, were intermittently ill and, even when well, were distracted by other pressing matters. Below the level of the Governors, who dominated the international relations of the United States and British central banks, were Harrison and Lubbock, but they were in less satisfactory positions to understand the overall problem; what is more important, the record gives no indication that either of them, or indeed anyone within the central banks, was asked or volunteered to explore the strengths and weaknesses of the existing international financial arrangements or to propose means by which these arrangements could be made more viable. Outside the central banks, there was no dearth of advice about how the international financial system should be improved. But outside observers were at best incompletely informed about the central problems. Even the Chancellor of the Exchequer was kept in the dark about certain crucial facets of the Bank of England's operations.[108]

Moreover, Norman did not welcome unsolicited advice or the probing of outsiders into the affairs of the Bank of England. His attitude was only partly a

---

[107] *On October 22, 1927, Gaspard Farrer of Barings wrote to Strong that "no amount of gold which we can afford to keep will suffice if ever serious doubts as to our stability arise—transfer by capitalist and speculator would be overwhelming".*

[108] *For example, in his memorandum of May 24, 1928 on the Currency and Bank Notes Bill, Strong registered his "almost consternation" at the discovery that no member of the British government had been made aware that the Bank of England held more than $200 million in New York.*

142

reflection of the traditional feeling that the bank's operations should not be subject to public scrutiny. As the defense of sterling ran into increasing difficulties, the wisdom of the return to the 1914 parity and the judgment of those responsible for the return were increasingly brought into question. Perhaps inevitably Norman and Churchill, who of course were the main targets of public criticism, responded by closing ranks: nothing was fundamentally wrong; the well-seasoned arrangements of 1844 were working well; the critics were generally either knaves or fools.[109] Hence the authorities rejected the suggestion for official investigation into Britain's monetary problems, a suggestion repeatedly made by Reginald McKenna and taken up by the Labor Party.[110] Indeed, to head off such an inquiry, the authorities proposed to appoint a committee of experts who, it was hoped, would support the views of the Treasury and the Bank of England,[111] but even such a group was apparently never appointed.

Thus, an expert and wide-ranging investigation of British monetary problems was not conducted in the relatively favorable circumstances of 1927-28, when it could still perhaps have had useful results, but was delayed until after the election of the Labor Party in June 1929. By November 1929, when the Committee on Finance and Industry was appointed, headed by Lord Macmillan, the international economic climate had already taken a decided turn for the worse, and by July 1931, when the committee's report was finally published, sterling was on the brink of disaster. The worst fears of those who had opposed the inquiry were then realized, because the *Macmillan Report's* estimates of the magnitude of London's short-term liabilities probably contributed to the crisis of confidence that was soon to break sterling's link with gold.

---

[109] *Norman letter to Strong, March 14, 1927. See also Strong memorandum of May 24, 1928, on Bank of England-Bank of France relations, especially page 14.*

[110] *See, for example, McKenna's speech delivered on January 28, 1927 and reprinted in the* Monthly Review *of the Midland Bank for January-February 1927, page 6.*

[111] *Crane memorandum on conversation with Sir Otto Niemeyer, February 18, 1928.*

7. Mounting Strains — Declining Cooperation

. . . reconstruction needs an outside body of some sort which can continue for many years to exercise a wide and impartial authority behind anything the Central Banks may do.

Write me your ideas before your fears take effect and competition squeezes out cooperation.

Norman letter to Strong,
April 17, 1927.

*   *   *   *   *

Now that budgets are balanced, debts are less menacing and currencies are reorganized, the principal European nations are being influenced by the feeling of strength and security which they have obtained, and the old evils of cut-throat competition are again showing themselves. It even enters into the policies of the banks of issue. My belief is that the time has arrived to keep out of any complications of the sort which the European banks of issue are likely to encounter. We have discharged our moral obligation to Europe, and there seems to me to be no further occasion for entering into arrangements which might embarrass us in any way, politically or financially.

Benjamin Strong,
August 17, 1928.

Beginning in the summer of 1928 the international economy became subject to strains with which the governments in the major countries were unprepared to cope. Nowhere did the authorities deal effectively with the difficulties in their domestic economies; what they did do often exacerbated the problems of other countries, led to retaliation, aggravated existing frictions, and rendered increasingly remote the possibility that their common economic problems could be tackled on a cooperative basis. The one major international effort of 1929-30 was directed toward the final settlement of reparations on a basis that could have succeeded only if prosperity in the major countries and equilibrium in the international economy had been maintained. Both of these conditions disappeared in 1930-31. Unsupported by the requisite government policies and equipped with instruments designed to deal only with relatively minor disturbances, the major central banks, even when they were willing to cooperate, could do little more than stand on the sidelines and watch the disintegration of the international economic system.

144

In its timing and form, reparation settlement was heavily influenced by problems that had become pressing in Germany and France. In Germany, there was of course continuous agitation to reduce the annuities which were scheduled to total at least $596 million equivalent in the year ended August 1929 (two and a half times the amount paid in 1924-25) and which were contributing to a growing budgetary deficit. Indeed, there was concern that the annuity might go even higher because, under the so-called prosperity index of the Dawes Plan, the payments required were linked to specified indicators of German economic activity. At least as important were pressures for the elimination of Allied controls over the Reichsbank, the German railroads, and the post office and above all for the evacuation of the Rhineland.

In France, the government wished to settle the amount and duration of the annuities it was to receive from Germany before it ratified the war debt agreements it had negotiated with Britain and the United States in 1926 and which called for substantial cash payments to those countries if the ratification were not completed before August 1929. In addition, the French government wished to capitalize part of its share of reparations, ostensibly in order to reduce its internal debt. Probably a more fundamental reason was that the French authorities wished to shift part of Germany's reparation obligation from the Allied governments to private creditors on the theory that Germany would be less likely to renege on a "commercial" debt than on a "political" one.[1]

As a result of negotiations in Paris during February-June 1929 and at the Hague in August 1929 and again in January 1930, both Germany and its creditors partially gained their objectives. The Allied controls over, and occupation of, Germany were to be ended. Germany's reparation obligation for the year beginning April 1930 was reduced to a little over $400 million. Although the annuities were to continue thereafter for fifty-seven years, the amount required was appreciably smaller than under the Dawes Plan. Moreover, Germany's immediate problems were alleviated through the flotation of a $300 million international

---

[1] *The plan, which was implemented through the flotation of the Young Loan, was to assign a specified part of the annual reparation payments to the servicing of a bond issue that was to be raised by the German government in the United States and in the principal financial markets of Europe. The proceeds of the loan were distributed primarily to France, Britain, and Germany.* Moreau Diary, *March 22, 1928, page 519;* Thomas Balogh, *"The Import of Gold Into France",* Economic Journal, *September 1930, page 452; BIS First Annual Report, May 19, 1931; Gustav Stolper,* German Economy: 1870-1940, Issues and Trends *(New York: Reynal and Hitchcock, 1940), page 175.*

loan—called the Young Loan after Owen D. Young who played a prominent role in the negotiations in Paris and at the Hague. Of the proceeds of this loan Germany was to receive one third, an amount that was expected both to help finance its budgetary deficit and also to supply part of the foreign exchange required to transfer reparations in the year beginning April 1930. For their parts, France and the other creditor countries were assured of reparation receipts that would at least equal their net war debt payments.[2]

While the reparation settlement alleviated some international financial difficulties, it aggravated others. Germany lost most of the transfer protection that it had been accorded under the Dawes Plan. The Young Plan added to Germany's obligation to service the Dawes Loan the further unconditional obligation to transfer $146 million equivalent annually to service the Young Loan and other portions of the reparation annuities that were expected to be capitalized. The remainder—which amounted to three fifths of the scheduled payments in the year beginning April 1930 and to a somewhat larger proportion in later years[3]—could be postponed up to two years by the German authorities if in their judgment "Germany's exchange and economic life may be seriously endangered by the transfer . . . ."[4] This was in sharp contrast to the Dawes Plan arrangements under which (1) a threat to the exchange stability of the reichsmark was grounds for the complete suspension of reparation transfer, (2) no time limit was specified, and (3) the responsibility for making the suspension rested with a technical body—the Transfer Committee—appointed by the Reparation Commission and indirectly by the Allied governments. Whereas the Dawes Plan made transfer protection complete and removed it as far as possible from the political sphere, the Young Plan not only severely reduced the extent of transfer protection, but—in an international situation that was still charged with tension—gave the responsibility for invoking this protection to the German government. The door was thus opened to recriminations and charges of bad faith, to further worsening of relations between the debtor and creditor powers, and to an aggravation rather than an alleviation of the pressures that were to afflict the reichsmark in the years immediately ahead.

---

[2] Federal Reserve Bulletin *(April 1930), pages 172-249;* Reports of the Agent General, *September 1, 1928 to May 17, 1930, Vol. I, page 213; and BIS* First Annual Report, *May 19, 1931.*

[3] Federal Reserve Bulletin, *April 1930, pages 181 and 184.*

[4] Ibid., *page 175.*

A more positive outcome of the Hague negotiations was the establishment in mid-May 1930 of the Bank for International Settlements. This institution, designed to facilitate the transfer of reparations and to promote international financial cooperation, was equipped with resources adequate to smooth out the relatively minor exchange disturbances characteristic of a prosperous and balanced world economy, but was never intended to cope with difficulties of the magnitude of those which arose in the early 1930's. It started off with a major handicap. The Federal Reserve System was not permitted to join because membership was thought by the United States Government to conflict with the official American position regarding reparations. To assure itself of close relations with the world's major capital market, the BIS therefore invited the participation of a group of United States commercial banks. In addition, the central banks of Britain, France, and Germany and of eighteen other countries as well as a group of Japanese commercial banks participated. Even so, the resources of the BIS were relatively small. Its capital totaled $100 million, of which only $21 million was paid up before the end of 1931. Its assets totaled $412 million equivalent at the end of May 1931, when they reached their peak for 1930-31, an amount that was about the same as Germany's reparation obligation for that year. And of course only a small proportion of these assets was available to support any single currency. The bulk of its assets was held in dollar investments, while another substantial proportion was placed in sterling. Under extreme pressure the bank might have provided as much as $100 million in short-term support for a threatened major currency, i.e., support on the same scale as the Federal Reserve was authorized to give under the November 2, 1927 resolution of the OMIC.

STRAINS DURING THE BOOM: JULY 1928-OCTOBER 1929

Even while the Paris and Hague conferences were still in session, economic changes occurred that led to the collapse of the reparation settlement and to the overwhelming of the efforts of the BIS and the major central banks to support the international financial system.

INTERNATIONAL IMBALANCE. The first phase of the international economic breakdown coincided with the final sixteen months of the New York stock market boom, i.e., July 1928 to the end of October 1929. During this period the pull of the booming American economy on investable funds drove New York money market rates to record levels and greatly decreased the net outflow of capital from the United States. Whereas during 1927 and probably also during the first half of 1928, the United States balance-of-payments deficit had been in excess of $1,000 million annually, it dropped to only $53 million in 1929. Especially before the October 1929 crash, foreigners added substantially to their dollar assets, with the consequence that the direction of gold flows shifted dramatically. While in the year ended June 1928 the United States sold some $500 million in gold to foreign countries, in the sixteen months ended October 1929 it bought almost $300 million.

The pressures that were being exerted on the rest of the world by the United States were augmented by the other major surplus country, France. Although France's payments surplus was sharply reduced from the $500-600 million levels of 1927 and 1928, it remained somewhat above $100 million in 1929. Moreover, the $383 million in Bank of France swaps that were outstanding in mid-1928 matured during the second half of the year. Under the policy followed by the French authorities after June 1928, foreign exchange acquired by the Bank of France on account both of these maturities and of the payments surplus was converted virtually entirely into gold. Hence, although the Bank of France did not run down its large preexisting foreign exchange holdings in the sixteen months ended October 1929, it raised its gold reserves during this period by $434 million, partly as a result of domestic dishoarding but mainly by purchases from abroad.[5]

The pressure emanating from the United States and France was felt throughout the world. In an effort to counter the pull of the New York market and to replace capital that was no longer flowing from the United States, monetary policy was tightened nearly everywhere. Among the hardest hit by the change in the international economic climate was Germany which had been so dependent on the inflow of foreign, and especially American, capital in earlier years. To the extent that it could no longer borrow abroad, Germany was faced with the need to restrict spending at home in order to expand exports and so fulfill its reparation obligation. Indeed, German credit conditions had been tight for much of the year before mid-1928. The Reichsbank discount rate, which had been set at 7 per cent in October 1927, remained at that level throughout 1928 (see Chart 7), while Berlin market rates, fluctuating on either side of the 7 per cent level, were well above those of any other major European center. As a result, when the inflow of American capital declined, Germany was able to recoup much of

---

[5] *Quesnay letter to Goldenweiser, November 29, 1928 (Federal Reserve Board Papers).*

CHART 7

CENTRAL BANK DISCOUNT RATES
UNITED STATES, UNITED KINGDOM, GERMANY, AND FRANCE
DECEMBER 1927–APRIL 1931

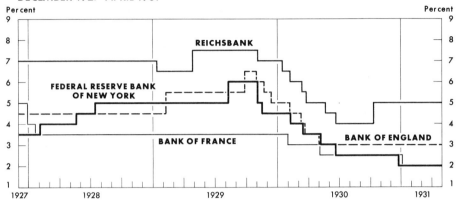

Sources: Board of Governors of the Federal Reserve System, Banking and Monetary Statistics (Washington, D.C., November 1943); R.G. Hawtrey, A Century of Bank Rate (London, 1932); A. Parchman, Die Reichsbank (Berlin, 1933).

the shortfall by borrowing in various European markets and especially in London and Paris.[6] The German credit stringency was accompanied not only by a continued high level of capital inflow but also by a rapid export rise, with the consequences that the Reichsbank's published international reserves increased $120 million during the July-December 1928 period. Early the following January the Reichsbank discount rate was reduced to 6½ per cent. Thereafter, however, the further tightening of credit conditions both in other European markets and in the United States severely restricted the inflow of funds to Germany, and a heavy volume of short-term balances was withdrawn in April when difficulties arose at the Paris reparation conference.[7] Although the Reichsbank discount rate was

---

[6] *Sir Henry Clay,* Lord Norman *(London: Macmillan & Co., Ltd., 1957), pages 244-45; Gardner memorandum to Goldenweiser, December 14, 1928, pages 4-6 (Federal Reserve Board Papers); Reports of the Agent General, September 1, 1928 to May 17, 1930, Vol. 1, page 107; and C. T. Schmidt, German Business Cycles, 1924-1933 (New York: National Bureau of Economic Research, Inc., 1934), page 71.*

[7] Infra, *pages 165-66.*

raised to 7½ per cent toward the end of April and Germany's trade balance was strengthened by the curtailment of domestic spending, the Reichsbank's published international reserves were still 10 per cent lower in October 1929 than they had been ten months before.

Britain was also hard hit by the change in the economic climate. Much of the demand for funds that could no longer be satisfied in New York was shifted to London. Despite an increasingly stringent Bank of England monetary policy, the amount of new issues floated in London on behalf of overseas countries remained substantial in the year ended June 1929. When the Bank of England's policy, together with various market disturbances, finally brought a sharp reduction in the flotation of new issues after mid-1929,[8] many countries found it necessary to draw down their existing London balances.[9] Consequently, sterling came under considerable pressure. Whereas in the year ended July 1928 the Bank of England's gold and dollar balances[10] had increased $163 million to their peak for 1924-31, in the following sixteen months they dropped $298 million to their lowest level prior to the summer-1931 crisis. In August 1929, when the pressure was especially severe, Norman had told the Committee of Treasury that unless conditions improved Britain might be forced, along with other countries, to abandon the gold standard.[11]

DIFFICULTIES OF COOPERATION. A variety of difficulties prevented the major central bankers from cooperating on any significant scale to deal with these pressures. Even if they had wished, they could not have isolated themselves from the conflicts in which their countries were engaged. Norman, Moreau, and Schacht all became involved in greater or less degree in the frequently acrimonious negotiations over reparations.[12] At the same time, the determination of the United States Government to keep out of the reparation controversy minimized Federal

---

[8] Infra, *page 159.*

[9] *BIS* Ninth Annual Report, *1939, page 81.*

[10] *The gold figures used are those reported by the Bank of England. The dollar balances include those on the books of the Federal Reserve Bank of New York and those reported to the Federal Reserve Bank of New York by the only United States commercial bank at which the Bank of England is known to have held a deposit.*

[11] *Clay,* op. cit., *page 252.*

[12] *Hjalmar Schacht,* My First Seventy-Six Years (London: Allan Wingate, 1955), *pages 233-39; Clay,* op. cit., *pages 268 and 364; and* The Economist, *January 19, 1929, page 100.*

Reserve involvement in European monetary problems. Beyond this, Harrison's relations with his European counterparts were almost certainly constrained as a result of the struggle for System leadership that developed between the New York Reserve Bank and the Board after Strong's death in October 1928.

Monetary policy difficulties. In the literature, this struggle has usually been discussed as if it took the form primarily of a controversy over the appropriate means of handling the stock market boom, with the New York Reserve Bank advocating the traditional discount rate-open market approach and the Board supporting direct control over the end use of Federal Reserve credit.[13] Actually the controversy also involved a deeper conflict between the needs of the international financial system and those of the United States domestic economy. The Federal Reserve had been able to cooperate fully and successfully in 1924-25 and again in 1927 primarily because the monetary policy required to deal with the domestic recessions of those years also fostered the System's international financial objectives. In 1928-29 this harmony was lacking. While speculative profits and very high call money rates were drawing funds to New York from all the world, few other signs of inflationary pressures were visible in the United States. Industrial production expanded rapidly until July 1929, but wholesale prices remained stable, and during the previous months significant declines were reported both in construction and in new orders for durables. The business outlook was especially clouded by the expectation among many thoughtful observers that the stock market bubble was certain to burst sooner or later and by the fear that the speculative collapse would have repercussions throughout the economy.

The policies advocated to deal with this complex situation were poles apart, Norman and his colleagues being at one extreme, the Board of Governors at the other, while Harrison attempted a reconciliation that leaned nearer to Norman than to the Board. Uppermost in Norman's mind, of course, were the international repercussions of New York's high call money rates and the decline in the outflow of United States capital. These threatened the gold standard generally and sterling in particular.[14] Accordingly, having postponed action during the

---

[13] *See, for example, Milton Friedman and Anna J. Schwartz,* A Monetary History of the United States, 1867-1960 *(Princeton: Princeton University Press, 1963), pages 254-55; E. A. Goldenweiser,* American Monetary Policy *(1st ed.; New York: McGraw-Hill, Inc., 1951), pages 152-53; and C. O. Hardy,* Credit Policies of the Federal Reserve System *(Washington, D. C.: The Brookings Institution, 1932), pages 131-36.*

[14] *Clay, op. cit., pages 244-49.*

autumn of 1928 in the vain hope that the pressure would ease after the turn of the year, Norman traveled to the United States in late January 1929 to urge joint corrective measures. On February 4, after he had had discussions in New York, Norman clearly hoped that the Federal Reserve discount rates would soon be increased, that this move would be accompanied by a rise in the Bank of England rate, and that Federal Reserve rates at least would be increased further if necessary to break the speculative activity on Wall Street.[15] The results that Norman expected from this course of action are not recorded. However, it is clear almost beyond doubt that he saw an incisive tightening of Federal Reserve policy and the breaking of the stock market boom as steps toward both the decline of United States interest rates to the levels that had prevailed in 1925-27 and also the revival of the American capital outflow. If the Federal Reserve acted decisively, the strain on the Bank of England's reserves would be severe but short and would be repaid in the restoration of an international economic balance that would in the longer run be favorable to sterling. The British strategy was clearly stated by Walter Stewart, an American economist who had become Adviser to the Governors of the Bank of England and had accompanied Norman on the trip from London. A member of the Board staff, who discussed the strategy with Stewart, concluded that the British felt Federal Reserve discount rates should[16]

> be raised, at some unspecified time by a full one per cent with a view to breaking the spirit of speculation, and then subsequently if necessary by another one per cent, in order to provoke liquidation, and then after a fall in the stock market similar rate action at the first sign of the next revival. By thus prostrating the stock market and insuring that thereafter, as in the last three-quarters of 1926, there would always be stock for sale on rallies, we should be cutting at the root of the present situation and could rather promptly reduce rates thereafter and buy securities. I take it that such action would be received abroad as earnest evidence of the right spirit of international cooperation. It is not high rates that any European country shudders at; it is persistence of high rates.

Without doubt, Norman was prepared to argue that such an incisive and cooperative raising of discount rates as he proposed would serve the long-term interests not only of sterling and the international financial system generally but

---

[15] *Clay, op. cit., pages 246-47; Hamlin Diary, February 4, April 18, and June 28, 1929.*

[16] *Memorandum of February 7, 1929 on visit with Mr. Stewart on February 6, 1929, page 4 (Goldenweiser Papers 1929-31, Library of Congress).*

of the United States economy as well. Harrison and his colleagues at the New York Reserve Bank eventually came to share Norman's view but only after a searching debate and as a last resort. A move in the Federal Reserve discount rates to 6 per cent and perhaps even to 7 per cent or more would clearly have involved an extraordinary degree of stringency for the American economy. Already in the early months of 1928 Federal Reserve policy had become progressively tighter. By August 1, 1928 the discount rates of eight of the banks were at 5 per cent, and heavy sales from the Open Market Investment Account had squeezed the money market, with the consequence that member bank borrowings from the Federal Reserve were equivalent to almost half of member bank reserves.

Returning from Europe at the beginning of August 1928, Strong had seen the problem in all its complexity. He was deeply concerned to avoid: (1) "a calamitous break in the stock market, a panicky feeling about money, a setback to business because of the change in psychology", (2) "a precipitous decline in the exchanges, especially sterling, which would weaken the bank position abroad", (3) "embarrassment to the smooth operation of the Dawes Plan", and (4) "restriction upon our exports". For all these reasons, he felt that there were "many advantages in having the period of dear money as short as possible". He reiterated his doubts about any attempt to deal with the speculative tendencies in the stock market: "a gradual unwinding of the situation is quite possible and is the best bet".[17] Two weeks later, when he was back in New York but under doctor's orders to rest at home, his views had crystallized. He felt that some of the difficulties that were being experienced might have been avoided if monetary policy had been tightened more vigorously at the beginning of 1928 but now it was too late to tighten further. On the contrary, he was worried about the lagging effects of monetary policy: high rates now might have effects six months or a year later in the "curtailment of construction and other business activities which might affect business unfavorably". And he concluded that the "time has come to take some of the pressure off the money market without disclosing our hand more than is inevitable".[18]

The adoption in August of a System program along the lines indicated by

---

[17] *Strong letter to Stewart, August 3, 1928, pages 4 and 6. Most of this interesting letter to Stewart is published in L. V. Chandler.* Benjamin Strong, Central Banker *(Washington, D. C.: The Brookings Institution, 1958) pages 460-62.*

[18] *Strong memorandum to files, August 17, 1928, page 8 (Harrison Papers).*

Strong and the repercussions of this program during the fall and early winter of 1928-29 were major factors in Harrison's subsequent decision to advocate cooperation with Norman. The easing of the pressure on the money market gave new life to the stock market boom. Call money rates rose to new highs. In Harrison's view, the threat both to the international financial system and to the domestic economy had become greater; the longer the boom continued, the worse the repercussions would be both internally and externally.[19]

Harrison elaborated the views of the New York Bank to the Federal Reserve Board in Washington on February 5, 1929. The Reserve Bank's ultimate objective, he stated, was to get to a lower level of interest rates as speedily as possible. The continuation of the present high rates for very long "would not only have a directly detrimental effect on our domestic business and commerce, but would force penalty rates of discount abroad and a possible consequent depression which would indirectly but seriously affect our export markets". The stumbling block was that the total volume of credit (in which he included loans extended not only by banks but also by corporations and individuals) was expanding too fast. So long as this expansion continued, the System could not achieve its objectives by simply going into reverse, i.e., by reducing discount rates and by buying securities in the open market. The question that the System had to decide was[20]

> whether we want to let the present situation go along until it corrects itself or whether we should increase discount rates and through sharp incisive action quickly control the long continued expansion in the total volume of credit so that we might then adopt a System policy of easing rates.

Harrison also made clear that, if an increase in some or all Federal Reserve discount rates were decided upon, it was his feeling that the move should not be simultaneous with a Bank of England rate increase. Although a simultaneous move "would have the greatest effect upon the control of credit", Harrison "feared lest such concerted action might be misinterpreted and severely criticized to the point of militating against our effective cooperation with foreign banks of issue".[21]

---

[19] *Harrison letter to Platt, April 17, 1929, especially pages 3-4.*

[20] *Harrison conversation with the Federal Reserve Board on February 5, 1929 (Harrison Papers).*

[21] *Harrison conversation with Mellon on February 5, 1929 (Harrison Papers).*

154

The crucial question of course was whether the New York Reserve Bank's cure would be worse than the disease, whether incisive increases in Federal Reserve and Bank of England discount rates could break the stock market boom without at the same time doing serious damage to economic activity generally. Although this question was certainly uppermost in the minds of Harrison and his colleagues at the New York Bank, their answer is not easy to document, perhaps for the understandable reason that they were reluctant to have it recorded that the breaking of the speculative boom was a prerequisite for the achievement of their ultimate objectives. In its discussions with the Board, the New York Bank minimized the immediate effects on business on the ground that the proposed discount rate increase would be unlikely to raise significantly the already high cost of business borrowing and argued that business could "better afford to pay a higher rate for a short time than even present rates over too long a period".[22] In a cable to one of his directors in mid-March, Harrison revealed his views more clearly:[23]

> We have tried everything but the bank-rate and I personally feel that apart from all other considerations outside [i.e., money market] rates themselves now justify using that.

> With nearly $1,000,000,000 in discounts in the Federal Reserve System I believe we still have control and that sharp incisive and if necessary repeated increases will be effective.

> Of course such a procedure may be costly and will require courage but will it be more costly or require more courage than to do nothing in the face of the likelihood of a long continuation of present or even higher market rates with their inevitable effect upon economic and monetary conditions both here and abroad[?]

The fact is that Harrison and his colleagues at the New York Reserve Bank felt that, if an early breaking of the stock market boom had adverse effects (hopefully short-term ones) on the United States economy, these would be a small price to pay for avoiding the disastrous consequences for both the domestic and international economies that would result from a prolongation of the speculative excesses and from the inevitable and violent collapse of the speculative bubble.

---

[22] *Unsigned memorandum included in a letter from Harrison to Governor Roy A. Young, April 9, 1929, page 4 (Harrison Papers).*

[23] *Harrison to Young, unnumbered cable, March 15, 1929 (Harrison Papers).*

A fundamental difference in viewpoint as well as the struggle for leadership led to the split between the New York Bank and the Board in the early months of 1929 and to the disapproval of the 6 per cent discount rate established by the New York Bank on February 14 and on ten occasions during the following spring. Situated in the political capital, removed from New York's international financial markets, the Board gave low priority to the needs of the international financial system and focused its attention primarily on those of the domestic economy. Thus, to cite only one illustration, the Board's famous direct action letter of February 2, 1929 ignored the difficulties that were being experienced by foreign countries as the result of the New York stock market boom and concentrated exclusively on the threat presented to United States trade and industry by the "extraordinary absorption of funds in speculative security loans".[24] The interaction of the Board's concern with domestic problems and its assertion of leadership is strikingly illustrated in a memorandum in which a member of the Board staff summarized a discussion that he had with Governor Roy A. Young on March 6, 1929. Young was not ready to approve sharp increases in discount rates to break the speculative boom, according to this memorandum, chiefly because he was still hopeful that the market would break without the need for any further System action.[25]

> His inclination against advances is partly because he thinks they do influence business and do not affect speculators, and partly, I am afraid, his desire to do it his own way and not the New York bank's way. He feels that the New York bank directors made an incredible blunder when . . . they passed the resolution that they wanted their discount rate advanced right away, if at all. By doing that they accomplished what they had never accomplished before—they made the Board actually turn down their recommendation. Regardless of the merits of the immediate situation, this is a great accomplishment because it raises the prestige of the Federal Reserve Board in the system . . . it places the Board in the position of protecting American business against high rates, which are wanted partly in view of the international situation.
>
> International concessions are not popular with Congress nor with the people . . . .
>
> The Governor feels that Harrison unquestionably has a commitment (which I believe probably amounts to nothing more than the desire to play the world game)

---

[24] *The Board's letter of February 2, 1929 to the Federal Reserve Banks is published in the* Federal Reserve Bulletin, *February 1929, page 94.*

[25] *Unsigned memorandum on talk with Governor Young on March 6, 1929, pages 3 and 4 (Goldenweiser Papers).*

to Norman to use his influence towards the adoption of radical rate advances. That's the trouble with Harrison. He always presents a plausible story—a good argument, and when he is all through he leaves an impression that he has an ulterior motive. I think the impression is even more potent than the reality.

A day earlier Charles Hamlin recorded Young as saying that he felt Harrison "lived and breathed for Norman".[26]

The result of the deadlock between the New York Reserve Bank and the Board was a System policy that achieved the aims of neither. The Board's stand against discount rate increases did not prevent the reversal of the easier policy that had been followed in the latter part of 1928. The rate at which the New York Bank bought 91-day acceptances was increased ¼ per cent to 4⅞ per cent on January 4, 1929 and was subsequently increased in several steps to 5½ per cent on March 21, 1929. Consequently, Federal Reserve bills "bought" declined much more than seasonally in January-July and the effect of this decline was accentuated by System sales of Government securities. Since the effect of these changes was only partly offset by declines in currency circulation, gold inflows, and increased borrowing at the Federal Reserve, member bank reserves were slightly lower on the average in July than they had been the previous December. Net borrowed reserves had increased to $1,054 million in July, compared with $806 million in January (the first month for which these data are published). But while the credit stringency had adverse repercussions on the outflow of capital from the United States and on construction and other business expenditures, it failed to dampen the stock market boom.[27] The rate of increase in Standard and Poor's composite stock index was almost as large in the seven months ended July 1929 as in the second half of 1928. Rates on new call loans moved steadily upward, from an average of 7.61 per cent in the final quarter of 1928, to 8.07 per cent in January-March 1929, to 8.69 per cent in April-June, and to 9.41 per cent in July. The combined effects of the mild reversal of Federal Reserve policy and the continued stock market boom only increased the strength of New York's pull on foreign and domestic capital.

The increasing credit stringency, together with a growing conviction among the members of the Federal Reserve Board that "direct action" was ineffective, led

---

[26] *Hamlin Diary, March 5, 1929, page 186.*

[27] *See, for example, OMIC, preliminary memorandum, April 1, 1929, pages 4 and 5.*

to a significant change in monetary policy early in August. For Harrison and his colleagues at the New York Reserve Bank the objective remained a significant reduction in the structure of market rates but the tactics were changed. At a meeting with the Federal Reserve Board on August 2, he indicated that the time had passed when this objective could be attained through incisive increases in discount rates and proposed an alternative twofold program. In order to satisfy seasonal credit needs and generally to reduce market rates, the System should pump out funds through market purchases of securities. At the same time, the System would discourage any excessive expansion of credit and any impression that the lid was off by increasing discount rates to 6 per cent. When some members of the Board, who had previously been opposed to the discount rate increase, indicated that they would approve provided that the increase was accompanied by a reduction in the rate at which the New York Reserve Bank bought acceptances, Harrison accepted the compromise.[28] Accordingly the acceptance rate was reduced ⅛ per cent to 5⅛ per cent, and effective August 9 the long sought discount rate increase was approved by the Board.

The results of this change in Federal Reserve policy were highly satisfactory to Harrison when he assessed them early in October. He could hardly have been surprised that the stock market continued to rise during August and early September, and he was pleased to note that credit conditions were easing. In the three months ended in October the System bought some $260 million in bills and, other transactions largely canceling each other out, member bank discounts dropped by $211 million while reserve balances rose $52 million. In October net borrowed reserves were down to $843 million while the average rate for new call loans at 6.10 per cent was 3.31 percentage points lower than in July. Writing to Pierre Jay on October 7, 1929 Harrison summed up his impressions:[29]

> the policy which we adopted early in August, of putting out funds through the bill market under the protection of an effective six per cent rate, has thus far worked much better than I had even dared hope. Bills have gone up, discounts have gone down, and the total volume of Federal Reserve credit has expanded only in proportion to the historic seasonal line. If we can continue this program so that the total volume of discounts in the System will gradually decline to a figure much

---

[28] *Harrison conversations on August 2, 8, and 9, 1929 (Harrison Papers), and unsigned memorandum of August 2, 1929 (Goldenweiser Papers).*

[29] *Harrison letter to Jay, October 7, 1929 (Harrison Papers).*

less than we have averaged during the past year, we will have perhaps taken the first step looking toward a more natural relationship between discounts and the total volume of Federal Reserve credit. On August 1, those discounts were over 85 per cent of the total of reserve credit, a higher percentage than at any time since 1920, and only by decreasing this percentage can we hope safely to pave the way for an easing in the money situation.

In the meantime, the Bank of England had been acting to alleviate the pressure on sterling. As Norman had forewarned when he was in New York, the bank rate was raised to 5½ per cent on February 7, 1929 from the 4½ per cent at which it had stood during the previous twenty-two months. Bank of England operations kept the London money market tight, bill rates were held close to the discount rate, and sterling was thus kept out of serious difficulties throughout most of the first half of the year. In the late spring and early summer, however, the election of a Labor government, continued conflicts over the reparation settlement, the transfer of French balances from London to New York, and the increasing credit stringency in the United States led to a renewed and serious strain on sterling. The exchange rate against the dollar was at or only a little above the gold export point from the beginning of June to mid-September, and the Bank of England's gold holdings declined $133 million. Although Norman did not wish to raise the bank rate again while the Hague conference was in session, he intimated to Harrison that a rise was likely after the conference ended.[30] The Hatry scandal[31] which broke in London on September 20 provided a suitable occasion for action: six days later the bank rate was raised to 6½ per cent and during the following two weeks seven other foreign central banks also raised their rates.

The Bank of England action coincided with and, to an undeterminable but probably small extent, contributed to the ending of the New York stock market boom and to a consequent turn of events that was to bring sterling welcome relief for a few months and deepening difficulties thereafter. The danger signals had of course been flying in the American economy for some time before mid-September.[32] A 2 per cent decline in the industrial production index for

---

[30] *Norman cables to Harrison, Nos. 209, 211, and 250, August 15 and 16, September 7, 1929.*

[31] *Details of this complex stock fraud are discussed in* The Economist, *September 28, 1929, pages 562-63, and February 22, 1930, pages 417-18.*

[32] Supra, *page 151.*

July was announced to the press on August 31, and on September 22 the New York papers carried an investment service advertisement warning investors about "overstaying a bull market".[33] In the circumstances, it was hardly surprising that the stock market turned gently downward during the third week in September.[34] Significant declines occurred on the days following the announcements of the Hatry scandal and the increase in the Bank of England discount rate, but the market steadied immediately thereafter and the decline was mild until the third week in October.

In the meantime international payments flows were responding to the change in market expectations and in interest rate relationships. The margin of the London acceptance rate above the corresponding rate in New York, which had been small throughout the previous summer, widened to more than 1 per cent after the bank rate increase, while the margin in favor of New York on call money rates narrowed sharply. At the same time, there were indications that foreign balances were being withdrawn from the New York call loan market.[35] The premium on three-month forward sterling, which had appeared in mid-1928 when the pull of the New York market began to be strongly felt in London and which stood at ½ per cent per annum on September 14, 1929, had almost disappeared by the month end. In October, the premium on sterling had changed to a progressively growing discount. Spot sterling, which had fallen to a low of $4.84½ on the day following the announcement of the Hatry scandal, was above $4.85 a week later and above $4.87 on October 19. On October 24, before the news reached London that the panic had already begun on the New York stock market, Norman cabled Harrison to indicate his gratification at the turnaround in the markets:[36]

> Recent liquidation in your stock market and reduction in call money rates have been satisfactory and have helped to re-establish international position.

---

[33] *J. K. Galbraith, The Great Crash, 1929 (Boston: Houghton Mifflin Company, 1955), page 97.*

[34] *Standard and Poor's Corporation, Daily Stock Price Indexes, 1926-1957 (New York, 1957), pages 10-11; C. A. Dice and W. J. Eiteman, The Stock Market (3rd ed.; New York: McGraw-Hill, Inc., 1952), page 349, gives the peaks shown by various indexes of industrial shares as September 3, 7, and 19.*

[35] *OMIC, preliminary memorandum, September 24, 1929, pages 4-5.*

[36] *Norman cable to Harrison, No. 297, October 24, 1929 (Harrison Papers).*

Market operations to support sterling. The difficulties of monetary policy cooperation were paralleled in the field of Federal Reserve foreign exchange operations during the sixteen months ended October 1929. Operations to support sterling were frequently discussed but very little was done. While changes in the international political and economic climate and in the leadership of the Federal Reserve doubtless contributed to this result, central bank policy also played a role. Early in the period, as previously noted, the Bank of England's international assets were at their peak for the years 1924-31. Nevertheless, when sterling came under pressure early in August 1928, Harrison proposed to buy sterling both to support the British currency and as part of the program to ease United States monetary conditions. However, the suggestion came to naught. The New York Reserve Bank insisted that the proceeds be placed in sterling bills which were chronically scarce in London; on the other hand, the Bank of England was reluctant to add to the demand for such paper at a time when it was striving to keep short-term rates as close to the bank rate as possible.[37] In addition, Norman seems to have felt that part of the pressure should be reflected in gold losses that would impress the public with the continuing need for a strict monetary policy and that he could afford to absorb the rest of the pressure by running down the Bank of England's unreported dollar balances which at the time were ample.[38] He may also have wished to conserve the external assistance that was available to him until the need for it was more urgent. After the turn of the year another difficulty arose. The Federal Reserve was again squeezing the money market and was running out of open market ammunition. Government securities in the Open Market Investment Account were down to $40 million on April 1, enough to offset the expansionary effects on the cash base of only a modest amount of sterling purchases.[39]

As the pressure on sterling mounted during the summer of 1929, the need to surmount these technical difficulties became urgent. On August 9, Harrison telephoned to Norman that sterling had weakened somewhat upon the announce-

---

[37] *Harrison cables to Lubbock, Nos. 176, 183, and 201 of August 2, 15, and 31, 1928; Lubbock cable to Harrison, No. 145, August 14, 1928; and testimony of Sir Robert Kindersley,* Macmillan Evidence, *Vol. I, Question 1269.*

[38] *Norman cable to Harrison, No. 165, September 5, 1928.*

[39] *Harrison cable to Norman, No. 15, January 16, 1929 (Harrison Papers); OMIC preliminary memorandum, April 1, 1929.*

ment of the increase in the New York Reserve Bank's discount rate, and suggested the possibility of Federal Reserve purchases of sterling in the amount of $25-50 million. He indicated that, although bills were preferred, he would be satisfied if the sterling were invested half in bills and half "employed" at interest.[40] After a few days' consideration, Norman accepted Harrison's proposal. The fifty-fifty formula was agreed upon, and it was decided that any purchases should be made only when sterling was at the gold export point to New York.[41] Harrison was also concerned about exchange risks, particularly in view of the fact that Norman himself had repeatedly expressed fears about the future of sterling. When all other details had been settled, therefore, Harrison cabled that he assumed that the Bank of England "would be prepared if necessary at any time to repay us in gold or in dollars at New York for any sterling which we might buy", to which Norman replied curtly "of course sterling is repayable in gold. That is the gold standard."[42] Apparently Harrison was satisfied by the response, and no arrangements were made to cover the forthcoming sterling purchases in the forward market.[43] Shortly thereafter, the directors of the New York Reserve Bank, acting under power conferred by the Federal Reserve Act, authorized sterling purchases of up to $25 million.[44] In the event, only £3.3 million ($16 million) was bought during late August and early September. The rise in sterling following the September 26 increase in the Bank of England discount rate ended the need for further operations and the whole amount was repaid on November 22.[45]

Longer term financing. Norman also discussed the possibility of longer term financing with Harrison and with various New York commercial bankers during the spring and summer of 1929. As foreigners turned increasingly to London for funds, the Bank of England received credit applications that revealed a need

---

[40] *Harrison conversation with Governor Norman on August 9, 1929 (Harrison Papers).*

[41] *Norman cable to Harrison, No. 205, August 13, 1929; Harrison cable to Norman, No. 224, August 14, 1929.*

[42] *Harrison cable to Norman, No. 224, August 14, 1929; Norman cable to Harrison, No. 209, August 15, 1929.*

[43] *Harrison conversation with Young on August 16, 1929 (Harrison Papers).*

[44] *Unsigned memorandum on meeting of the Board with Kenzel and Harrison, August 15, 1929 (Goldenweiser Papers); Harrison conversations with Young on August 16 and 19, 1929 (Harrison Papers).*

[45] *See cables between the Federal Reserve Bank of New York and the Bank of England, August 22-September 6 and November 20-24, 1929.*

not so much for sterling as for dollars. On May 10 Norman wrote Harrison that he expected such applications to increase, especially if New York interest rates remained high. As to the means by which the needed dollars could be obtained, Norman saw several possibilities:[46]

first, that the advances should as far as possible come direct from you whence, by the sale of Bonds, they would eventually be repaid: secondly, that the advances should come from us European Banks which would lead to further increases of Bank Rates in Europe. Unless you think there is yet another possibility—that the Bank of France or we or some others should lend the money here and ourselves directly re-borrow from the Federal Reserve Bank: this obviously raises a number of questions!

The American response to Norman's suggestion was generally very sympathetic. Although Harrison indicated that Norman's third possibility should be considered only as a last resort, he suggested that another gold credit might be arranged along the lines of that negotiated between the Federal Reserve and the Bank of England in April 1925. In addition, officers of J. P. Morgan & Co. made it clear that their institution would be more than willing to do anything that it could to help. But, by mid-August, when these offers of help were made definite, Norman's situation had changed. He told Harrison that he was not in a position to consider another 1925-type credit, and he discounted as unfounded all rumors that the British government was about to obtain a large loan from the New York market.[47]

The available records do not indicate what lay behind the shift in Norman's position, but an explanation may well be found in the attitude of the Labor government toward the level of the Bank of England's fiduciary issue. A year before when the Conservative government had set the fiduciary issue at £260 million, members of the Labor opposition had criticized the figure as too low and had argued in addition that the arrangements for changing the level of the issue were unduly cumbersome.[48] Having come to power at the beginning of June 1929,

---

[46] *Norman letter to Harrison, May 10, 1929 (Harrison Papers).*

[47] *Harrison cables to Norman, Nos. 171 and 224, May 23 and August 14, 1929; Harrison memorandum on Federal Reserve Board meeting, August 14, 1929; unsigned memorandum on Board meeting with Kenzel and Harrison, August 15, 1929 (Goldenweiser Papers); Leffingwell cable to Grenfell, August 15, 1929 (Lamont Papers).*

[48] Supra, *page 141.*

the Labor government apparently decided to deal with the pressures on sterling not through foreign borrowing as Norman had originally contemplated but by increasing the fiduciary issue. At any rate, early in August 1929 Norman did ask the Bank of England's Committee of Treasury to consider whether such an increase would be advisable in order to release gold for the defense of sterling.[49] As events turned out, sterling's subsequent recovery made the adoption of special measures unnecessary during the rest of 1929 and 1930, but these preliminary discussions laid the groundwork for the changing of the fiduciary issue and the credits from the Federal Reserve and Morgan's that were thrown into the unsuccessful attempt to save sterling during the summer of 1931.

THE ROLE OF THE BANK OF FRANCE. The international monetary problems of Britain and Germany were complicated during the sixteen months ended October 1929 by pressures not only from the United States but also from France, whose authorities were preoccupied with safeguarding their nation's interests in the reparation settlement and were reluctant to increase the large balances that they had accumulated in London during 1927 and early 1928.[50]

Ordinary financial relations were almost certain to be disturbed by the reparation negotiation in which France and Germany were the principal antagonists, but there is evidence that the disturbances were aggravated during the latter part of 1928 and early 1929 by official measures to strengthen the bargaining positions of the main contenders. Moreau, who had no compunctions about using financial power to support the aims of his government, did nothing to discourage the substantial flow of French funds that was responding to the high interest rates then prevailing in Germany.[51] He may even have contributed to the flow through

---

[49] *Clay, op. cit., page 252.*

[50] Supra, *pages 111, 117, and 118.*

[51] *Moreau's attitude toward the use of financial power can be copiously illustrated from his Diary which, however, ends in mid-1928. Toward the end of January 1928, Moreau was upset because the Bank of England seemed to be stealing a march on France in negotiations with Yugoslavia. He wrote in his Diary on January 27:*

> *If the Bank of England takes away from us these customers, whom we are anxious to hold for political reasons, I shall show my displeasure by buying gold in London.*

On February 6, 1928 Moreau discussed with Poincaré the conflicts between the Bank of France and the Bank of England in numerous Continental countries and told him, according to the Diary:

> *We now have powerful means of exerting pressure upon the Bank of England. Would it not be advisable to have a serious discussion with Mr. Norman, to try to divide Europe into two zones of financial influence, allocated respectively to France and to England?*

164

the transfer of Bank of France funds from New York and London. Large balances in Berlin would give France leverage over Germany in the forthcoming negotiation.[52]

Schacht, too, was preparing. He was aware that much of the inflow to Germany in the second half of 1928 consisted of French balances,[53] and he knew from experience that the French were unlikely to be squeamish about employing such financial weapons as they possessed to attain their reparation objectives. The settlement in gold of the balance-of-payments surplus that Germany enjoyed in the latter part of 1928 therefore accorded not only with Schacht's gold standard principles but was a necessary precaution against the possible, if not the probable, withdrawal of French balances. Of course, the bulk of the gold was taken from London. Norman, seeking to relieve the pressure, suggested that Schacht increase his holdings of sterling. But Schacht could only have cooperated at the cost of weakening his own position.[54]

The test came during the third week in April 1929 when the Paris conference became deadlocked over the amount and duration of the annuities to be paid by Germany. To be sure, the January reduction in the Reichsbank discount rate and nervousness about the outcome of the conference had been accompanied by increasing pressure on the mark. The Reichsbank's gold and reported foreign exchange dropped $40 million during the first quarter. As political tensions rose, some $60 million more was lost in the first half of April. On April 18, shortly after the conference breakdown, Pierre Quesnay of the Bank of France told an American at the conference that $200 million would be withdrawn from Germany by noon the next day.[55] Schacht, who headed the German delegation to the conference, related that[56]

the big banks of Berlin received from various French financial institutions letters, couched in almost identical terms and referring in unmistakable terms to

---

[52] *Gardner memorandum to Goldenweiser, December 14, 1928, page 5 (Federal Reserve Board Papers).*

[53] *Clay, op. cit., page 244.*

[54] Ibid., *page 245.*

[55] *S. M. Crocker, "Notes on the Young Plan", page 147 (Young Papers). Quesnay said this to Fred Bate, Secretary to Young Committee.*

[56] *Hjalmar Schacht,* The End of Reparations *(New York: Jonathan Cape and Harrison Smith, 1931), page 89.*

the Paris negotiations, announcing a curtailment of the credits which had been put at Germany's disposal.

How far the withdrawals of balances from Germany were politically motivated, as Schacht believed,[57] or were merely the market's response to the deadlock is unclear. Whatever the underlying causes, the last two weeks of April saw a further $110 million drop in the Reichsbank's reported international reserves and an increase in its discount rate to 7½ per cent. However, the storm was quickly over. By mid-May the deadlock had been broken, Norman was organizing central bank assistance for the Reichsbank, but already funds were flowing back to Germany, the Reichsbank's foreign exchange reserves were again rising, and no help was in fact required.[58]

Only $128 million of the Bank of France's $434 million gold gain in the sixteen months ended October 1929 can be attributed to the withdrawal of French balances from Germany during the Paris conference. Another $177 million was acquired during the latter part of 1928 largely from domestic dishoarding and from the United States. The remainder was acquired during July-October 1929 when London was hit by heavy buying from Paris and when British net exports of gold to France totaled $129 million after having been negligible throughout the previous year.

The official French view was that the gold movement from Britain was merely the natural result of the international movement of funds. In its annual report of 1929, the Bank of France declared:[59]

> From June to December we never took the initiative in acquiring gold by means of foreign bills. We were obliged, in fulfillment of our obligation to regulate the currency, to accept all gold of foreign origin which was offered to us over the counter for francs, but we did not at any time intervene in the exchange market to accelerate the pace of these gold imports. The bank has opposed no obstacle whatever to the free play of the money market under the régime of the gold standard.

But this was merely gold standard rhetoric which concealed more than it revealed. In particular, it concealed the extent to which the gold movement arose,

---

[57] Schacht, My First Seventy-Six Years, *page 238.*

[58] Norman cables to Harrison, Nos. 100 and 115, May 6 and 16, 1929 (Harrison Papers).

[59] Bank of France, Annual Report, 1929, published in the Federal Reserve Bulletin (March 1930), page 113.

as in May 1927, from French institutional arrangements and financial policies—from the Bank of France's lack of authority to conduct open market operations, from the commercial banks' reluctance to discount at the central bank, and from the piling up at the central bank of surplus Treasury and other official receipts from the public. A large rise in such official balances did in fact occur during the summer of 1929, while the expansion of the French economy and increases in wages and consumer prices led to a significant rise in note circulation during the whole second half of the year. Since only a small part of the consequent pressure on the commercial banks was offset by increases in discounts and advances at the Bank of France, the Paris market acted to avoid stringency by drawing down its London balances. Sterling was sold for francs, the exchange rate for the British currency fell to the gold export point to Paris, and French commercial banks thus met their cash needs by selling gold to the Bank of France.[60]

Undoubtedly it was true that the Bank of France was obliged to buy, at a fixed price, all gold offered to it, but the statement quoted above from the bank's 1929 annual report sidestepped an important question. Since the bank retained full authority, under the June 1928 monetary law, to operate in the foreign exchange markets, it had a choice of meeting the Paris market's cash needs either as it did, through the purchase of gold, or by acquiring sterling and thereby keeping the British currency above the gold export point. However, the latter was hardly an inviting alternative for the Bank of France, which considered that it was already extending too much help to the London market. At the end of June 1929, indeed, Bank of France holdings of sterling probably stood well above the £70-80 million that Moreau had agreed to hold in June 1927.[61] The conflict that developed at the Hague conference between the British and the Continental delegations and the increasing questioning in the markets about the future of sterling can only have stiffened the Bank of France's resolve to avoid any further increase in its sterling commitment. Indeed, this commitment was reduced, some $100 million having been transferred to New York in the four

---

[60] *The factors behind France's absorption of gold during 1929-30 are discussed by R. G. Hawtrey,* The Art of Central Banking *(London: Longmans, Green and Co. Ltd., 1932), Chapter I, especially pages 28-32; Balogh, op. cit., pages 442-60; League of Nations,* International Currency Experience, *pages 38 and 39; and W. A. Brown, Jr.,* The International Gold Standard Reinterpreted, 1914-1934 *(New York: National Bureau of Economic Research, Inc., 1940), Vol. II, pages 766-67.*

[61] Supra, *page 119.*

months to the end of October 1929. Even so, on the latter date the Bank of France still held £97 million in London.[62]

FALSE HOPES: NOVEMBER 1929-JUNE 1930

In the eight months that followed the New York stock market crash, there seemed a good chance that the vision shared by Harrison and Norman in February 1929 might be realized. Although production and prices were declining nearly every-where, the contraction was fairly mild in Britain while in France, contrary to the prevailing trend, the economy continued to expand. United States production, after declining sharply in the second half of 1929, made a modest recovery in the early months of the new year. It was clear that a considerable recession was in progress, but this was the price that Harrison and Norman had felt might have to be paid in order to eliminate the speculative boom and restore the equilibrating outflow of long-term capital from the United States.

In fact, the crash brought a dramatic about-face in the exchange and inter-national capital markets. In the following four months, foreign balances in New York were repatriated in substantial volume. The major foreign currencies swiftly recovered. Both the French franc and sterling were close to or at the gold import point during much of November and December, and gold moved once again from New York to London and Paris. Then in January-June 1930 there was a major revival of new issues for foreign account on both the New York and London markets. Germany was one of the main beneficiaries of this revival which, together with a growing merchandise trade surplus, raised the gold and reported foreign exchange holdings of the Reichsbank by mid-1930 to its 1924-31 peak. Moreover, despite the revival in capital outflows, Britain continued to gain gold in January-June 1930 when the gold inflow into the United States was also resumed. Unfortunately, as noted below, these British and American gains were largely at the expense of primary producing countries whose external positions were becom-ing increasingly desperate.

The revival of international capital flows was sought by the major central bankers with rare harmony. They agreed that the revival was necessary for the

---

[62] *Crane memorandum to Harrison, November 30, 1929, "Report of Trip to Europe", September 11-November 20, 1929, pages 24 and 25.*

168

success of the Young Plan and for the maintenance of exchange stability. In addition, each had special reasons of his own. For Norman, the renewed American outflow was desirable because it supported sterling and facilitated the reopening of the London capital market. For the German authorities, foreign funds were needed to cover the deficits both in the government budget and in the country's balance of payments. Moreau sought to encourage an outflow of French capital to enhance both Paris' position as an international financial center and the political leadership of France in Europe, while Harrison saw the revived outflow of American funds as a means to foster United States exports and thus counter the contraction in domestic spending.

The revival in capital flows was facilitated by the virtually simultaneous easing of monetary policy in the major financial centers. With America slipping into depression, the Federal Reserve was no longer hampered by the conflict between domestic and international aims. Within the System, to be sure, some emphasized the need to liquidate unsound positions that had been built up during the preceding boom and warned, especially when the stock market was staging an ephemeral but spectacular recovery in April 1930, against the revival of the speculative fever. Measures to support foreign central banks were also somewhat inhibited by continuing suspicions in Washington that Norman, and perhaps Moreau, too, had undue influence on the New York Reserve Bank.[63] Even so, the reversal of Federal Reserve policy was remarkably swift, the change being led by the New York Reserve Bank. Its discount rate was reduced to 5 per cent on November 1, 1929, to 4½ per cent two weeks later, and in four additional steps to 2½ per cent on June 20, 1930. At the same time, open market operations quickly changed direction. Over $400 million of Government securities was bought in the eight months beginning November 1, 1929, more than the amount that was sold when the markets were being squeezed during January-August 1928. During January-June 1930 a heavy reduction in note circulation and the renewed rise in the gold stock acted together with open market purchases to pump out reserves and to facilitate a sharp reduction in member bank borrowings at the Federal Reserve. In June 1930 net borrowed reserves had dropped to $197 million from more than $900 million a year earlier, member bank reserves were slightly higher, while the total of currency held by the public and commercial

---

[63] *Hamlin Diary, January 20, 1930, page 90.*

169

bank deposits was only slightly lower.[64]

In Europe, too, monetary policy was eased significantly, although the change was not so large as in the United States. The Bank of France's discount rate, which had been at 3½ per cent since the beginning of 1928, was reduced to 3 per cent at the end of January 1930 and to 2½ per cent on May 1. Moreover, the effects of the continued rise in note circulation were more than offset in January-May by an apparently fortuitous rundown of official deposits at the Bank of France, which led to a distinct easing of money market conditions.[65] In the fiscal area, the government, at the request of the Bank of France, acted during the winter of 1929-30 to reduce a variety of taxes that were discouraging the outflow of French long-term capital.[66] Of necessity, the movement toward ease in Germany and Britain was considerably more cautious than in the United States and France. Both the Reichsbank and the Bank of England acted more or less in step with the New York Reserve Bank, but their discount rates were kept generally above New York's. By June 1930, when the discount rates in New York and Paris were down to 2½ per cent, London's and Berlin's stood, respectively, at 3 per cent and 4 per cent.

The easing of monetary policy, combined with the sharp decline in economic activity, brought a major drop in money market rates in all the major centers. In the capital markets, however, the reaction was less satisfactory. In New York, yields on United States Government and other prime long-term securities were significantly lower in January-June 1930 than they had been a year earlier but yields on lesser quality bonds were virtually unchanged. Elsewhere, the cost of long-term borrowing was still at about the same level as in the first half of 1929, even for the British government; in Paris, it was distinctly lower but, despite official efforts, the market for the general run of foreign issues remained all but dead.[67]

Even so, the revival of international lending during the first half of 1930 was remarkable. The total of new issues for foreign account floated in the United

---

[64] *Friedman and Schwartz, op. cit., pages 712, 713, and 739; Board of Governors of the Federal Reserve System*, Banking and Monetary Statistics, *page 371.*

[65] *Hawtrey, op. cit., page 29.*

[66] *Bank of France,* Annual Report, *1930, published in the* Federal Reserve Bulletin *(March 1931), page 147.*

[67] The Economist, *May 10, 1930 (Banking Supplement), pages 13-14, and August 9, 1930, page 278.*

States was $701 million, second only to the record amount issued in January-June 1928. Similarly, in Britain new issues for overseas countries totaled $331 million, an amount that had been exceeded only in the first halves of 1928 and 1929. In both markets, the issues (apart from the Young Loan) were primarily on behalf of non-European governments, those raised in New York being largely for the Western Hemisphere, Australia, and Japan, those in London for British Empire countries.

On two occasions, the Paris market did come to life when it played a significant but not entirely helpful role in the flotation of securities to support the Young Plan. In accordance with agreements negotiated earlier in the year, the BIS shares were issued on May 20 and the Young Loan on June 12 and 13 in Paris as well as in London and other European centers and in New York. In Paris the response was very large, both issues being heavily oversubscribed.[68] Unfortunately the ease that had prevailed earlier in the Paris market was already giving way to renewed stringency, and this stringency was accentuated by large transfers of funds to the Bank of France in subscriptions for the new issues. As in earlier periods, the stringency in Paris was relieved by a flow of funds from London so that, after a three-month lull, gold again began to move from Britain to France in substantial volume. This being the outcome, there must have been serious doubts, at least at the Bank of England, whether the benefit of French official participation in such international efforts was not heavily outweighed by the cost.

STRAINS DURING THE DEPRESSION: JULY 1930-MAY 1931

DETERIORATION. Hopes that the depression would be mild and that a renewed outflow of United States capital would restore the international economic balance were undermined by the further deterioration of the international economy during the eleven months that followed the flotation of the Young Loan. The mild recovery of United States industrial production in early 1930 proved abortive; from April on, output dropped sharply as it also did in Germany. In France, too, economic expansion gave way after mid-1930 to a gradually deepening depression. Especially in Britain, Germany, and the United States, unemployment

---

[68] The Economist, *May 24, 1930, page 1160;* The Commercial and Financial Chronicle, *June 14, 1930, page 4107, and June 21, 1930, page 4296.*

171

became a major problem, even on occasion a threat to political stability. Primary producing countries, too, suffered from declining exports to the industrial countries and from continued high levels of raw material and food production. The decline in primary commodity prices steepened and, with the worsening of the primary producers' terms of trade, the pressure on their international positions became severe.

As the economic climate worsened, confidence in the international financial markets was hit by a series of shocks. Defaults on foreign bonds increased. The currencies of several primary producers were devalued. Eastern European and South American governments were overthrown by coups.[69] In the United States, the stock market resumed a sharply downward course and import duties were raised over protests both from abroad and from a large body of American economists. Confidence was further weakened in the United States, Britain, and Germany by rapidly rising budget deficits and in the United States and France by a growing number of bank failures. In Germany, the summer of 1930 saw an ugly outburst of nationalism, and September, the rise of the Nazis from an insignificant minority to a major national party. With the ink on the Young Plan hardly dry, the markets began to hear rumors during the fall that the German government would ask for a reparation moratorium.

For their parts, the monetary authorities in the major countries, having eased credit policies very considerably in the eight months following the crash, did little more. No further discount rate reductions were made until, at the turn of the year, the New York Reserve Bank and the Bank of France both cut their rates to 2 per cent;[70] thereafter, the New York Reserve Bank went to 1½ per cent early in May 1931 and the Bank of England followed with a reduction in its rate to 2½ per cent. In both the United States and Britain, the central banks followed an extremely cautious open market policy. From late June 1930 on, Harrison vigorously advocated a policy of open market purchases that aimed, through the pumping of funds into the money market and the further reduction of short-term interest rates, to support a revival of the bond market.[71] But this

---

[69] *Report of the Chairman of the Open Market Policy Conference to the Governors' Conference, April 27, 1931, pages 3-4.*

[70] *Harrison conversations with Harvey and Lacour-Gayet on December 22, 1930 (Harrison Papers).*

[71] *Harrison letter to Seay, July 3, 1930.*

172

proposal was not accepted. In the eleven months ended May 1931, System purchases of bills and Government securities totaled only $31 million which, together with gold purchases of $239 million, did little more than offset the drain on member bank reserves from increased currency circulation. At the end of the eleven months that saw an increasing number of bank failures, rising currency hoarding, and a significant decline in bank deposits, member banks still showed net borrowed reserves of almost $100 million. In Britain, the Bank of England, which previously had at least partly offset the effects of gold movements on bank reserves, reversed its policy. During the eleven months beginning July 1930 open market sales reinforced the cash drain that resulted from the outflow of gold so that bankers' balances at the Bank of England in May 1931 averaged 5 per cent lower than a year earlier.

The monetary policies of the major countries combined with the continued decline in production and prices and the rise in defaults, devaluations, and political disturbances to kill the revival of the long-term capital flow. In the year beginning July 1930, new issues for foreign account fell in both Britain and the United States to only about one third of the rate in January-June 1930.

The international disequilibrium again became manifest. Despite the enlarged outflow of long-term capital during the first half of the year and a slight decline in its current account surplus, the United States payments balance changed from a $53 million deficit in 1929 to a $598 million surplus in 1930, and the surplus seems to have run at an even higher rate during January-May 1931. France's surplus was almost $300 million in 1930, compared with $125 million the year before. Germany's position, on the other hand, moved into deficit, the Reichsbank's gold and reported foreign exchange balances dropping by about one fifth in the eleven months ended May 1931. Britain, too, was under severe pressure, especially from France, to which it exported almost $300 million in gold during the eleven months, somewhat more than South Africa's production of gold during the whole of 1930. However, Britain succeeded in passing on much of this pressure to other countries, notably the primary producers which, being in desperate straits themselves, were heavy sellers of gold not only in New York but also in London. Consequently, the decline in the Bank of England's gold holdings was comparatively modest.

CENTRAL BANK COOPERATION: MUCH ACTIVITY; LITTLE ACCOMPLISHED. Although the international economy was visibly deteriorating, the threat of an imminent and major crisis was required to open the way for significant measures of central bank cooperation. In the absence of such a threat, much of the eleven months immediately prior to the outbreak of the 1931 crisis was given over to bickering and sparring for position. The Micawberish attitude of the Hoover Administration and the continuing struggle over leadership within the System prevented any vigorous initiative on the part of the Federal Reserve. With little freedom of action, Harrison had to tread carefully.[72] The kind of intimacy that had existed between Strong and Norman disappeared. Although Harrison visited the major European central banks in April and again in November 1930 and Norman came to New York in the spring of 1931, the Federal Reserve was not represented at the BIS monthly meetings and remained perforce on the periphery of the discussions among the European central bankers. And of course these discussions, being affected by continuing political tensions between Germany and France, were far from harmonious. Minor irritations added to the strains—as when the Bank of England failed to mint an adequate supply of fine gold bars and instead offered standard bars which the Bank of France considered unacceptable.[73]

Short-term support for the reichsmark and sterling. The only currency support operations of which we have any record in the eleven months ended May 1931 occurred after the September German national elections in which the Nazis scored large gains. In the month that followed, Germany suffered a heavy outflow of funds as the result of which the Reichsbank lost some $250 million in gold and foreign exchange, mostly in the first few days after the election.[74] Apart from vigorous intervention by the Reichsbank itself, operations to support the reichsmark apparently were undertaken only by the BIS. But the form of this support was curious and the scope small. Although by far the largest share of the BIS assets was held in the United States, its dollars were not employed. Rather, despite the delicate condition of the British currency at the time, the

---

[72] *Harrison was continually being sniped at from the Board. Some of its members objected on legal grounds to the New York Reserve Bank's foreign exchange operations. Others felt that Harrison should not go abroad without the Board's consent and, foreshadowing subsequent amendments to the Federal Reserve Act, that legislation should be adopted to subject any consultations between the New York Reserve Bank and foreign central banks to the supervision of the Board. Hamlin Diary, October 22, 1930 and March 26, 1931, pages 99 and 199.*

[73] *Moreau letter to Harrison, June 13, 1930; Allan Sproul memorandum to files, January 21, 1931, pages 7 and 8.*

[74] *BIS cable to Federal Reserve Bank of New York, No. 130, September 23, 1930; Luther letter to Sackett, February 27, 1931, page 11.*

BIS chose to sell sterling for dollars and to transfer the proceeds into reichsmarks, switching about $2 million equivalent in this manner between September 23 and October 1.[75] Although this support was given on a short-term basis, the continued weakness of the German currency made it impracticable for the BIS to reduce its reichsmark assets until special arrangements were made for their partial liquidation during 1932.[76]

Toward the middle of September 1930 Harrison cabled Norman that sterling had suffered a sudden drop in New York which was not explicable on seasonal and other technical grounds alone and raised the question whether the rate could be most conveniently supported through the Bank of England's sales of dollars or Federal Reserve purchases of sterling.[77] Initially Norman indicated his preference for the first alternative but subsequently agreed that Federal Reserve sterling purchases would be helpful. Acting under their statutory power, the New York Reserve Bank's directors on October 9 authorized sterling purchases of up to £5 million. There were the usual difficulties about investing the sterling in commercial bills which the Bank of England said it could not obtain at the moment without "breaking the rate".[78] On this occasion, the New York Reserve Bank took a flexible position, and it was agreed that the proceeds would be placed in deposits at the Bank of England with the understanding that these would be converted "into bills as and when they can be obtained without inconvenience to you". It was also understood that the operation would not be reversed until after the turn of the year when sterling was expected to be stronger.[79]

Under these arrangements, the New York Reserve Bank acquired sterling with the prime objective, as on earlier occasions, of preventing the London market from losing gold to New York. Initially the support operations were quite vigorous, purchases being made at the rate of £500,000 daily between October 14 and 17. Purchases were suspended when sterling rose somewhat above the gold export point to New York but were resumed during the final week of

---

[75] *McGarrah cable to Harrison, No. 9, September 23, 1930; BIS cables to Federal Reserve Bank of New York, Nos. 130, 132, 136, September 23, 24 and 30, 1930.*

[76] *Roger Auboin,* The Bank For International Settlements, 1930-1955, *Essays in International Finance (Princeton: Princeton University Press, May 1955), page 9.*

[77] *Harrison cables to Norman, Nos. 216 and 218, September 12 and 16, 1930.*

[78] *Harvey cable to Harrison, No. 230, October 9, 1930.*

[79] *Harrison cable to Harvey, No. 244, October 10, 1930.*

October. By the end of the month, £4.7 million had been acquired (all of which had been invested in bills) and authority was obtained to acquire £5 million more.[80] However, the feeling was strong at both the New York Reserve Bank and the Bank of England that £10 million should be the ceiling.[81] O. M. W. Sprague, who had succeeded Walter Stewart as Adviser to the Governors of the Bank of England, told Allan Sproul who visited him at the Bank of England in early December 1930 that,[82]

> Except in connection with a temporary condition, such purchases merely postpone the setting in motion of the forces which will really correct the underlying situation. In this case they would foster the willingness of England to take her difficulties sitting down, instead of standing against them.

Using its additional ammunition conservatively, the New York Reserve Bank acquired only £2.5 million during November and December so that at the year-end its holdings totaled £7.2 million. Although sterling was under considerable pressure at times during January 1931, no more was acquired by the Federal Reserve, and with the concurrence of the Bank of England the whole amount was gradually liquidated during February and March at rates that were only fractionally higher than those at which it was bought. Even so, the objective of the operation was attained: London lost virtually no gold to New York during six months of considerable strain.[83]

The Bank of France, too, supported sterling during the autumn of 1930, acting apparently during early November when the failure of several French banks precipitated difficulties in the Paris market and heavy withdrawals of French funds from London.[84] However, the Bank of France's intervention was limited to averting what appeared to be a critical situation.[85] Once the emergency had

---

[80] *Harrison letter to Young, October 17, 1930; Harrison letter to Seay, October 31, 1930, pages 3-4.*

[81] *Harrison cable to Case, No. 2, November 14, 1930, page 1 (Harrison Papers).*

[82] *Allan Sproul memorandum to files, January 21, 1931, page 8.*

[83] *Crane letter to Young, March 20, 1931.*

[84] The Economist, *November 8, 1930 pages 853-54; Crane letter to Black, November 21, 1930.*

[85] *Apparently the demand for cash in Paris was so great that it could not be met either by selling gold to, or borrowing from, the Bank of France. Gold could not be shipped fast enough from London. In order to prevent a money panic, the Bank of France pumped funds into the market by buying sterling balances.*

passed, it quietly sold most of the sterling to private bankers and resumed its passive role in the exchange markets.[86] In the three months beginning November 1930, British gold exports to France totaled $178 million.

The search for longer term solutions. The eleven months before the outbreak of the international financial crisis in the summer of 1931 saw an intensified search for longer term means to reduce the pressure on the reichsmark and sterling. In Germany, the conservative Brüning government was convinced that no solution was possible unless the payment of reparations was stopped and debated only the strategy and timing to attain this objective.[87] At the same time, Luther, who had succeeded Schacht as President of the Reichsbank, carried on without much hope a desperate attempt to stave off a new financial crisis. The German government was virtually at the end of its international credit. Between April and November 1930, it had obtained almost $350 million of long- and medium-term funds from abroad under the Young Loan and from international consortia headed by Kreuger and Toll and Lee-Higginson. Despite repeated attempts at retrenchment, the budgetary deficit was still increasing, and at the end of 1930 foreign short-term claims on Germany were still more than three times as large as the Reichsbank's total holdings of gold and foreign exchange, a ratio that was only slightly smaller than it had been a year earlier.[88]

From Luther's point of view, the one hopeful aspect was that United States commercial bankers, who held almost two fifths of Germany's short-term debt to foreigners in March 1931,[89] were deeply worried about the soundness of their claims. An official of Lee-Higginson, in Berlin to discuss yet another loan to the German government, told the American ambassador, Frederic M. Sackett, late in January 1931 that "the short loans to Germany were now in such volume that they could not be called or renewals refused without great danger to the financial situation in the United States".[90] A month later, Luther sent Sackett a memo-

---

[86] *Allan Sproul memorandum to files, January 31, 1931, on report of conversation with Cariguel of the Bank of France, pages 31-34.*

[87] *E. W. Bennett, Germany and the Diplomacy of the Financial Crisis, 1931 (Cambridge: Harvard University Press, 1962), pages 9-26.*

[88] *Report of Committee Appointed on the Recommendation of the London Conference (Basle, August 18, 1931), hereafter referred to as Wiggin Report.*

[89] *Wiggin Report, page 3; Board of Governors of the Federal Reserve System, Banking and Monetary Statistics, page 585.*

[90] *Quoted in Bennett, op. cit., pages 38-39.*

randum that provided detailed statistics showing the weakness of Germany's short-term position, emphasized that the country's financial difficulties were insoluble so long as reparations continued, and proposed, merely as a palliative, a long-term loan to fund perhaps $350-475 million equivalent of Germany's short-term liabilities.[91] Sackett, deeply disturbed, passed the information he had received from the American bankers and Luther on to Washington where copies of at least one of his dispatches were sent to President Hoover and Secretary of the Treasury Mellon. Luther himself sent a copy of his memorandum to Harrison. Not surprisingly the proposal for a refunding loan fell on barren ground, but Sackett's dispatches nurtured the seeds that were to grow during the following four months into President Hoover's moratorium on reparations and war debts.

Means of strengthening the position of sterling were also under intensive discussion during the latter part of 1930 and early 1931. In mid-November, when sterling was under severe pressure from the withdrawal of French balances in London, Pierre Quesnay, who had become the General Manager of the BIS, was urging that Britain float a long-term loan in France in order to reduce its short-term liabilities to foreigners.[92] Early in December, Norman discussed the question with Clément Moret, who in September 1930 had succeeded Moreau as Governor of the Bank of France. As he related it to Harrison, Moret told Norman that[93]

> public opinion in France, as well as the Government and the Bank of France, would look very favorably upon the issue of English private loans in France, or upon French participation in an English conversion operation, if such a course were technically possible of adoption. Nor did I hide from Mr. Norman that if he thought well of it, I should certainly be disposed, as has been done in the past, to facilitate the rediscount of sterling bills by French banking groups, which bills they would acquire by agreement with financial institutions in London.
>
> Our conversations did not result [in] any concrete solution: nevertheless I was very glad, for my part, to talk in all frankness with Mr. Norman, and I hope that what I said will again have given him the impression that we here are disposed to cooperate fully and loyally with the Bank of England.

---

[91] *Luther letter to Sackett, February 27, 1931.*

[92] *Sproul memorandum to files, January 21, 1931, page 6.*

[93] *Moret letter to Harrison, December 10, 1930, pages 4-5.*

However, Norman was bent on a different course. Early in February 1931 he presented to the BIS governors a proposal that in some ways anticipated the International Bank for Reconstruction and Development. This proposal, which apparently originated with Sir Robert Kindersley, envisaged an International Corporation with headquarters in Switzerland or Holland, subscribed capital of £25-50 million, authority to issue bonds up to three times the amount of subscribed capital, the proceeds of the bond issues to be loaned to various governments and other official and private entities that could not obtain needed funds through customary channels and that could offer good security. The crux of the proposal was that, whereas France and the United States were expected to absorb the bulk of the bonds issued, the corporation was to be managed, under the initial version, by a board to which each subscriber of a specified amount of capital could appoint a director. Under a version that Norman espoused later, the BIS was to assume the entire responsibility for the organization and management of the corporation and would appoint its president and a majority of its directors.[94]

This proposal, as Norman described it to Harrison, was a trial balloon:[95]

> the BIS is already slipping to the bottom of a ditch and in that position seems likely to do no more than helpfully perform a number of routine and Central Banking transactions. A change of direction and of spirit is needed in order that it may also fulfil the hopes for its wider usefulness which were expressed, although perhaps vaguely, in the Young Plan: to these the German Directors are forever drawing attention and to their non-fulfillment they may in the future attribute difficulties which arise.
>
> Some such scheme as the one we have under discussion would serve as a good occasion to enable the BIS to kill the two birds with one stone. But frankly I can find little hope of this scheme (or any other designed to open up the Capital Markets) being entertained by the [BIS] Board: there are a number of reasons for my doubts but perhaps the principal obstacle is the unwillingness, which we have seen in certain quarters, to support a scheme of which the control and the funds are truly international.

Norman had reasons to be gloomy. Except for Luther, the governors of the

---

[94] *Unsigned memorandum of February 2, 1931 sent by Norman to Harrison under cover of letter dated March 3, 1931 (Harrison Papers); McGarrah cable to J. P. Morgan, March 12, 1931.*

[95] *Norman letter to Harrison, March 3, 1931.*

BIS had shown little interest in the proposal, and both the French and the Americans were decidedly cool. The reaction of the major Paris commercial banks, to which the plan had been transmitted by the Bank of France, was that the scheme was too big, that its chances of realization were very small, and above all that, as the Paris market was expected to furnish most of the funds, it would be necessary to have full French control over the institution. This reaction was entirely shared by the Bank of France.[96]

The views of the New York Reserve Bank were reflected in a memorandum to Harrison from J. E. Crane, Deputy Governor in charge of the foreign function. The proposal, Crane wrote, was impractical; international control raised serious difficulties and would not "dissipate present reluctance in New York to purchase foreign securities"; the Corporation would have only "second grade clients". As for the role of the BIS in the plan, Crane stated that "it has always been felt that these larger functions were rather visionary and inflationary in character and should be left severely alone for the present.[97] J. P. Morgan and his colleagues cabled Gates McGarrah, President of the BIS, in a similar vein, adding that the New York market "is not accustomed to this form of international organization of credit" and would be unwilling to surrender its judgment to such an institution which would, in any case, be open to political influence abroad and to invite attack from politicians in the United States. Morgan's was opposed to "the intervention of artificial agencies" and felt that the best results would be obtained in the long run if new foreign issues "have to meet the tests of the market at the time of issue on their own merits.[98]

While the considerations behind the failure of the Kindersley proposal are clear enough, the reasons why Norman did not take up Moret's offer are largely a matter for conjecture. Our records reveal nothing about the conditions attached to Moret's offer except that the French insisted, not unreasonably, that any British bonds issued in Paris be denominated in francs. This condition the British authorities were unwilling to accept,[99] presumably because it implied doubts

---

[96] *Lacour-Gayet letter to Crane, February 24, 1931.*

[97] *Crane memorandum to Harrison, "Kindersley Plan—Bank for International Settlements", March 12, 1931.*

[98] *J. P. Morgan, T. W. Lamont, and S. P. Gilbert cable to McGarrah, March 13, 1931.*

[99] *Hamlin Diary, December 20, 1930, page 132A.*

about the position and future of sterling. They doubtless felt also, on the basis of the May-June 1930 experience, that any sizable flotation in Paris would only increase both the withdrawal of French balances from London and the movement of gold from Britain to France and thus offset much, if not all, the benefit that might otherwise be obtained from a loan. Although these problems would not have arisen under the alternative proposals[100] that Moret discussed with Norman, it would be surprising—in view of the moves that the German government was making at the time toward a reparation moratorium and a customs union with Austria—if France had not employed all its bargaining strength to obtain firm commitments of political support from Britain.[101] In London, however, the government was unwilling to give up its freedom of action, and the proposal for an International Corporation that, as the memorandum presented to the BIS indicated, would grant loans "on a purely business basis" seems to have been an attempt to obtain at least indirect support for Britain's financial position while at the same time avoiding new political commitments.

One final puzzle remains. Available records give no sign that, during the eleven months before the outbreak of the crisis, Norman discussed the possibility of raising long-term funds in New York—where they could almost certainly have been obtained on terms that would have been acceptable to the British authorities. Although Norman was in the United States from March 27 to April 14, 1931, there is no indication that the subject was mentioned. The explanation seems to be that by mid-March, when it was clear that the Kindersley proposal was dead, the international financial climate seemed to be improving. Norman was more hopeful about the German outlook.[102] Both sterling and the reichsmark were strengthening somewhat on the exchange markets, and the heavy movement of gold from Britain to France had temporarily stopped. In the four months following their low point at the end of January 1931, the Bank of England's gold and dollar reserves increased by $59 million. It would have been easy that spring to hope that the worst was over.

---

[100] Supra, *page 178.*

[101] *Bennett,* op. cit., *pages 44-62 and 83-85.*

[102] *Harrison letter to Stimson, April 21, 1931 (Harrison Papers).*

INTRODUCTION

The brief respite enjoyed by sterling and the reichsmark in the spring of 1931 belied the dangers ahead. The foundations on which the international financial system had been built were already weak, and the forces of destruction were poised. The network of financial claims that bound the international economy together was under severe strain as a result of the world depression. This network had been built on confidence among investors—mainly in the United States and Britain—that, if they made allowances only for ordinary business risks, they could obtain the relatively high earnings offered abroad without placing their capital in jeopardy. However, as prices, production, and incomes declined, the basis for this confidence became increasingly tenuous. Public authorities, whose revenues were declining sharply, defaulted on bonded indebtedness. Banks, which had borrowed abroad to enlarge their investable funds, found their assets frozen in firms on the verge of bankruptcy. All over the world those who held bank deposits, both in their own countries and abroad, became nervous about the safety of their funds. The authorities, in their attempts to stave off financial panic and to restore confidence, increased interest rates and/or cut government spending in a futile attempt to balance budgets but succeeded only in making matters worse by smothering any remaining incentive to invest and by further reducing already diminishing incomes.

Even before the spring of 1931 the deepening deflationary spiral had been accompanied, as noted in Chapter 7, by an increasing number of defaults and devaluations. However, these had occurred mainly among the primary producing countries. The major shock to the system came with the breakdown in the industrial heart of Central Europe where both United States and British investors had especially heavy commitments. Locked into loans to firms afflicted by the depression, the Credit-Anstalt,[1] Austria's largest commercial bank, had short-term liabilities to foreigners totaling $100 million on May 11, when its difficulties were announced to the public.[2] The bulk of these liabilities were to British and

---

[1] *Abbreviation for Oesterreichische Credit-Anstalt für Handel und Gewerbe.*

[2] *Morgan & Cie. to J. P. Morgan & Co. (cable) message from L. Fraser for S. P. Gilbert, May 26, 1931.*

United States interests, but significant amounts were also owed to Germany, France, and other European countries.[3] Thus all the major countries were involved, but the most susceptible to trouble was Germany which itself had short-term liabilities to foreigners that probably totaled between $2½-3 billion at the end of March 1931 and whose largest creditors (as in the case of Austria) were the United States and Britain.[4] The danger was plain. A chain of deposit withdrawals, panicky runs on the banks, and moratoria could spread from Austria to Germany and even to Britain and the United States. The threat to exchange stability was especially grave because in Austria, Germany, and Britain short-term liabilities to foreigners were a multiple of total official gold and foreign exchange reserves, because all but relatively small amounts of these reserves were tied up as cover for liabilities of the central banks, and because—given the psychology of businessmen at the time—recourse to special measures to release additional reserves for the defense of the currency was more likely to aggravate than to alleviate market fears and uncertainties.

GERMANY AT LOGGERHEADS WITH FRANCE

The authorities in the major countries recognized almost as soon as the Credit-Anstalt difficulties were announced that they were confronted with a serious international financial crisis, but their efforts to deal with this crisis cooperatively were thwarted by a fundamental political conflict, i.e., by Germany's drive to throw off the obligations imposed on it under the Versailles Treaty and by France's insistence that these obligations be fulfilled.

By the spring of 1931 immense pressures had built up in Germany to throw off what were regarded as the shackles of the Versailles settlement on which all the country's ills were blamed. Industrial production in the second quarter was down one third from the level of two years before; almost two fifths of the industrial labor force was unemployed; street fights between extremists of the right and left were increasing. The Brüning government which, backed by the army, had been ruling by decree since October 1930 was desperately seeking diplomatic

---

[3] *Morgan Grenfell & Co. cable to J. P. Morgan & Co., May 20, 1931; McGarrah cable to Harrison, No. 13, May 27, 1931.*

[4] Wiggin Report, *pages 1-10.*

victories to increase its domestic political support.[5] Accordingly, it risked increased French hostility by announcing in mid-March arrangements under which Germany and Austria proposed to form a customs union and subsequently by pressing for immediate and substantial relief from reparations.

In both Britain and the United States, there was understanding and some sympathy for the problems and aims of the Brüning government. Indeed, ever since the Balfour note of 1922 British governments had advocated an all-round cancellation of reparations and war debts. However, bankers in both London and New York were worried lest German invocation of the relief provisions of the Young Plan[6] precipitate heavy withdrawals of foreign-owned deposits from Germany and lead to the freezing of their reichsmark claims. This prospect was especially frightening to the authorities in the United States where bank failures had been rising sharply during the spring of 1931.[7] The solvency of some of New York's great banks that were heavily committed in Germany might become suspect and thereby add to the already severe strain under which the American banking system was operating. It was to avert this new threat to the already depressed United States economy and to take the initiative in the fight against the depression that President Hoover on June 20 proposed the one-year postponement of payments of interest and principal on intergovernmental debts and reparations—which became known as the Hoover moratorium.

The authorities in London and Berlin immediately accepted the President's proposal, but in Paris the announcement from Washington was received with consternation and anger. The French reaction was only partly attributable to the fact that the United States Government had announced a proposal under which France would lose almost $100 million during the coming year (i.e., the excess of its reparation receipts over its war debt payments) and had done so unilaterally and virtually without consulting the authorities in Paris. The reaction also stemmed from bitterness that the United States Government, in its haste to protect American interests, had given away a major bargaining counter, i.e.,

---

[5] *Hans Luther,* Vor dem Abgrund 1930-1933 *(Berlin: Propyläen Verlag, 1964), pages 159 and 163.*

[6] Supra, *page 146.*

[7] *Milton Friedman and Anna J. Schwartz,* A Monetary History of the United States, 1867-1960 *(Princeton: Princeton University Press, 1963), page 309; McGarrah letter to Fraser, June 9, 1931; Harrison cable to Norman, No. 181, May 27, 1931; E. W. Bennett,* Germany and the Diplomacy of the Financial Crisis, 1931 *(Cambridge: Harvard University Press, 1962), page 138; and Luther,* op. cit., *page 164.*

the granting of reparation relief which the French themselves might have employed in their efforts to force Germany to drop the proposed customs union with Austria. More fundamentally still, the reaction arose from France's deep-seated belief that, to the extent that Germany threw off the obligations of Versailles, French security would be increasingly threatened.[8] France, as we shall see, would fight intransigently to safeguard its security against a resurgent Germany; it would also go to great lengths to offer financial cooperation to maintain a status quo that Germany now found intolerable.

CENTRAL BANK COOPERATION: HALF MEASURES TO SUPPORT AUSTRIA AND GERMANY

In dealing with the 1931 crisis the major central bankers were hobbled not only by fundamental political conflicts but also by a number of other handicaps. As no comparable international financial difficulties had occurred before, the authorities had no previous experience by which to guide themselves. They were still only partly aware, moreover, of the magnitude of the potential trouble. It was not until May 20 that Norman and Harrison had roughly reliable data on the extent of London's and New York's claims on the Credit-Anstalt. Harrison had fairly accurate data on the short-term claims of the major New York banks against Germany, but he did not learn the magnitude of London's short-term claims against Germany until the latter part of July.[9] The first figures he saw on London's short-term liabilities to foreigners were from the *Macmillan Report* which was published on July 13. But more than mere information was lacking. A conception of the kind of dramatic cooperative action that was required to restore confidence and thus stop the mounting financial crisis had yet to be developed. The Bank of England, from which leadership might ordinarily have been expected, was in no position to organize an adequate cooperative effort. As already noted, the French authorities, who had large resources at their command, would make them available only on conditions that were politically unacceptable to Germany and Austria. The Federal Reserve, too, had large resources, but in May 1931 Harrison was still guided by the stabilization expe-

---

[8] *Bennett, op. cit., pages 169-72.*

[9] *Cable received on July 21, 1931 from "responsible friends" in London by the Grace National Bank and made available to Harrison.*

riences of the 1920's. It was not until the end of July, when sterling was coming under increasing pressure, that Harrison began to grope toward action on a scale approaching the magnitude required to deal with the crisis.

These many difficulties were reflected in the handling of both the Austrian and German crises. Although central bankers understood the close monetary links between Austria and Germany, the difficulties in the two countries were not treated as an organic whole but separately. However, a country-by-country approach could have been successful only if the assistance to Austria had been given in sufficient amount and with sufficient promptness to restore full confidence in the stability and convertibility of the currency and had thus prevented the crisis from infecting Germany. Neither condition was fulfilled. Instead, heavy reliance was placed on arrangements under which Austria's foreign creditors agreed not to withdraw their outstanding claims on the country. Unfortunately the standstill arrangements—as they came to be called—had an effect contrary to that intended by the central bankers. By freezing the creditors into their Austrian assets, the standstill arrangements created doubts about the ability both of the creditor institutions to meet their own deposit liabilities and also of the creditor countries to convert their currencies into gold and foreign exchange at the existing exchange rate. Consequently, Austria's difficulties were transmitted to its weakest creditor, Germany, whose difficulties were similarly treated with inadequate central bank credits and standstill arrangements, thereby insuring that the trouble would spread to the next weakest creditor, Britain, from which the infection spread, after the severing of sterling's link with gold, to the United States.

SUPPORTING THE AUSTRIAN SCHILLING. All the weaknesses that were to lose the battle against the 1931 crisis were evident in the international attempt to support the Austrian schilling. By almost every standard, the amount of the central bank credits was too small. Arranged under the leadership of Gates W. McGarrah, President of the BIS, and granted by the BIS and the central banks of Britain, France, Germany, the United States, and seven other countries, they totaled only $14 million.[10] This was of the same order of magnitude as the stabilization

---

[10] *The Federal Reserve agreed to take up to $1.4 million of the credit but, because more central banks agreed to participate than had been expected, the share that the Federal Reserve was actually asked to contribute totaled only $1.1 million. Harrison letter to Norris, May 22, 1931; BIS cable to Federal Reserve Bank of New York, No. 348, June 14, 1931; and Memorandum of Agreement between Federal Reserve Bank of New York and BIS, May 30, 1931.*

credits that had been granted to the various Central and Eastern European countries during the 1920's but, considering that the foreign short-term claims on the Credit-Anstalt alone were $100 million at the beginning of May and that perhaps $20 million was withdrawn in the first two weeks of the crisis, credits of this magnitude were clearly inadequate to restore confidence in the circumstances of May 1931.[11]

Moreover, there was a three-week delay between the onset of the crisis on May 11 and the making available of the credits to the Austrian National Bank on May 31. It is true that almost as soon as the crisis broke McGarrah began to sound out the major central banks about aid to Austria.[12] By May 14, when he approached Harrison, the Reichsbank, the National Bank of Belgium, and the Bank of England had agreed to participate.[13] On the following day, in response to Harrison's request, the Federal Reserve Board approved Federal Reserve participation up to a maximum of $3 million.[14] That the credit was delayed for another two and one-half weeks is probably attributable only in small part to the negotiations to obtain the participation of seven other central banks, including the Bank of France. The delay was attributable mainly to the need to arrange the standstill among the Credit-Anstalt's principal creditors in Berlin, London, New York, and Paris and to persuade the Austrian government to guarantee the eventual repayment of the Credit-Anstalt's foreign obligations.[15]

From one point of view these were reasonable precautions. Having agreed to extend assistance insufficient in amount to restore confidence in the schilling, the central bankers were exposed to the danger that their credits to the Austrian National Bank would in effect be used to finance the withdrawal of foreign short-term loans to Austria. However, while the haggling over the terms of the standstill and the Austrian government guarantee continued, the pressure on the schilling, which had virtually ceased during the third week in May, was

---

[11] *The stabilization credits granted during the 1920's to Czechoslovakia, Hungary, Poland, and Rumania were in the $10-25 million range. Morgan & Cie. cable to J. P. Morgan & Co. for S. P. Gilbert, May 26, 1931 and Morgan Grenfell & Co. to J. P. Morgan & Co., May 20, 1931.*

[12] *Fraser cable to Harrison, No. 3, May 11, 1931.*

[13] *McGarrah cable to Harrison, No. 6, May 14, 1931.*

[14] *Meyer letter to Harrison, May 15, 1931.*

[15] *BIS cable to Federal Reserve Bank of New York, No. 319, May 28, 1931; Austrian National Bank letter to Federal Reserve Bank of New York, May 28, 1931.*

renewed on a substantial scale.[16] In the last statement week of the month the Austrian National Bank lost one-third again as much foreign exchange as it obtained from the central bank-BIS consortium. Some three fifths of the credits were drawn as soon as they became available at the end of May, but the pressure on the schilling continued albeit with somewhat diminishing intensity.[17] The remainder was drawn on June 5, and on June 8 the Austrian National Bank requested a second $14 million credit.[18] Under BIS leadership this too was arranged by June 14, but subject to the condition that the Austrian government negotiate a $21 million, two- to three-year foreign loan, the proceeds of which would be employed to strengthen the position of the Credit-Anstalt.[19]

Negotiations for this loan, of which a substantial part was expected to be taken up in Paris, were initiated but promptly bogged down when it became evident that the French made the abandonment of the customs union a condition for cooperation.[20] The situation was further complicated by stiff opposition within the Austrian cabinet to the guarantee of the Credit-Anstalt's foreign liabilities. The fall of the Austrian government was imminent. Meanwhile, rumors of these difficulties had reached the exchange markets and the schilling again came under heavy pressure. On June 16 Norman telephoned Harrison that the position in Vienna was critical, that unless the Austrian government immediately obtained the loan and the Austrian National Bank the second credit, the Austrian commercial banks would close on June 18, and that the moratorium would probably spread to adjoining countries including Germany. The situation, Norman said, was too pressing and serious to wait upon the ordinary placing of the Austrian government bonds. Accordingly, the Bank of England had that day, on its own account, extended the entire amount of the loan to the Austrian government. Norman expressed the hope that this emergency credit, which was for seven days and renewable on a week-to-week basis, would "avoid a crisis in

---

[16] *Morgan & Cie. letter to J. P. Morgan & Co., May 26, 1931.*

[17] *BIS cable to Federal Reserve Bank of New York, No. 324, May 31, 1931. Draft Report on Arrangements in connection with Austrian Situation, Basle, June 3, 1931.*

[18] *BIS letter to Federal Reserve Bank of New York, June 5, 1931; Harrison conversation with Norman on June 8, 1931 (Harrison Papers).*

[19] *McGarrah letter to Fraser, June 9, 1931; BIS cable to Federal Reserve Bank of New York, No. 348, June 14, 1931.*

[20] *Gannon letter to Wiggin, June 13, 1931; Bennett, op. cit., pages 149-50.*

Central Europe . . . afford the Austrian government some time to turn around and to negotiate for the sale of its bonds" and "save the ship before she sinks".[21]

The immediate objective of the central bankers was achieved. The Austrian banks remained open, the parity of the schilling was maintained and, although the Austrian government fell on June 16, the succeeding government respected the guarantee extended to the Credit-Anstalt's foreign obligations. For a time the standstill arrangements were fairly well observed. But these arrangements led to other forms of direct control over Austria's financial markets. The agreement of foreign banks to maintain their credits was followed almost inevitably by pressure for, and the eventual adoption of, exchange controls in order to prevent capital flight by Austrian nationals, to collect Austrian foreign exchange receipts, and to ration foreign payments in order to facilitate the reduction of the country's external obligations.[22] The first steps were thus taken to break up, and fundamentally change, the system of unrestricted multilateral payments that had been restored during the 1920's.

THE FAILURE OF EFFORTS TO SUPPORT THE REICHSMARK. The cooperative effort to support the reichsmark fell into three distinct phases. The first effort followed immediately upon the announcement of the Hoover moratorium proposal on June 20, was complicated to only a minor extent by political conflicts, and was rewarded with a definite but brief success. The second, stimulated by the renewed attack on the reichsmark that began at the end of June, involved an attempt to organize central bank support on a hitherto unparalleled scale, was thwarted by the prevailing political conflicts, and led the central bankers to pass the problem of supporting the German currency on to their respective governments. In the third phase, the problem was tackled at the highest governmental level. However, since the political differences were found irreconcilable, the problem was passed on to an international committee of experts who in due course returned it unsolved to the governments.

First phase: the central bank credit to the Reichsbank. The central bankers' fears that Austria's difficulties in May and June would infect Germany proved

---

[21] *Harrison conversation with Norman on June 16, 1931 (Harrison Papers).*

[22] *Morgan Grenfell & Co. cable to J. P. Morgan & Co., May 28, 1931;* H. S. Ellis, Exchange Control in Central Europe *(Cambridge: Harvard University Press, 1941), pages 33-39. Laws establishing exchange control were enacted in October 1931. H. C. Hageman memorandum to Crane, March 9, 1933.*

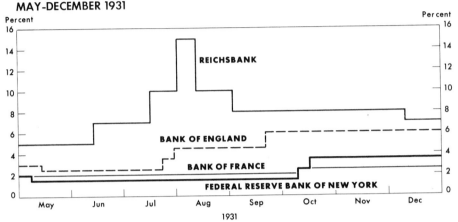

CHART 8

CENTRAL BANK DISCOUNT RATES
UNITED STATES, UNITED KINGDOM, GERMANY, AND FRANCE
MAY-DECEMBER 1931

Percent

REICHSBANK

BANK OF ENGLAND

BANK OF FRANCE

FEDERAL RESERVE BANK OF NEW YORK

May Jun Jul Aug Sep Oct Nov Dec

1931

Sources: Board of Governors of the Federal Reserve System, Banking and Monetary Statistics (Washington, D.C., November 1943); R.G. Hawtrey, A Century of Bank Rate (London, 1932); A. Parchman, Die Reichsbank (Berlin, 1933).

only too well founded. On May 26, when it was still uncertain whether Austria would be forced to close its banks and when the central bank credit to the Austrian National Bank was still pending, rumors spread through the exchange markets that a German bank moratorium was imminent. Berlin stock market prices declined sharply, and in the foreign exchange market the reichsmark dropped below the gold export point.[23] Subsequently it became known that, despite the government's earlier retrenchment efforts, the national budget was still showing a substantial deficit. New taxes were decreed and new cuts were announced in official salaries and in payments to the four million unemployed.[24] On June 13 the Reichsbank increased its discount rate to 7 per cent from 5 per cent

---

[23] *Norman cable to Harrison, No. 152, May 28, 1931;* The New York Times, *May 27, 1931; and* Bennett, op. cit., *page 117.*

[24] *Ellis, op. cit., page 165; League of Nations,* Monthly Bulletin of Statistics, *December 1931.*

190

(see Chart 8). However, these official measures led to intensification of domestic political agitation and to widespread expectations both that the German government would soon declare that it could no longer meet its reparation obligations and that this declaration would precipitate the long feared financial crisis.

In the resulting uncertainty, German capital moved abroad and foreigners hastened to reduce their commitments in Germany. The Reichsbank lost some $250 million in gold and foreign exchange in the first three weeks of June. On June 19 when it was clear that the Reichsbank's eligible international assets would be insufficient to meet its note cover requirements for the June 23 statement,[25] Luther approached Norman for a credit from the Bank of England, the Federal Reserve, and/or the BIS. Although the announcement of the Hoover moratorium on the following day brought respite from the pressure on the reichsmark, Luther indicated on June 22 that he still needed $80-100 million in order to meet his legal minimum during the period June 24-July 16 when the bank was faced with substantial temporary demands for currency and foreign exchange.[26] Norman, who had kept Harrison informed by daily telephone calls and cables, indicated that he was reluctant to lend additional funds since the Bank of England was already heavily committed in Austria and Hungary[27] but that, since the situation was "critical and dangerous", he would agree to a $100 million credit to the Reichsbank against commercial bills provided the Federal Reserve participated on a fifty-fifty basis.[28]

Harrison was in full agreement with the need for such a credit but insisted that the participation be broadened, particularly to include the Bank of France. Long-standing Federal Reserve policy would in any case have required that an invitation be extended to the Bank of France, but there was another even stronger reason for Harrison's position. He had learned from Governor Meyer of the Board that the Washington administration, including apparently the President, was dubious that *any* credit should be extended to the Reichsbank on the grounds

---

[25] *The statement was published four times each month and not necessarily on the same day of each week.*

[26] *Harrison conversations with Norman on June 19, 23, 24, 1931 and with Lacour-Gayet on June 23, 1931 (Harrison Papers).*

[27] *The Bank of England had participated with the Federal Reserve, seven other central banks, and the BIS in a $10 million, three-month credit to the Hungarian National Bank. The Bank of England's share, like that of the Federal Reserve, was $2 million. The agreement on the credit was dated June 18, 1931.*

[28] *Harrison conversation with Norman on June 23, 1931 (Harrison Papers).*

that such assistance might remove the pressure on the French government to accept the proposed moratorium on intergovernmental debts and reparations. Harrison himself was skeptical that the extention of the proposed credit would have such an effect but indicated that he would make it a condition for Federal Reserve participation that the Bank of France participate in substantial amount. However, even after he had been reassured on this point, Meyer remained hesitant. According to Harrison's notes of a telephone conversation on June 23, Meyer asked[29]

> whether I thought that the credit would be repaid. I said my own judgment was, and Norman was firmly of the opinion, that the credit would be repaid on July 16, unless, of course, negotiations relative to the debts completely broke down, in which event I said that he must realize that we ran the risk of a frozen credit in the Reichsbank. I stated, however, that even if the credit should become frozen, I did not feel that there was much risk of ultimate loss. In any event, I felt that the risks of not participating were greater than the risks of doing so . . . .

Meyer then asked whether it would not be better for the Board to authorize participation up to only $35 million rather than the $50 million for which the New York Reserve Bank had asked and Harrison explained that, although he did not expect to extend more than $35-40 million, he wanted some leeway.

> Governor Meyer then asked what was the hurry and why couldn't he take it up with the Board tomorrow or give them more chance to think it over. I told him that I only knew what Norman told me, that it was essential that they have the credit as of tomorrow, and if that was so we had to act tonight, and I asked him if he would not try to please arrange for approval or disapproval tonight so that I might cable Norman.

Meyer then agreed to consult the members of the Board. At 7 p.m. on June 23 Meyer advised Harrison that the Board had approved a credit of up to $50 million. At the same time that Harrison was making these arrangements, he was also in touch with Lacour-Gayet of the Bank of France and with McGarrah of the BIS. The upshot was that by June 24 the $100 million credit to the Reichsbank had been put together with the BIS and the central banks of Britain, France, and the United States participating to the extent of $25 million each.[30]

---

[29] *Harrison conversation with Meyer on June 23, 1931 (Harrison Papers).*

[30] *Norman cable to Harrison, No. 191, June 24, 1931.*

Even so the credit was not available in time to be included in the Reichsbank statement for June 23, but the $5 million deficiency in the reserve requirement was made good by an overnight deposit in that amount made with the Reichsbank by the Bank of England.[31]

Second phase: the attempt to raise a second central bank credit for the Reichsbank. The announcement of the central bank credit to the Reichsbank on June 25 reinforced the effect of the Hoover moratorium proposal on the exchange markets. The reichsmark strengthened, and for a day or two the Reichsbank apparently lost no reserves in exchange operations.[32]

However, the calm was short-lived. As June drew to a close, uncertainty increased whether the French would accept the President's proposal. Moreover, on July 2-3 there was news of the failure of a major German textile concern to which the Darmstädter und Nationalbank (Danat Bank) had large loans outstanding.[33] A run on the Danat and other banks began, and with it a renewal of the pressure on the reichsmark in the exchange markets. The story is told in the use of the central bank credit. The first $4 million drawing was not made until June 27; by June 29, no more than $12 million had been drawn. In the next three days $64 million was drawn. Even so, the Reichsbank's eligible international assets were below the 40 per cent minimum ratio on July 3.[34] On July 4, the credit was exhausted and the Reichsbank was obliged to draw the full amount of a $50 million line of credit that had been arranged in the twenties by its affiliate, the Gold Discount Bank, with a group of New York banks under the leadership of the International Acceptance Corporation.[35] These drawings enabled the Reichsbank to show a $69 million reserve gain in the two weeks ended July 7 but, despite the announcement on July 6 of an agreement between the United States and French governments on the Hoover proposals, the Reichsbank lost some $71 million in gold and foreign exchange during the following week, with the consequence that its July 15 statement showed reserves substantially below the legal minimum.

---

[31] *Harrison conversation with Norman on June 23, 1931 (Harrison Papers).*

[32] *Luther, op. cit., pages 173 and 178.*

[33] *Bennett, op. cit., page 220.*

[34] *See various cables between the Federal Reserve Bank of New York and the BIS, the Reichsbank, and the Federal Reserve Board between June 26 and July 4, 1931.*

[35] *Reichsbank cable to Harrison, No. 195, July 4, 1931.*

The imposition of direct controls over the exchanges, on which major reliance was eventually placed, played a secondary role in the initial efforts to deal with this renewed outbreak of the crisis. True, Harrison was in touch with the major New York commercial bankers on July 3 or earlier and was able to tell Luther on July 7 that the New York banks were generally maintaining the amount of their credits to Germany at the level outstanding on June 20.[36] It seems probable that parallel standstill efforts were being made by Norman in London, but on this the evidence is not entirely clear.

At this stage, however, the main effort lay in hectic negotiations to raise a new central bank credit for the Reichsbank. On July 8 Norman telephoned Harrison that he had heard from Luther that[37]

> the position in Berlin is now desperate; that they lost another $10,000,000 in exchange today and that Luther is going to London tomorrow by aeroplane just for one hour; that they would travel to Dover together and that Luther would then go on to Paris to see Governor Moret, and he, Norman, to Basle.
>
> Norman said that judging by his conversation with Luther this afternoon, Luther will . . . ask that the central bank credit shall be renewed, and will further ask for an additional credit in "an unlimited amount" otherwise, he will say, Germany will collapse . . . . Norman then mentioned that while Luther had referred to an unlimited credit it was, of course, out of the question and that he gathered from the conversation with Luther that they would need accommodation anywhere from $500,000,000 to $1,000,000,000 to avoid a complete breakdown. Governor Norman mentioned that he would be willing to join in such a credit, which Luther said must be for at least six months, provided we and the Bank of France participated, and that he felt that the character of the credit or the terms must be made to suit Paris and New York, inasmuch as the powers of the Bank of England are so much broader than ours, and that he was therefore able legally to participate in any arrangement that would be adaptable to our own needs.

In the ensuing conversation Harrison stressed that, if any such large credit were contemplated, he would consider it only on condition that (1) the private bankers in the major international financial centers agreed to maintain their existing credits to Germany and to take participations in the new central bank credit and (2) that the new credit be guaranteed by the Reichsbank, the Gold Discount Bank, and the German government. With all these points Norman agreed. Finally Harrison told Norman that

---

[36] *Harrison conversation with American bankers July 3, 1931 (Harrison Papers); Harrison cable to Luther, No. 107, July 7, 1931.*

[37] *Harrison conversation with Norman on Germany, July 8, 1931 (Harrison Papers).*

I was very skeptical about the idea of a credit in any event; that I felt the chief difficulty was a flight from the reichsmark by German nationals and that the Reichsbank should resort to much more drastic credit control than apparently was the case. Governor Norman said he thought Luther was now rationing credit very strictly, but he was not sure how effective or how broad it was. He thinks the difficulty is that they need Dr. Schacht there; that Luther does not seem to have the force necessary to do the trick. In any event, I insisted that these credit restrictions should be adopted, in my judgment, before we could fairly be asked for a sizable new credit. Norman generally agreed with this position.

Governor Norman mentioned that the next published statement of the Reichsbank will be as of Tuesday, July 14, and that if anything was to be done it should be done before that time.

Later the same day Harrison dispatched cables to Norman, Luther, and Moret in which he reiterated his view that much of the pressure on the reichsmark was attributable to German capital flight which he felt could be curbed by a firmer Reichsbank credit policy.

In the negotiations of the next five days both Harrison and Norman changed their positions regarding the second Reichsbank credit. As the prospects for a collapse of the Germany currency increased, Harrison worked desperately for the adoption of a program that would enable him to recommend that a second credit be granted. On the other hand, Norman, after initially favoring the credit, turned flatly against it and in this was supported by Moret.

Moret's position reflected that of his government. Having surrendered one major bargaining counter when they agreed to the Hoover moratorium, the French authorities were determined to exploit the reichsmark crisis to force Brüning to agree to France's terms. Repeatedly in the conversations of July 10-21, French officials urged the German government to agree (1) to drop the customs union proposal, (2) to resume the full payment of reparations at the end of the moratorium year, (3) to refrain in the meantime from using for military purposes any of the funds that in the absence of the moratorium would have been paid in reparations, and (4) to suspend agitation for the revision of Germany's eastern frontier. If Germany would do so, the international political atmosphere would clear.[38] Such an improvement, the French pointed out, not only would reduce the pressure on the reichsmark but also would put the French government in a position to come to the aid of Germany with substantial financial

---

[38] *Luther,* op. cit., *page 187; Bennett,* op. cit., *pages 230, 231, and 264-65.*

assistance. However, until Germany accepted France's terms, the Paris authorities were prepared to wait in the belief that Brüning would find that he had no alternative and in the knowledge that France's position was strong—the French banks had withdrawn most of their credits to Germany during the previous fall and winter. What the French failed to foresee was that Germany would escape the acceptance of France's terms and would at the same time avoid a complete currency debacle through the adoption of exchange controls.

While the considerations behind the French position were clear from the beginning, those behind the shift in Norman's position became apparent only gradually. When Harrison telephoned on Thursday, July 9, the day Luther was to arrive in London, Norman reported that the Bank of England directors were doubtful about the granting of a second credit to the Reichsbank because they, like Harrison, felt that the pressure on the reichsmark was due more to the outflow of German capital than to the withdrawal of foreign funds; because they were uncertain whether the Reichsbank could or would adopt a more stringent monetary policy; the proposed credits were "altogether too big and political rather than financial"; the French would require political conditions to which the British could not agree; and because the Bank of England did not wish to participate in a credit that would facilitate the continued payment of reparations to France.[39] Norman's final objection was especially significant. In view of the United States-French agreement three days earlier to suspend intergovernmental payments for a year, it could only have meant that he was opposed to a credit granted on the understanding that reparations would be resumed at the end of the moratorium year.

In the course of the following week indeed it became unmistakably clear that, whereas French policy aimed to perpetuate the status quo, Norman backed by Snowden was working for a new order. Both the Governor and the Chancellor felt intensely that the whole Versailles system of reparations and war debts was one of the fundamental causes of the crisis and that, unless the governments could agree to eliminate the system forthwith, there was little that the central banks could do to alleviate the pressure on the reichsmark.[40]

---

[39] *Harrison conversation with Norman on Germany, July 9, 1931 (Harrison Papers).*

[40] *Harrison conversations with McGarrah and Fraser on July 14 and with Norman on July 16, 1931 (Harrison Papers); Cochran cable to Castle,* Papers Relating to the Foreign Relations of the United States, 1931, *Vol. I, page 255.*

However, Norman and Snowden were deceived in hoping that the deepening of the crisis would bring France and the United States to accept the need for a fresh start.[41] Such a reversal in the French position was not in the cards. It is true that the involvement of the New York banks in Germany gave the United States authorities an interest in helping to support the reichsmark, but they would not have done so without the participation of both Britain and France whose positions, as we have seen, were irreconcilable. Above all, any suggestion of going beyond the one-year moratorium was flatly rejected by the Hoover administration. At this stage indeed the position of the United States was much closer to that of France than to that of Britain.

Luther's flying trip to London and Paris was thus in vain. News of its failure intensified the pressure on the reichsmark.[42] On July 11-12 Harrison received desperate messages from the German authorities appealing for large credits and for a Federal Reserve statement of confidence in the reichsmark.[43] To all of these, Harrison's response was that he could do nothing until the German authorities had presented a program to support their currency that was satisfactory to Norman and Moret who on July 12-13 were to meet in Basle to discuss the German crisis.[44]

In view of the diametrically opposed positions of the major countries, the Basle meeting could hardly have avoided a deadlock. Moreover, Luther was exhausted from his trip to London and Paris and from hectic discussions in Berlin that began on Sunday and continued until 3 a.m., Monday, July 13 when he flew to Basle.[45] Once there Luther indicated that the Reichsbank was doing all it could to support the currency and reiterated his request for an additional loan of unspecified amount. However, Leon Fraser, the BIS's vice president, felt Luther had presented no program worthy of the name; he had indeed been "quite helpless" during the entire meeting. For their parts, Norman and Moret were prepared only to renew the first central bank credit to the Reichsbank. They indicated that any new loan to Germany would have to be supplied primarily

---

[41] *Luther, op. cit., page 186.*

[42] The Economist, *July 18, 1931, page 104.*

[43] *Kiep to Harrison with copy of cable from Berlin, July 11, 1931; Harrison conversation with Kiep at 10 a.m. and 12 noon on July 12, 1931.*

[44] *Harrison cable to Luther, No. 116, July 12, 1931.*

[45] *Luther, op. cit., page 193.*

by governments. If such a loan could be arranged, they would be prepared to support it with additional central bank credits. Relaying this information to Harrison by telephone, McGarrah asked whether the United States Government would participate in such a loan and if so for how much.[46]

Harrison's personal reaction was that the proposal for a government loan was "futile" and that the United States Government felt it had already "done a great deal" under the Hoover moratorium. He emphasized that[47]

> time is the essence and it would undoubtedly take all the governments a long while; that our own government, certainly, could not make such a loan without the approval of Congress and there would be no session of Congress until December, and that any plan proposing government loans would seem to me to be disingenuous, and would be considered as an effort to pass the buck back to the United States, realizing it is likely that we would not be able to make the loan anyway. McGarrah agreed with this and said he was quite conscious of the fact that it might be an effort to "put the baby on our doorstep".

However, Harrison also felt that, unless prompt and substantial support were received from abroad, the German currency would collapse, and this view was shared by McGarrah. Accordingly, Harrison suggested to McGarrah that it might be possible to avoid the delays and political dangers inherent in a government loan by arranging a private loan to the Gold Discount Bank from the commericial banks in the major financial centers and to supplement this private loan with an additional central bank credit to the Reichsbank. McGarrah indicated that he felt this to be a constructive suggestion and that he would discuss it immediately with Luther and perhaps also with the others at the meeting.[48]

By 5:20 p.m. New York time (11:20 p.m. Basle time) Harrison had heard nothing further from Basle. He then telephoned Norman. Called from the meeting, which was still in session, Norman indicated that the deadlock was unbroken. In Harrison's record of the conversation, Norman then said[49]

---

[46] *Harrison conversations with McGarrah at 10:35 a.m. and 3:45 p.m. on July 13, and with McGarrah and Fraser on July 14, 1931 (Harrison Papers).*

[47] *Harrison conversation with McGarrah at 3:45 p.m. on July 13, 1931 (Harrison Papers).*

[48] *Harrison conversations with McGarrah at 10:35 a.m. and 3:45 p.m. on July 13, 1931 (Harrison Papers).*

[49] *Harrison conversation with Norman at 5:20 p.m. on July 13, 1931 (Harrison Papers).*

that he was leaving in an hour to go back to London and that the board was going to adjourn. I said, if that is true, what is going to happen? He said nothing is going to happen—absolutely nothing. I said I thought it was a great pity that they should adjourn before something was done. He said: "Well, what have you to suggest?"

Harrison then repeated the proposal that he had made earlier in the day to McGarrah to which Norman's response was merely to reiterate that the German problem was

too big for the central banks, and the governments must interest themselves in it, and he did not see anything that the central banks could do at this time. He said he had to go back to the meeting as they were still in session and that he was leaving in an hour for London. He seemed tired, disgruntled and discouraged.

Third phase: the London Conference. There was ample ground for discouragement. On July 13—the very day of the Basle meeting—the failure of the Danat Bank was announced. Thereupon the German government decreed a two-day holiday for the Berlin bourse and all commercial and savings banks. When the financial markets and banks reopened on July 16, the Reichsbank discount rate was increased to 10 per cent, and the first of an ever-growing number of exchange control regulations had already been promulgated.[50] Until the last moment, moreover, it was uncertain whether a conference of the major governments could be arranged because Pierre Laval, the French Prime Minister, and President Hoover would not agree to send representatives until they had received assurances from Prime Minister MacDonald that the conference would deal only with the immediate emergency and would avoid (contrary to the hopes of Norman and Snowden) any discussion of "fundamental questions", i.e., reparations and war debts.[51]

As discussions about the terms of reference for the conference continued, the French government made a major bid for the preservation of the status quo. It proposed on July 16 that a $500 million ten-year government-guaranteed loan be floated on Germany's behalf on the Paris, London, and New York markets. It was also made clear that the Bank of France would participate in additional central bank credits to the Reichsbank pending the flotation of the

---

[50] *Ellis, op. cit., page 166.*

[51] *Stimson conversation with Hoover, July 17,* Papers Relating to the Foreign Relations of the United States, 1931, *Vol. I, page 273; Harrison conversation with Mills on July 16, 1931 (Harrison Papers); and Bennett, op. cit., page 256.*

bonds.[52] The reception for the loan proposal was completely negative. Hoover's reaction was that he would not call a special session of Congress to obtain authority for such a loan and that, even if he did, Congress—which had come under the control of a coalition unsympathetic to his administration as the result of the November 1930 election—would not grant the authority.[53] Norman rejected the proposal on the ground that, if the British government guaranteed a loan for Germany, it could hardly avoid extending the same favor to India, Australia, and other British dominions.[54] Beyond this, sterling was already feeling the devastating repercussions of the German crisis and was in no position to stand the strain of additional assistance to support the reichsmark. Even if sterling had been strong, however, it is virtually certain that the British authorities would not have participated in a loan whose aim was to perpetuate the status quo. In any event, Germany would not make the necessary political concessions as became evident in the discussions that took place in Paris between Brüning and Laval on July 18-19.[55]

In view of this response, no more was heard of the French loan proposal when the representatives of the major powers met in London on July 20-23. Indeed, this conference was unable to move significantly beyond the positions that had previously been reached by the central bankers. The conference recommended that the central bank credits to the Reichsbank, which had already been renewed until August 6, be extended for three months beyond that date.[56] It put the sanction of the governments behind the efforts that Harrison and Norman were already making to prevent the withdrawal of outstanding private credits to Germany,[57] and it recommended that the BIS establish a committee of experts "to enquire into Germany's immediate further credit needs and to study the possibility of

---

[52] *Harrison conversation with Mills on July 16, 1931 (Harrison Papers); Bennett, op. cit., pages* 256-57.

[53] *Stimson memorandum of July 15,* Papers Relating to the Foreign Relations of the United States, 1931, *Vol. I, page 261; Bennett, op. cit., pages 259-60.*

[54] *Harrison conversation with Norman on July 16, 1931 (Harrison Papers).*

[55] *Bennett, op. cit., pages 263-74.*

[56] *See particularly the stenographic notes of the London Conference, July 20-23,* Documents on British Foreign Policy, 1919-1939, *2nd Series, Vol. II, pages 435-84; BIS cable to Federal Reserve Bank of New York, No. 429, July 15, 1931.*

[57] *Harrison conversation with Norman at 9:30 a.m. on July 15, 1931 (Harrison Papers); Harrison cables to Norman, No. 231 and No. 234, July 15 and 16, 1931.*

converting a portion of the short-term credits into long term".[58] A month later this committee, of which Albert Wiggin of the Chase National Bank was chairman, made a report that in effect handed the problem of Germany's credit needs back to the governments. But by this time Germany was learning to live without additional foreign loans behind a mounting barrier of exchange controls. The center of the crisis had moved to London.

THE ATTACK ON STERLING

Britain was in a weak position to resist the attack on sterling largely because the Labor government was unable to resolve the conflict between the need for domestic economic recovery and the requirements of external stability. The Labor Party itself was split. Snowden was as fully committed to the defense of sterling's gold parity and to the balancing of the government's budget as his Conservative predecessors but, in seeking these objectives, he was obliged to deal with strong opposition from Labor Party colleagues led by Arthur Henderson, the Foreign Minister. While this opposing group did not advocate the abandonment of gold, it refused on domestic welfare grounds to accept the policies that Snowden insisted were necessary for the protection of sterling. Many within the Labor Party were suspicious that the well-being of the workers was being sacrificed to the international interests of the City of London, and all were highly sensitive to Britain's growing industrial distress. In the two years that Labor had been in power, industrial output had declined about one fifth and unemployment had more than doubled to 22 per cent of the labor force in June. Snowden had nevertheless rejected proposals for greatly expanded public works. Even so, government expenditures rose. Moreover, with the continued contraction of economic activity in 1931, revenues declined, the consequence being that Snowden's hopes for budgetary balance were disappointed. The upshot was that Snowden satisfied neither those who favored spending to relieve unemployment nor those who felt that budgetary balance was essential to avoid financial disaster.

At the same time Britain's external position failed to show any fundamental improvement. In the two years ended the second quarter of 1931, imports had

---

[58] *Report of the Committee appointed on the Recommendation of the London Conference, 1931, published in* Documents on British Foreign Policy, 1919-1939, *2nd Series, Vol. II, page 485.*

dropped sharply but the decline in exports was sharper still. Long-term capital outflow was reduced but so were earnings from shipping, tourism, insurance, and investments abroad. Although London's short-term liabilities to foreigners had been reduced, they were still in the neighborhood of £600-700 million in mid-1931, four to five times as large as the Bank of England's gold reserve.[59]

THE FIRST ATTACK. The first phase of the attack on sterling began on Monday, July 13, when the central bank governors were deadlocked at Basle and when the failure of the Danat Bank was announced. On that day sterling, which had been at or close to parity with both the dollar and the French franc for the past two months, dropped sharply on the exchange markets. On July 15 the rate was $4.84¼, well below the gold export point to New York. On the following day, Norman telephoned Harrison that "the situation now looks very bad . . . the whole thing is 'boiling up' ".[60] In the two weeks ended July 29 the Bank of England lost $200 million in gold and dollars, one quarter of its international reserves.

The major immediate cause of the attack was the closing of the Berlin banks, accompanied by the virtual freezing of foreign assets in Germany where British interests had short-term claims of around $300 million.[61] Although the magnitude of these claims became generally known only later, it was understood in the markets in mid-July that London's commitment in Germany was large and that the merchant banks, which typically financed a substantial proportion of their foreign investments with funds borrowed from abroad, were heavily involved.[62] To make matters worse, estimates of London's large short-term liabilities to foreigners also became available to the public for the first time on July 13 when the *Macmillan Report* was published. The market was thus flooded with doubts not only about the solvency of individual British banks but also about whether the authorities would be able to maintain the convertibility of sterling at the existing parity. Beyond this there were fears on the Continent that the runs suffered by

---

[59] David Williams, *"London and the 1931 Financial Crisis"*, The Economic History Review, *Vol. 15 (April 1963), page 528.*

[60] *Harrison conversation with Norman at 3:50 p.m. on July 16, 1931 (Harrison Papers).*

[61] *Report of the Committee appointed on the Recommendation of the London Conference, Annex V, August 18, 1931; Parliamentary Debates (Great Britain, House of Commons), September 21, 1931, column 1294.*

[62] *David Williams, "The 1931 Financial Crisis", The Yorkshire Bulletin, Vol. 15 (November 1963), page 107.*

the Austrian and German banks would spread to yet other countries, and these fears led commercial banks in Belgium, France, Holland, Sweden, and Switzerland to attempt to bolster their liquidity by drawing down their London balances.[63] Doubts and fears quickly snowballed. Rumors spread that Norman was demanding the imposition of a moratorium on payments by British banks, and that the government would levy a tax on capital to deal with the crisis. These rumors not only aggravated the withdrawal of foreign balances but stimulated some outflow of British funds as well.[64]

BRITAIN'S RESPONSE. The distraction of the German crisis and the split in the Labor Party resulted in a hesitant initial response by the British authorities to the attack on sterling. On July 16, when the Bank of England had already lost £7 million in gold but when it was still possible to be hopeful about the forthcoming London Conference, Norman cabled Harrison:[65]

> We were perplexed this morning about change in bank rate because exchanges are still so disorganized that 2½ per cent is hardly justified. But to cope with such disorganization would require 7 per cent or 8 per cent rather than 3½ per cent and as no more gold is being withdrawn we hope to ride at least another week.

But, although the London Conference failed and the pressure on sterling intensified, the bank increased its discount rate only 1 point on July 23 and a week later by another 1 point to 4½ per cent, at which level it remained unchanged until after the suspension of the gold standard. Meanwhile, the government did nothing more than promise on July 30 that it would "take every possible step to ensure that the proud and sound position of British credit shall be in no way impaired". Thereupon Parliament adjourned in the expectation that it would not reassemble until October when the government planned to present its budgetary retrenchment program.[66]

---

[63] *Willard Hurst, "Holland, Switzerland, and Belgium and the English Gold Crisis of 1931". The Journal of Political Economy, Vol. 40 (October 1932); Snowden statement on July 21, 1931 to London Conference and Tyrrell cable to Vansittart, No. 174, July 16, 1931, published in* Documents on British Foreign Policy, 1919-1939, *2nd Series, Vol. II, pages 451 and 203.*

[64] *Hugh Dalton, Call Back Yesterday: Memoirs 1887-1931 (London: Frederick Muller, Ltd., 1953), Vol. I, page 255; G. L. Harrison, "The Credit Crisis of 1931", dated November 20, 1931, memorandum prepared for the Governors Conference in December 1931.*

[65] *Norman cable to Harrison, No. 223, July 16, 1931.*

[66] Parliamentary Debates *(Great Britain, House of Commons), Vol. 255, Statement to the House of commons by the Chancellor of the Exchequer, July 30, 1931, columns 2512-15.*

At this point, the cause of inaction was partly pure physical exhaustion. Norman collapsed on July 29 and was almost entirely out of action until after the crisis was over. Partly it was because Snowden was waiting for the report of a committee, headed by Sir George May, which had been appointed the previous February to review the government's finances. Snowden hoped apparently that this report, which predicted an enlargement in the budgetary deficit that was regarded as huge, would convince his reluctant colleagues to accept drastic financial retrenchment. At the same time, the authorities hesitated to borrow abroad, partly because they felt that such borrowings would remove the pressure on the government to eliminate the budget deficit, and partly because they were loath to approach France, which Harrison insisted should participate in any credits to support sterling.[67]

CENTRAL BANK CREDITS TO THE BANK OF ENGLAND. It is doubtful whether, in the circumstances, sterling could have been saved by even the most drastic combination of measures that the authorities of the day could have adopted, but the program that actually was adopted was definitely a second best, even by the standards of mid-1931. While the total amount of the credits obtained was considered very substantial, they were not granted in a single impressive package but in two separate arrangements. The first set of credits was unaccompanied by any additional measures to check the pressure on sterling, and the second set, which was accompanied by the formation of a new government pledged to the elimination of the budgetary deficit, was only announced after it was known in the markets that the first credits had been virtually exhausted.

The handling of the crisis was a source of frustration and disappointment to the central bankers. Harrison and apparently also Moret had hoped that the central bank credits could be granted simultaneously, or at least in conjunction, with large market loans to the British government.[68] But the latter could hardly be floated in New York or Paris until the British government had dealt with the budgetary deficit. To Norman this was painfully clear. When toward the end of

---

[67] McGarrah cable to Harrison, No. 27, July 28, and Norman cable to Harrison, No. 247, July 28, 1931; Harrison conversation with Norman on July 29 and with Lacour-Gayet, August 7, 1931 (Harrison Papers); Sir Henry Clay, Lord Norman (London: Macmillan & Co., Ltd., 1957), page 385; and Bennett, op. cit., pages 281-82.

[68] Harrison conversations with Lacour-Gayet on August 6 and 7, 1931 (Harrison Papers).

July Harrison telephoned to ask about the possibility of such a loan, Norman replied that[69]

> there was absolutely nothing to it; in the first place, Parliament was adjourning and there was no time for action; in the second place, the home political situation was not satisfactory and no such loan was possible . . . . you cannot make a loan unless your house is in order.

In the meantime, however, the pressure on sterling was increasing and the need for action was becoming urgent. Shortly after the failure of the London Conference, the Bank of England approached both the Federal Reserve and the Bank of France to obtain market support for sterling. On July 23 the directors of the New York Reserve Bank authorized purchases of sterling of up to £5 million on terms similar to those adopted under earlier arrangements.[70] Apparently because the main pressure was coming from Continentals who were offering sterling in their own markets, the opportunity to operate under this arrangement was not great; by August 8 when the last purchase was made, only £2.1 million ($10.2 million) had been acquired by the New York Reserve Bank.[71] In contrast, Bank of France sterling purchases, which were undertaken against dollars pledged by the Bank of England, were far larger, apparently totaling some $60 million equivalent in the period up to August 7.[72]

The Bank of England also overcame its reluctance to approach foreign markets for loans. Sir Robert Kindersley was dispatched on July 25 to Paris where he discussed with Moret the possibility of a £20-30 million rediscount credit for six to nine months against sterling bills.[73] As Norman described it, the credit might have been either between the two central banks directly or between groups of London and Paris commercial banks or a combination of both. On July 28, Norman indicated that he had expected to ask the Federal Reserve Bank of New York to make a similar arrangement in favor of the Bank of England but for a

---

[69] *Harrison conversation with Norman on July 29, 1931 (Harrison Papers).*

[70] *Harrison cable to Norman, No. 243, July 23, 1931; McClelland letter to Crane, July 24, 1931; and Harrison memorandum for files, July 24, 1931 (Harrison Papers).*

[71] *Compilation (apparently by Sproul) of Bank of England dollar sales and Federal Reserve Bank of New York sterling purchases, July 23-September 18, 1931.*

[72] *Harrison conversation with Lacour-Gayet on August 7, 1931 (Harrison Papers).*

[73] *Norman cables to Harrison, No. 243 and No. 247, July 27 and 28, 1931.*

larger amount and for a longer period.[74] However, the inability of the British government to agree on a budgetary retrenchment program, the complications of raising a loan from the Paris commercial banks, and above all the need for immediate action swept these proposals aside. On July 30 Harrison was urging that the Federal Reserve and the Bank of France act alone. He telephoned Lacour-Gayet:[75]

> We are the two banks with the greatest gold supplies in the world, and a credit granted by us, in which we each take equal shares without any other participants, would have an electrifying effect, in my judgment, and would do more than anything else to convince the world of our constructive cooperation in the interest of the gold standard . . . .

The Federal Reserve credit to the Bank of England was approved on July 30 by both the New York Reserve Bank's directors and by the Federal Reserve Board. Although Sir Ernest Harvey, the Deputy Governor who had taken over the leadership of the Bank of England after Norman's collapse, had hoped for a substantially larger amount and was supported in this by Harrison and by at least one of the directors of the New York Reserve Bank,[76] the amount granted was $125 million. Harrison made it clear to the Bank of England that this was the maximum that could be obtained from the Federal Reserve. If more were required, the British authorities should approach their New York commercial bankers who would, Harrison indicated, promptly provide additional funds. At this stage, however, Harvey indicated that the Federal Reserve credit, together with an equivalent one from the Bank of France, would be enough.[77] The assistance was in the form of lines of credit on which the Bank of England could draw dollars and francs as required. As each drawing was made, the Bank of England was to deposit in the account of the central bank concerned prime sterling commercial bills of not more than ninety days' maturity, having at least two satisfactory bank signatures and the guarantee of the Bank of England. The credits were for three months, with the understanding that they could be renewed for a further period of three months, and carried interest on the amounts drawn

---

[74] *Norman cable to Harrison, No. 247, July 28, 1931.*

[75] *Harrison conversation with Lacour-Gayet on July 30, 1931 (Harrison Papers).*

[76] *Memorandum on meeting of board of directors of the Federal Reserve Bank of New York, July 30, 1931 (Harrison Papers); Hamlin Diary, July 30, 1931, page 115.*

[77] *Harrison conversation with Harvey on July 30, 1931 (Harrison Papers).*

206

at the rate of 3⅜ per cent per annum. Provisions were made safeguarding the lenders against exchange risks and against the erection of any legal obstacles to repayment in gold at maturity.[78]

The $250 million credits were announced on Saturday, August 1, in singularly unpropitious circumstances. On the previous day the May Committee published its report indicating that under existing policies the British budgetary deficit in the 1932-33 fiscal year would be £120 million, the largest since 1920, and that the prospective deficit in the following fiscal year would be substantially larger. At the same time the Bank of England fiduciary issue was increased by £15 million which, in conjunction with the gloomy May report, was interpreted in the markets as a sign of inflation while the credits themselves were interpreted as a sign of weakness.[79]

To make matters worse, when the London market opened on Tuesday, August 4, after the long Bank Holiday weekend, the Bank of England failed to draw on the credits or even to support sterling firmly with its own resources. This lapse was apparently due to the feeling at the bank that the strain on sterling should be primarily reflected in gold losses that would jolt the government into action and that would perhaps provide a basis for a further increase in the discount rate.[80] It was also due to the insistence of the Bank of France that the Paris commercial banks participated in each drawing on the French tranche of the credit.[81] Since such participation would reveal to the Paris market the extent to which the credit was being utilized and since the agreements with the Bank of France and the Federal Reserve provided that the two lines of credit be used pari passu, the Bank of England felt unable to draw on either of its new facilities.

In the absence of firm official support, the sterling exchange rate declined slightly on August 4 and on the following day broke badly in London, New York, and Paris[82] (see Chart 9). Rumors flooded the markets that the Bank of France had withdrawn its support for sterling and that it would not cooperate as long as

---

[78] *Agreement between Federal Reserve Bank of New York and the Governor and Company of the Bank of England, August 1, 1931; agreement concluded on August 1, 1931, between the Bank of France and the Bank of England.*

[79] *Clay, op. cit., page 386.*

[80] *Harrison conversation with Lacour-Gayet on August 7, 1931 (Harrison Papers).*

[81] *Crane cable to Harrison, No. 4, August 10, 1931.*

[82] The Economist, *August 8, 1931, page 254.*

CHART 9

SUPPORTING STERLING IN CRISIS: A PARTIAL VIEW
JULY 13–SEPTEMBER 21, 1931

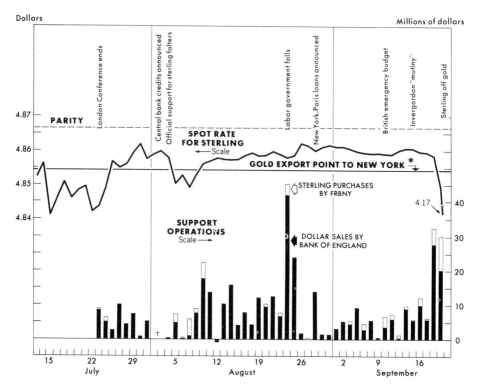

Note: Support operations include Bank of England dollar sales, as reported in daily cables to the Federal Reserve Bank of New York, and purchases of sterling by the New York Reserve Bank. All told, these operations amounted to somewhat over $400 million in the period July 23-September 19, 1931, roughly two fifths of the more than £200 million ($972 million) reserve losses officially stated to have been sustained by the British authorities during the two months before sterling went off gold. The chart does not include other support operations, particularly those conducted on the basis of the credits extended by the Bank of France and the Paris market. The sterling exchange rate shown in the chart is the average of noon buying rates for cable transfers in New York as certified by the Federal Reserve Bank of New York to the Secretary of the Treasury.

*The gold export point from London to New York, roughly approximated by the line in the chart, was defined as that exchange rate below which it was advantageous for holders of sterling to purchase gold from the Bank of England, ship the metal to New York, and sell it to the United States authorities in order to acquire dollars.

† Bank holiday weekend.

Norman remained head of the Bank of England.[83] Although vigorous support operations were quickly resumed under the market arrangements that had been concluded toward the end of July, negotiations to resolve the problem of drawing on the Bank of France credit dragged on until August 7 when it was decided that the entire $125 million equivalent would be drawn at once in the hope that the Bank of England could by this means conceal its operations from the Paris market.[84] In the meantime, however, as Lacour-Gayet lamented, the "moral effect" of the credits was being lost.[85] Pressure on sterling, which had been light on August 4, became heavy in the days that followed. A fair, though incomplete, notion of the hectic developments in the exchange markets is given by the daily total of support operations in the form of Bank of England dollar sales and Federal Reserve sterling purchases, comparable data for support operations in other forms being unavailable. These support operations, which amounted to only $0.5 million on August 4, mounted to $9 million on August 8 and to $22 million on August 10. They slackened somewhat thereafter, but they mounted to a peak of $45 million on August 24, the day the Labor government resigned.[86]

THE BANKERS' LOAN TO THE BRITISH GOVERNMENT. Most of the story of the raising of the loans to the British government from New York and Paris commercial bankers in the latter part of August has already been told, most notably by Sir Henry Clay's biography of *Lord Norman* and in Reginald Bassett's *Nineteen Thirty One*.[87] Accordingly, it is not necessary to recount the details of Snowden's and MacDonald's conversion to the view that additional loans would have to be raised in New York and Paris, the approach to private bankers in those centers, the communications from the bankers to the effect that loans could be raised only if the British government were to adopt a program of budgetary reform that had the full approval and support of the Bank of England and the

---

[83] Papers Relating to the Foreign Relations of the United States, 1931, *Vol. I, page 18; Sproul conversation with Catterns, August 5, 1931; and Hurst, op. cit., page 640.*

[84] *The agreement was facilitated when the Federal Reserve waived its right to pari passu drawings with the Bank of France. The Paris commercial banks eventually participated to the extent of half the credit. Crane cable to Harrison, No. 4, August 10, 1931; Bank of France Annual Report, 1931 published in Federal Reserve Bulletin (March 1932), page 162; and Harvey cable to Harrison, No. 280, August 7, 1931.*

[85] *Harrison conversation with Lacour-Gayet on August 6, 1931 (Harrison Papers).*

[86] *Crane cables to Harrison, No. 292, August 11, 1931, and No. 24, August 24, 1931; Clay, op. cit., page 386; Reginald Bassett, Nineteen Thirty-One (London: Macmillan & Co., Ltd., 1958), page 155.*

[87] *See especially Clay, op. cit., pages 387-95; Bassett, op. cit., Chapter 9.*

City of London generally, the refusal of the Henderson faction to accept Snowden's budget balancing proposals which included a 10 per cent cut in relief payments to the unemployed, the resignation of the Labor government, the subsequent bitter allegations that Snowden's budgetary proposals had been adopted under pressure from foreign bankers, and particularly that the Federal Reserve Bank of New York had informed the British government that further credits would be granted to the Bank of England only if economies in the dole were enforced and the British government's subsequent flat denials that these allegations contained any truth.

The part of the story that has not hitherto been published relates to Harrison's efforts both to obtain substantial additional funds to support sterling and to avoid entanglement in the bitter political controversy that, as he was fully aware, was then raging in Britain. It has already been noted that, repeatedly during the latter part of July, Harrison had urged Norman and Harvey to encourage the British government to approach the New York market for a long-term loan. Although Norman was dubious, Harvey on July 30 indicated not only that he heartily agreed with Harrison's suggestion but that he had already raised the question with the British Treasury.[88] Throughout early August the Bank of England exerted its utmost efforts to hasten the formulation of the government's proposals to reduce expenditure and balance its budget and, foreseeing that its efforts might soon bear fruit, the bank approached Harrison on August 13 for advice on the raising of a foreign loan for the British government.[89] Harrison's response was that such a loan "should be arranged jointly in Paris and New York since it is essential that Paris and London should work together", and that it should be arranged "promptly after the announcement of a strong budget program". Harrison himself did not venture to say how much might be raised but other senior officers of the bank guessed that "perhaps $250,000,000" could be obtained in New York if sterling were kept strong and if the government were to announce "a very convincing budget reform".[90]

On August 22 Harrison received from Harvey an outline of Snowden's proposal for balancing the budget, and on the following day he discussed these proposals with Norman who was recuperating at the Château Frontenac in Quebec.

---

[88] *Harrison conversation with Harvey, July 30, 1931 (Harrison Papers).*
[89] *Crane cable to Harrison, No. 4, August 10, 1931; Burgess memorandum to files, August 4, 1931.*
[90] *Burgess cable to Crane, No. 10, August 14, 1931.*

Harrison told Norman that Morgan's had received messages from London indicating that MacDonald would resign if either Morgan's or Harrison himself felt the program inadequate. Harrison then told Norman, according to his record, that:[91]

> both Morgan's and I thought that was not a fair question to put up to us; that while we were certain that a very definite budgetary program must be put through if they are to float a loan here, nevertheless it was impossible for us at this distance to determine whether the proposed program was adequate enough . . . . Norman agreed with this one hundred per cent . . . . He said that was obviously a question to be determined in London; that we could not do so here. I told him that Morgan's had finally cabled them to ask whether the program was satisfactory to the Bank of England and the City, including their own partners; that I thought that was the best way they could leave it. To this Norman also agreed. I then mentioned I had asked Harvey several times whether he thought the program was adequate and while he generally implied he thought it was, I got no definite answer from him. Norman intimated that I probably would not get a definite answer from him but that he, Norman, felt that the program was inadequate; that we must not fool ourselves now; that any inadequate program would cause trouble in a year or so and that it is essential that we must force an economic adjustment now and not in a year or so from now; that the program, in his judgment, must be sufficiently drastic to place the cost of output and wages on a competitive basis with the rest of the world and unless that were done he was certain the program would not be adequate; that if the Government attacked the situation courageously and did enough by way of drastic readjustment then, in his judgment, they would not need a credit at all. I said the difficulty with that was that the time was so short and the central bank credit so nearly exhausted, it was a risky thing to take the chance on even a drastic budgetary reform checking the withdrawals. Norman allowed there was something in this point. The sum and substance of our conversation indicated pretty clearly, however, that Norman felt the proposed program was not sufficiently severe to avoid trouble later on and that there was no use in doing the thing halfway.

Inadequate though Snowden's proposals may have been, they proved too much for Arthur Henderson and his followers to swallow. The Labor government split and resigned, effective August 24. Late the same day a "national" government was formed composed of members of the Conservative and Liberal Parties and led by MacDonald (who remained Prime Minister) and Snowden as Chancellor of the Exchequer. The stage was thus set for the announcement that the new government would implement Snowden's proposals and for the raising of the loans in the New York and Paris markets. By August 25 the British authorities were assured that $200-250 million could be obtained in the New York market

---

[91] *Harrison conversation with Norman on August 23, 1931 (Harrison Papers).*

if a similar amount could be raised in Paris.[92] On that day Harrison called Lacour-Gayet. He learned that Harry Siepmann of the Bank of England had discussed with Moret a loan of $120-235 million but that Moret felt the amount should be nearer the lower than the higher figure. For his part Harrison emphasized that this time the job "must be done once and for all and not piecemeal", and that the loan should be adequate in amount "to do the trick" and long enough to avoid any "embarrassing maturity". He then asked Lacour-Gayet[93]

> how quickly it would be possible to place the credit in Paris. He said he thought three or four days. I told him that I thought it ought to be done immediately . . . . He, figuratively, threw up his hands and said it was not possible, that it was now 5 o'clock in Paris and that Moret has not even yet been authorized to speak to any of the private bankers. I was astounded at this, and Lacour-Gayet said that neither he nor Moret got any impression from Siepmann that there was any imminence about this credit; that he had come to talk in the most general terms; that he was now flying back to London, and that until they were authorized to talk to the private bankers there was nothing more he could do about it. I asked whether, if they got immediate authority to approach the private banks, it would be possible to talk to some of the bankers tonight. He said possibly, but that many of them have already left for the day and gone out of town. I urged upon him what I considered the imminence of the British position, especially as the Bank of England has only £1,000,000 left in the [central bank] credit. Lacour-Gayet said he could not understand that as there was $8,000,000 not used in the French tranche. I said I got the figures from Crane last night; that he indicated there was only £1,000,000 left in all, and that I felt in any event it was necessary to do something by tomorrow night or Thursday morning at the latest. I asked him whether, if they got authority to go to work at once, it might not be possible to do it by that time. He said he supposed it might be but it would be difficult to act in such a hurry. On the whole, he was most sympathetic and helpful in his attitude, but somewhat surprised at our thought that there was any such rush . . . .

Harrison and Lacour-Gayet discussed the loan further on August 26. Both agreed that it would be desirable to raise at least $200 million in each market. Harrison emphasized that to raise $100 million in each market would be misunderstood and would cause more questioning and doubt than it would do good. With this Lacour-Gayet agreed but felt nevertheless that, without a public issue, the Paris banks might be able to raise only $100 million. The French private banks, he said, were not so organized to take up as much as $200 million by

---

[92] *J. P. Morgan & Co. cable to Morgan Grenfell & Co., August 24, 1931; Harrison conversation with Lacour-Gayet on August 25, 1931 (Harrison Papers).*

[93] *Harrison conversation with Lacour-Gayet on August 25, 1931, pages 4-5 (Harrison Papers).*

themselves on short notice. On the other hand, a public issue would require considerable time to arrange and might lead—as had happened on earlier occasions—to stringency in the Paris market which would attract balances from London to Paris, the very thing that the loan was aimed to discourage.[94]

In the end, it proved possible to raise a one-year $200 million loan in Paris but only half the amount was obtained from the banks, the other half being provided by a public issue which was not floated until September 14. Nevertheless, agreement to provide the loan was announced on August 28 at the same time as the $200 million loan from a group of New York banks headed by J. P. Morgan & Co.[95] Thereafter Parliament reconvened on September 8, and on September 10 Snowden, as promised, presented an emergency budget under which revenues were increased and expenditures cut to the extent necessary to change the deficit anticipated in the government's accounts into a small surplus.[96]

THE FINAL ONSLAUGHT. Although the formation of the "national" government, the announcement of the New York and Paris loans, and the emergency budget were all well received in the principal foreign markets, the pressure on sterling was only temporarily relieved. Basic problems remained unresolved. In particular, the bitterness in British domestic politics was far from reassuring. The "national" government had been formed to deal only with the crisis; an election was promised as soon as the emergency had passed. The hostility of the opposition to Snowden's budgetary reforms intensified; allegations of a Bankers' Ramp spread despite the official denials.[97] A manifesto, published on August 27 jointly by the Labor Party and the Trades Union Congress, predicted that cuts in wages and salaries would "bring about embittered conflict and industrial chaos".[98] There was much private discussion within the Labor Party and elsewhere about whether sterling

---

[94] *Harrison conversation with Lacour-Gayet on August 26, 1931 (Harrison Papers).* Supra, *page 171.*

[95] *Crane cable to Harrison, No. 19, August 28, 1931, and Clay, op. cit., pages 397-98.*

[96] Parliamentary Debates *(Great Britain, House of Commons), Statement by the Chancellor of the Exchequer to the House of Commons, September 10, 1931, columns 297-313;* The Economist, *September 12, 1931, pages 460-62.*

[97] *The phrase "Bankers' Ramp" was used by dissident Labor Party members and others in Britain to describe the pressure that was alleged to have been exerted on the Labor government by foreign financiers. In rejecting these allegations in an August 25, 1931 speech, Prime Minister MacDonald used the phrase as synonymous with conspiracy. In Webster's Dictionary (third international) "ramp" is described as obsolete slang meaning swindle, confidence game, dupery.*

[98] *The text of the manifesto was published in* The New York Times, *August 28, 1931, page 8.*

would or should be devalued although little of this was reflected in the press.[99] Disturbances in the Royal Navy, arising from pay cuts made under the emergency budget, were magnified in the foreign press into a serious mutiny.

Long before the so-called mutiny, of course, Continental bankers had been drawing down their sterling balances in order to reinforce their cash positions and so safeguard themselves against the threat of new currency panics. Withdrawals from London by Dutch and Swiss commercial banks were particularly heavy because they, like their London and New York counterparts, had substantial commitments in Germany which were frozen under the standstill arrangements that were announced September 9. But there can be little doubt that the so-called mutiny, announced on September 15, precipitated the final onslaught against sterling. In the days that followed, prices on the London stock exchange and on the Paris, Amsterdam, and Zurich bourses declined sharply and continuously.[100] The British 5 per cent War Loan, widely held by foreigners, which had been quoted at 100½ on September 9, was down to 97½ ten days later. Especially in the Dutch financial markets, conditions approached panic as the banks curtailed credit and repatriated funds from London.[101]

The scanty evidence that exists suggests that only a small part of the pressure against sterling was on official foreign account. Central bankers were nervous but generally seemed to have refrained from withdrawing the bulk of their sterling balances.[102] At least one western European central banker approached the Bank of England about the beginning of September for a gold guarantee of his sterling balances, was refused, and invited to take gold then and there if he wanted it but after considering the matter decided not to withdraw his funds.[103] On the other hand, another important European central bank, which apparently held significant short-term balances in London, is known to have converted all but £300,000 into gold before September 20.[104]

---

[99] Crane, "Notes on Visit in England" included in Confidential Memorandum of European Visit, September 16, 1931, and The Economist, September 19, 1931, page 504.

[100] The Economist, September 26, 1931, page 554.

[101] Hurst, op. cit., pages 656-59.

[102] Hurst, op. cit., pages 643-47.

[103] Crane cable to Harrison, No. 20, September 3, 1931; Harrison conversation with Norman and Harvey on October 2, 1931 (Harrison Papers).

[104] Crane, Report of European Trip, November 21, 1932.

The information on the behavior of the French banks during the crisis is conflicting. Crane was told in the course of various visits to London and Paris that toward the end of August 1931 the Bank of France still held about £80 million in short-term sterling balances, that French private banks held about £40 million, and that by September 21 the Bank of France's balances had been cut to £65 million, a reduction equivalent to about one fifth the amount of the Paris credits.[105] Market gossip was that the Paris private bank balances were down to £10 million by the time sterling went off gold.[106] On the other hand, in his September 21 post mortem, Snowden went out of his way to chide the critics of the French banks, saying that his information was that "these banks have not played any part in the recent withdrawals from London, but have maintained their balances practically intact...."[107]

As the pressure against sterling built up in the early days of September, the Bank of England held the spot rate within a narrow band around $4.86, roughly ½ cent above the gold export point to New York. It also supported sterling in the forward market especially after September 8 when Harrison was informed that the London clearing banks would thereafter be free sellers of forward exchange.[108] These exchange market tactics, which drew severe criticism in New York, were based on the view that any decline in the spot rate or widening in the forward discounts would sap such confidence in sterling as remained, would impair the confidence-making effects of the budgetary measures to be announced by the Chancellor on September 10, and would jeopardize the success of the Paris market issue on September 14.[109] For a time, Harrison deferred to this view which was held by the authorities in both London and Paris but, when the same tactics were continued after the flotation of the Paris issue, he strongly emphasized to Harvey that the feeling in New York was that the maintenance of such a high rate was encouraging sales of sterling, that no one was "satisfied with continued

[105] *It seems clear that the £80 million, which was held almost entirely at London commercial banks, did not include the sterling counterpart of drawings on the credit from the Bank of France. Under the loan agreement the sterling counterpart was to be held at the Bank of England. Crane cable to Harrison, No. 14, August 23, 1931. See also Crane conversation with Moret, August 26, in his Confidential Memorandum of European Visit, September 16, 1931, and Crane, Report on European Trip, November 21, 1932.*

[106] *Hurst, op. cit., page 642.*

[107] Parliamentary Debates *(Great Britain, House of Commons), September 21, 1931, column 1297.*

[108] *Harvey cable to Harrison, No. 411, September 8, 1931.*

[109] Ibid.; *Harvey cable to Harrison, No. 402, September 4, 1931.*

use of the credit to maintain sterling at such a high point", and that sentiment generally "was questioning and restless". He also reported that Norman, whom he had just seen, was[110]

> much disturbed about the way the exchange situation was handled and he agreed with us that it was most important not to peg it, that every peg in past history had proved disastrous, that he saw no occasion for it at this time and that the chief reason he was hurrying home before he was quite ready to do so was to see if he could not make some headway in handling the exchange situation more satisfactorily.

However, it is doubtful whether, at this stage, any change in exchange market tactics would have made an appreciable difference. The pressure was again snowballing fast. By Wednesday, September 16, almost half of the New York and Paris loans had been either sold in the spot market or committed against forward contracts.[111] That day the Bank of England's gold and foreign exchange loss was £5 million; it was £10 million on Thursday, nearly £18 million on Friday, and £10 million on Saturday when the markets were open only half a day.[112] At the close of business on September 19, the Bank of England's holdings of gold and foreign exchange exceeded by only £5 million the total of its obligations under forward exchange contracts, the central bank credits, and the New York and Paris loans.[113] More than £200 million of gold and foreign exchange had been lost since July 13.[114]

The final onslaught came, as Snowden said on September 21, with "appalling suddenness". The balancing of the budget, which had been considered the key to the defense of sterling and for which MacDonald and Snowden had accepted the breakup of the Labor government, was in vain. Less than a week after the budget message, the British authorities were again confronted with an urgent need for new measures to save sterling. Without much hope, they approached Washington about the possibility of some new initiative on the part of the Hoover

---

[110] *Harrison conversation with Harvey on September 16, 1931 (Harrison Papers).*

[111] *Harrison conversation with Harvey on September 16, 1931, page 1 (Harrison Papers).*

[112] Parliamentary Debates *(Great Britain, House of Commons), Snowden statement in Parliament, September 21, 1931, columns 1293-99.*

[113] *Harrison letter to Glass, March 23, 1939 (Harrison Papers).*

[114] Parliamentary Debates *(Great Britain, House of Commons), Snowden statement of September 21, 1931 to the House of Commons, column 1295; Clay, op. cit., page 398; and Harvey cable to Harrison, September 20, 1931.*

administration toward the permanent elimination of reparations and war debts. The question whether additional credits might be obtained was also raised with both the United States and French governments. On neither count were the responses encouraging.[115] Nor did the British authorities feel there was anything they themselves could do. From New York and the Continent they had received advice that a further increase in the Bank of England discount rate would only increase the distrust of sterling and that a further tightening of credit could not operate quickly enough to stem the reserve losses.[116] The possibility of mobilizing British private holdings of foreign securities was considered and rejected on the ground that the resources that could thus be obtained would have been inadequate to check the huge reserve drain. On similar grounds, it was decided that the Bank of England should conserve its remaining gold which amounted to £136 million on September 16. Foreign balances in London were still a multiple of the Bank's gold holdings, and it was believed that the release of even a large proportion of these holdings would not have stopped the drain but would, as Snowden said, only have benefited those who were showing the least confidence in sterling.[117]

At 6:30 a.m. New York time on Saturday, September 19, Harvey telephoned Harrison to say that, in the absence of any alternative, the British authorities had come to the conclusion that they would suspend gold payments effective Monday, September 21. After some discussion of market operation, Harrison asked[118]

whether there was not anything left to do, especially in view of the fact that withdrawals today seem to have let up so much as compared with yesterday. He said he was afraid not, that they had reached the end of their tether and that so far as he could see there was nothing left to do. But, I said, you have $75 million left in the Paris credit and with that as a backlog and possible change in conditions and some restrictions, might they not be able to control the situation. He said that the $75 million left in Paris was but a drop in the bucket considering the rate of withdrawals yesterday, and that it was hard to tell at the time he was talking how much has been disposed of today; and that furthermore there was still a half hour

---

[115] *Harrison conversation with Harvey on September 16, 1931, page 4, and Harrison conversation with Harvey at 8:35 a.m. on September 19, 1931, page 2 (Harrison Papers). Osborne cable to the Marquess of Reading, No. 578, September 20, 1931,* Documents on British Foreign Policy, 1919-1939, 2nd Series, Vol. II, 1931, *page 262; and Clay, op. cit., page 398.*

[116] *Clay, ibid., page 387.*

[117] Parliamentary Debates *(Great Britain, House of Commons), September 21, 1931, columns 1295-96.*

[118] *Harrison conversation with Harvey at 6:30 a.m. on September 19, 1931, pages 3-4 (Harrison Papers).*

left to go without any assurances as to what the total already is. I asked him whether with some evidence of slowing up today there were not some restrictions which might be put in together with the $75 million leeway that might turn the tide. Harvey was of the definite impression that there was nothing left for them to do; that in 1914 they had many powers which they do not now possess and that he did not see any way of effectively stemming the tide. I said it seems a great pity to let it go and asked whether there was anything we could do within reason. Harvey replied that he thought we had already done a great deal and that he saw nothing else which we could do to help, that there was no alternative left.

The same day the Bank of England addressed a formal letter to the government advising that the bank be relieved of its obligation to sell gold at a fixed price under the provisions of the Gold Standard Act of 1925. This advice was formally accepted at a Cabinet meeting on Sunday, September 20. The suspension of the gold standard was announced to the public the same evening and on the following day, with the stock exchange closed, legislation was enacted by both houses of Parliament giving the government's decision the force of law.[119]

EPILOGUE

Britain's abandonment of gold came as an unexpected shock after two years during which numerous other difficulties had already weakened and depressed the international economy, and was a major factor in the final plunge of the depression to the depths of 1932. The sequence of events in this further twist of the deflationary spiral is clear. When the flight from sterling forced the British currency off gold, the repercussions on international liquidity were immediate. Those foreigners—and there were many—who elected to continue to hold London balances found the gold value of these holdings reduced by 30 per cent as a result of the drop in the sterling exchange rate between mid-September and the end of 1931. Others, stopped from obtaining gold in London, shifted into dollar balances in order to obtain the metal in New York. At the same time, other holders of dollar balances, mainly foreigners, were also converting their funds into gold. The United States gold stock consequently declined by 11 per

---

[119] *The text of the communications between the Bank of England and the government regarding the suspension of the gold standard is printed in Bassett, op. cit., pages 237-39. See also Clay, op. cit., page 398.*

cent in the four months ended December 1931. Federal Reserve gold holdings, which for years had been far in excess of the amounts required, dropped close to the legal minima.[120] Despite the depressed condition of the United States economy, the Federal Reserve felt obliged sharply to increase discount rates, the rate of the New York Reserve Bank being increased 2 percentage points to 3½ per cent, and to squeeze member bank reserves during the remainder of 1931. For similar reasons, similar policies were pursued abroad. The Bank of England increased its discount rate by 1½ per cent to 6 per cent upon the announcement of the abandonment of gold while the Reichsbank, after having reduced its rate from the 15 per cent established at the beginning of August 1931, maintained the rate at 8 per cent in the three months ended December 10. Even in France, in which much of the flight capital sought refuge and where the authorities were already pursuing a very conservative policy, the central bank signaled the beginning of an even more cautious course by increasing its discount rate early in October.

Under the impact of the sharp decline in international liquidity, more stringent monetary policies, and deepening business pessimism, financial difficulties multiplied and production and trade contracted further. Comparing the second half of 1931 with a year earlier, United States commercial bank suspensions rose 86 per cent while defaults on foreign dollar bonds increased seventeenfold. In most industrial countries the decline in industrial production which had slowed during the spring of 1931, accelerated during the following autumn and winter and unemployment reached new highs.[121] In the external sphere, international commodity prices continued to decline. Moreover, Britain's abandonment of gold inaugurated a period of fluctuating exchange rates that contributed, together with declining national income and expenditures and rising tariffs and other barriers, to the stifling of international trade. The upshot was that the value of world exports in 1932 was about one third lower than it had been the year before and only two fifths that of 1929. The collapse of a key currency thus signaled the end of the international financial system established in the 1920's and contributed substantially to the disruption of the international economy.

[120] E. A. Goldenweiser, American Monetary Policy (1st ed.; New York: McGraw-Hill, Inc., 1951), pages 121-23, 158-60.

[121] League of Nations, Statistical Year-book, 1931-32, pages 58-59, 176-86; 1932-33, pages 146-56.

Judged by its overall accomplishments in 1924-31, central bank cooperation deserves only mixed marks. For the period up to June 1928, the record has considerable merit. Cooperation facilitated the stabilization of several major currencies and numerous minor ones. The strains that arose after these stabilizations were manageable. Deficit countries such as Britain and Germany adjusted slowly, but the pace of economic change elsewhere was not so rapid or abrupt as to make these adjustment efforts hopelessly inadequate. The acute monetary difficulties that arose were handled, not without hard bargaining, by compromise and accommodation. Had world trade continued to expand and had the United States economy remained reasonably prosperous, exchange stability might have been maintained at a cost in terms of unemployment no greater than the deficit countries were willing to pay. It is even conceivable that, had the economic weather remained fair, some of the deficiencies in the cooperative arrangements—for example, the rather narrow limitations on the amount of official credit available or the one-sided burden that the adjustment process placed on deficit countries—might in time have been at least partially remedied.

On the other hand, the record of central bank cooperation in the period after mid-1928 must be judged a failure. This failure stemmed not so much from the deficiencies of central bank cooperation itself as from the inability of the authorities—including particularly those in the United States—to manage their domestic economies successfully. For the breakdown of the American economy immensely complicated the problems of central bank cooperation. In addition to destroying the opportunity for any gradual improvement in cooperative techniques, the collapse greatly accelerated the pace of economic change and intensified the pressures to which the international financial system was subjected. The rate at which incomes and prices dropped, export markets narrowed, trade barriers were erected, and the direction of capital flows shifted far outstripped the capacity and willingness of individual countries to adjust. And from these basic economic changes arose major political and monetary difficulties with which the fair-weather cooperative arrangements of the 1920's were completely unable to cope.

But part of the failure also stemmed from rigidities in the views of the authorities themselves. They, in common with most economists and the public generally, failed to understand until it was too late that the economic breakdown of 1929-31 had created problems that were entirely different from those of the early and mid-1920's. They, therefore, followed policies which had been successful in earlier years but which—applied in the circumstances of the Great Depression—sometimes aggravated the problems they were intended to solve or, when they did work in the right direction, were inadequate to deal with those problems. The latter was certainly true of the central bank credits that were arranged during the 1931 crisis. Even so, it is difficult to conceive of any extension or modification of central bank cooperation—within the realm of what was then considered possible—that would have been sufficient to maintain exchange rate stability in the circumstances of political and economic disintegration that prevailed. Indeed, the conclusion seems inescapable that the failure of central bank cooperation in 1929-31 was only part of the larger failure of the Western democracies to deal successfully with the economic and political problems of the time.

The requisites for successful international financial management in the complex conditions of 1924-31 were many. The most basic need was to develop economic tools that would insure stable growth without inflation in the major countries. But stable growth—although necessary—was not sufficient for success. It was also necessary for each national component to mesh with the rest of the world economy, and to do so on the basis of stable exchange rates and without resort to restrictions on trade and payments. Hence there was need to develop (1) more effective policy instruments by which each country could foster adjustments to economic changes elsewhere in the international system, (2) better arrangements under which—if need be—international credit could be provided to finance such adjustments as well as to maintain orderly conditions in the exchange markets and to deal with unforeseen emergencies, and (3) a generally agreed conception of the international economy that could provide criteria for the administration of adjustment instruments and credit facilities. Meeting these various needs would not, of course, have eliminated all the difficulties of international economic management in 1924-31. But their fulfillment would have improved the chances for handling the problems that arose under relatively calm conditions rather than under the overwhelming pressures of world depression and financial crisis.

CHRONOLOGY OF IMPORTANT EVENTS, 1919-31

1919:

June 28   Versailles Treaty is signed by representatives of the Allied and Associated Powers and Germany. It is declared in force, January 10, 1920, when the majority of those powers—but not the United States—ratified it.

1920:

January 16   The League of Nations holds its first meeting in Paris.

February 23   The Reparation Commission meets in Paris. It is a successor to another similar body formed during the Peace Conference in 1919.

July 16   The Spa Conference of Allied and German ministers agrees upon percentages for division of German reparation payments by the Allies.

1921:

May 11   Germany accepts total reparation obligation of $33 billion, as set by the meeting of the Allied Supreme Council in London.

August 25   German-American Peace Treaty is signed in Berlin by representatives of German and American presidents.

1922:

February 9   United States War Debt Refunding Act, which provides a basis for negotiations on war debts with the Allies, is signed by President Harding.

February 15   Permanent Court of International Arbitration established at the Hague with thirty-three member countries, but not the United States.

May 19   Twelve Resolutions of the Financial Commission of the Genoa
                Conference, which include calling a central bankers' meeting
                and establishing the gold exchange standard, are approved by
                the conference.

August 1   Lord Balfour announces that Great Britain, while favoring the
                surrender of its share of German reparations and the writing-
                off of the whole body of inter-Allied indebtedness, will seek to
                collect debt payments from the Allies and Germany only
                sufficient to pay its debt to the United States.

September 21   President Harding signs the Fordney-McCumber Tariff Act,
                which raises rates on many agricultural and manufactured
                products to protect the farmers and certain wartime industries.
                The act also provides for adjustments by the President to
                equalize costs at home and abroad.

December 29   Secretary of State Hughes in New Haven proposes an investi-
                gation by experts of Germany's capacity to pay reparations.

1923:

January 11   French and Belgian troops occupy the Ruhr, following the
                Reparation Commission's declaration of Germany's default on
                reparation payments.

February 28   British-American war debt agreement, as approved by the
                Senate, is signed by President Harding. It is ratified by Great
                Britain, June 19, 1923.

October 16   Rentenbank is established as a means to halt German inflation.
                The currency is stabilized on November 15, 1923 on the basis
                of one rentenmark equal to one trillion paper marks.

1924:

January 14   First Committee of Experts, with Dawes as chairman, begins
                to work to determine ways of balancing Germany's budget and
                reinforcing the stabilization of the German currency.

January 21	Second Committee of Experts, with McKenna as chairman, begins to estimate the amount of German capital abroad.
April 9	Two Committees of Experts publish their reports to the Reparation Commission.
August 16	Protocol of the London Conference, to put the Dawes Plan into operation, is signed by government representatives. By August 30, 1924 the necessary German legislation is passed, including that for the Reichsbank.
September 1	Dawes Plan for payment of German reparations goes into operation.

1925:

January 14	United States and Germany sign a separate agreement for payment by the latter of American costs of occupation and mixed claims. Conference of Allied Finance Ministers in Paris sign agreement for division of reparation receipts.
April 28	Churchill announces that Great Britain is returning to the gold standard at prewar parity.
July 31	French and Belgian troops evacuate the Ruhr, according to the London Protocol of August 16, 1924.
December 1	Locarno nonaggression pacts are signed by European government representatives. They are ratified by sufficient countries to be declared in force February 14, 1926.

1926:

January 30	British forces evacuate Cologne, as provided for in the London Protocol.
April 29	Secretary of the Treasury Mellon and Ambassador Bérenger sign French-United States debt agreement. It is ratified by France, July 26, 1929 and by the United States, December 18, 1929.

| May 1 | British coal strike, followed on May 4 by general strike, in protest of wage cuts by mine owners and the Royal British Coal Commission Report. The coal strike lasts seven months and the general strike nine days. |

| July 12 | Churchill and Caillaux sign British-French war debt agreement, which comes into force on July 27, 1929 after it is ratified by France. |

| September 8 | Germany is admitted to the League of Nations. |

1928:

| June 25 | French law, stabilizing the franc at one fifth the 1914 parity and establishing the gold standard in France, becomes effective. |

| August 27 | Kellogg-Briand Peace Pact, renouncing war as an instrument of national policy, is signed by fifteen government representatives. It is ratified by France, March 29, 1929, by the United States, January 16, 1929, and declared in force by President Hoover, July 24, 1929. |

| November 22 | Currency and Bank Notes Act, adopted July 2, 1928, comes into effect establishing final form of gold standard in Great Britain. |

1929:

| February 11 | Committee of Experts, headed by Young, meets in Paris to set final plan for German reparation payments. |

| June 7 | Young Committee submits its plan to the Reparation Commission. |

| August 31 | End of first Hague Conference to draw up plans for putting Young Plan into operation. |

| September 20 | Hatry stock scandal in Great Britain occurs as the New York stock market prices begin to weaken. |

225

| October 24 | New York stock market panic starts. |

1930:

January 20	Protocol is signed at second Hague Conference on German reparations, to put Young Plan into operation. Necessary German legislation is passed and countries ratify by May 17, 1930.
May 17	Young Plan goes into operation, Bank for International Settlements is established, and Dawes Plan ends.
May 19	The Reparation Commission is liquidated in accordance with the Young Plan.
June 17	Hoover signs Hawley-Smoot Act which raises United States tariffs to new highs.
June 30	The Rhineland is evacuated by Allied forces, according to the Hague Protocol.
November 6	Oustric stock scandal in France ruins several banks and many small investors.

1931:

March 21	Germany announces plans for an Austro-German customs union. Plans are abandoned, September 3, 1931.
May 11	Credit-Anstalt, largest bank in Austria with international investments, reports heavy losses.
June 20	Hoover proposes a year's moratorium in intergovernmental debt payments.
July 13	Macmillan Report is published revealing large foreign short-term claims on London.
July 13	Danat Bank is closed in Berlin, followed by closing of Berlin bourse and promulgation of exchange controls.

July 23   Seven Power Conference in London, to consider ways to provide capital for Germany, adjourns.

July 31   May Committee issues report on needed economy in British government expenditures.

September 15   British sailors "mutiny" in protest of economy measures of new national government.

September 21   Gold Standard Amendment Bill is passed in Great Britain to suspend the gold standard.

Index:

229

233